LEGAL CARE

AF795604

LEGAL CARE

ADVOCACY AND FRICTION IN FAMILY DETENTION

ERIN ROUTON

THE UNIVERSITY OF
ARIZONA PRESS
TUCSON

The University of Arizona Press
www.uapress.arizona.edu

We respectfully acknowledge the University of Arizona is on the land and territories of Indigenous peoples. Today, Arizona is home to twenty-two federally recognized tribes, with Tucson being home to the O'odham and the Yaqui. The university strives to build sustainable relationships with sovereign Native Nations and Indigenous communities through education offerings, partnerships, and community service.

© 2026 by The Arizona Board of Regents
All rights reserved. Published 2026

ISBN-13: 978-0-8165-5574-1 (hardcover)
ISBN-13: 978-0-8165-5573-4 (paperback)
ISBN-13: 978-0-8165-5575-8 (ebook)

Cover design by Leigh McDonald
Typeset by Sara Thaxton in 10.5/14 Warnock Pro with Gothic 13 Std and Helvetica Neue LT Std

Publication of this book is made possible in part by funding from the University of Houston.

Library of Congress Cataloging-in-Publication Data
Names: Routon, Erin, 1983– author
Title: Legal care : advocacy and friction in family detention / Erin Routon.
Description: Tucson : University of Arizona Press, 2026. | Includes bibliographical references and index.
Identifiers: LCCN 2026010561 (print) | LCCN 2026010562 (ebook) | ISBN 9780816555741 hardcover | ISBN 9780816555734 paperback | ISBN 9780816555758 ebook
Subjects: LCSH: Immigration advocates—United States—Social conditions | Immigration advocates—Job stress—United States | Immigration advocates—Employment—United States | Legal assistance to immigrants—United States | Noncitizen detention centers—United States
Classification: LCC JV6475 .R68 2026 (print) | LCC JV6475 (ebook) | DDC 305.9/069120973—dc23/eng/20260427
LC record available at https://lccn.loc.gov/2026010561
LC ebook record available at https://lccn.loc.gov/2026010562

Printed in the United States of America
∞ This paper meets the requirements of ANSI/NISO Z39.48-1992 (Permanence of Paper).

For those with hearts that fiercely bleed

CONTENTS

ILLUSTRATIONS

ACKNOWLEDGMENTS

I feel immensely privileged to have been surrounded and supported by many kind and thoughtful individuals throughout my time conducting this research and writing this book. These people have cared for me and my project, and for that, I am forever indebted.

Words cannot properly express my feelings about the advocates at the center of this story. The individuals who served the projects at these detention facilities were some of the most admirable people I have ever known and had the fortune to work alongside. These advocates were tireless, creative, and above all, caring individuals engaged in what was objectively heartbreaking work. As work with asylum seekers makes clear, reliving trauma is neither desirable nor easy, and yet, despite that, these advocates consistently and enthusiastically volunteered to recount their experiences in family detention in our interviews and conversations: their own trauma, joy, anger, and sadness. Unlike asylum seekers forced to divulge these sorts of things through legal processes, these advocates didn't have to do this with me, for my research, and yet, most folks I met did so. I feel lucky to have known them, and I hope that this book serves as an accurate and careful representation of the experiences and sentiments they shared with me.

This book derives from my doctoral research at my alma mater, Cornell University, where I was a student in the Department of Anthropology from 2013 to 2020. My time at Cornell shaped both my work and identity as a scholar, and I am extremely grateful for the opportunity to have studied there. I owe a great debt to my dissertation committee, who offered unrelenting support and invaluable feedback throughout the entirety of my project. I want to thank my dissertation committee chair and adviser, Dr. Sofia Villenas, for both her constant support and unparalleled kindness. Her constructive feedback and thoughtful questions were what simultaneously built my confidence in my work while also encouraging me to examine my experiences in detention from different angles. I wish to thank the others who served as committee members and advisers—Drs. Vilma Santiago-Irizarry, Adam Smith, and Chris Garces—for their support, flexibility as my research project shifted over the years of my graduate education, and the critical, necessary questions they posed to me. I also thank my adviser during my master's degree program in religious studies at the University of California, Riverside—Dr. Jennifer Scheper-Hughes—for her advice and support in getting my first research project on humanitarian aid work along the Mexico-U.S. border off the ground. Her insightful direction and encouragement in my early years as a would-be scholar played a critical role in what this book now represents. I am so grateful as well to the incredible institution at which I now teach, the University of Houston, for their support of publication of this project, and my previous employer, Harvard University, for their support in further developing my skills as a writer (in teaching writing to their undergraduates and continuing education students). I deeply appreciate everything that these institutions offered that led me here.

I want to express special appreciation for my little precious family: my tenacious cats, who accompanied me in fieldwork, and my beloved partner and fellow Cornell anthro alum, John Gorczyk. Over the past many years, he has read, provided feedback on, and edited countless iterations of this book (unpaid). He also performed an inordinate amount of emotional labor as I struggled with the secondary trauma of my fieldwork, listening supportively and patiently on the many phone calls that followed difficult days in detention, all while working on his own doctoral project in Bulgaria. Throughout my work, he did what I witnessed legal advocates doing every day: allowing me the space to express my vulnerabilities and reminding me of my own strength. I cannot imagine having done this research in the way that I did without his support, and I'm lucky to have such a kind and adventurous partner in life.

While legal advocates stand at the center of the ensuing chapters, this story is simultaneously about the parents and children imprisoned in these facilities. I am incredibly appreciative of the fact that they allowed me to play some small part in their lives, doing what I could to help them in their journeys. Memories of their courage, kindness, and resilience remain with me, as do their stories of pain and trauma, some of which were written, needlessly, as they crossed the Mexico-U.S. border. This book is but a small gesture meant to express the realities they faced in making their way to and through detention, and the indelible mark they leave on those who attempt to care for them.

Finally, I am the person I am and care about others in the way that I do because of my own family. I appreciate my mom and pop—Vickie and Randy—and sister and brother—Hilary and Brian—for modeling curiosity, creativity, strength, and care for others and for always being there for me, without fail, even when I was hundreds of miles away. I love y'all.

LEGAL CARE

INTRODUCTION

The Middle of Nowhere

The middle of nowhere is how just about everyone describes places like this. By that, they usually mean there aren't any big malls, no tall buildings, far too much dirt. It's full of sights like wooden fenceposts stringing together limp barbed wire and swaths of open land dotted by fading billboards with ominous religious pronouncements. It's too bright during the day, too dark at night, and traffic is determined by loose cattle and wide, unhurried farm machinery. I grew up in a place like this, and in the late summer of 2015, I find myself making my way through terrain that strangely reminds me of home.

Driving down a lonely dirt road, I lean into the steering wheel and squint to see the silver metal gate past a slight turn. They said to keep an eye out because there wouldn't be a sign. The dust kicks up in cream-colored clouds behind me, and the sun is starting to slip below the distant horizon, turning the sky to its usual vibrant, dusky hues. I think I'm lost. They had told us the road would come right after the detention center, but I never saw the center, just a wide paved path leading off beyond some small hill. I'm already sweating, partially because it's August in South Texas, but I'm also nervous. The next day will be my first day in an immigrant detention center, and the same distracting thoughts keep running through my head: What am I doing here? I'm not a lawyer, so I don't really know how to help people with their legal cases. Why would they even

FIGURE 1 The entrance to the "ranch," where staff of the Dilley Pro Bono Project resided. Credit Erin Routon.

want my help? I feel the chunky bits of the road knock the floorboards under my feet, kicking my mind back to the present concern.

I see what looks like the right spot, so I get out to drag the gate open just enough for me to pass through. I drive slowly along a narrow sandy road shrouded with cacti and mesquite trees until coming upon a white, one-story ranch-style home. There's a row of sparkling clean rental cars with out-of-state plates parked along the side. I rumble over the cattle guard at the entrance and park next to the others. I walk past a rusted barbecue to a back door by the covered patio carrying a tote bag with my notebook and stacks of orientation paperwork, a six-pack of Shiner beer in hand. The door swings open, and I'm enthusiastically welcomed by a group I will come to know well in the coming years, though the faces will change. I will also come to know this particular house, known by many who pass through this little town as "the ranch," eventually thinking of it as a kind of home, and the people who pass through it as an unexpected kind of kin.

What follows is a story of liminal space, of a "nowhere" place caught somewhere in the middle, and the people within it that, in many different ways, find themselves similarly caught. Even the place and people at this story's center find themselves at a crossroads. Called a baby jail by some, a migrant family detention center by others, and a residential facility by an influential few, it's all the same place. The people are "legal assistants" or "legal advocates" on paper and "warriors" among *compañerxs*. In my view, they are also caregivers, and this is a story about why I believe this to be so.

In recent years, the detention of migrant families in the United States and the often-associated practice of family separation have become increasingly familiar topics to many Americans. Yet, an understanding of the everyday realizations of these policies, practices, and spaces remains largely elusive. This is no accident: Many migration scholars have noted the complex, intentional productions of isolation and dislocation involved in migrant detention (e.g., Martin 2015; Loyd and Mountz 2018).[1] This book concerns itself with illuminating a particular aspect of migrant incarceration within the context of so-called family detention, which officially ended in 2021 with the Biden administration, only to then be revived again by the second Trump administration. My research focuses on the centrality of care in the labors, experiences, and particular social arrangements involving legal advocates providing pro bono aid to the asylum-seeking families held in those facilities.

I use the ensuing chapters to demonstrate several critical points. The foremost contention is that these legal advocates were not just legal actors but also caregivers and that they should be recognized as such, for reasons I will offer. While their work is not commonly recognized as care work in academic scholarship or even within the public sphere, my research demonstrated that this is a fruitful way to frame the totality of their diverse efforts and subjective experiences. I argue that care came to circulate throughout these spaces in unexpected ways, taking different shape depending on the particularities of distinct encounters, and

1. While recognizing distinctions between the concepts of incarceration and detention, I deploy them both throughout this book to refer to the same punitive processes and spaces. I agree with scholarship that affirms the euphemistic quality of "immigrant detention" (Furman, Epps, and Lamphear 2016; Wexler 2007), yet because of its continued dominance in the discourse around these spaces, I use it alongside "incarceration" and "carceral."

playing an important role in contentious relationships advocates had with administrative actors. In such ways, care resides within unexpected spaces, even those that are too often "presumed to be devoid of it," like carceral spaces (Sufrin 2017), and is realized in unexpected encounters. The care that advocates brought into being—what I deem "legal care"—was furthermore a form of resistance and contestation of the dehumanizing practices and violent ideologies that moved throughout detention, articulated, albeit differently, through care as well. The contours of their care were inscribed by the "frictions" emerging from their work and even existence within these spaces. Additionally, despite their efforts and privileges as nonprisoners, family detention made its wounding mark on legal advocates, in part informed by these frictions. As such, these caregivers were engaged in the simultaneous resistance of myriad institutional and structural violences that define administrative incarceration and asylum legal processes, while they were also themselves implicated, in some ways "caught," within those very constructions.

THE FACILITIES

In late 2014, standing against the backdrop of a clear, bright sky and flanked by officers and American flags, then–Secretary of Homeland Security Jeh Johnson told the crowd of reporters, "Frankly, we want to send a message that our border is not open to illegal migration, and that if you come here, you should not expect to be simply released" (Preston 2014). Johnson's symbolic message referred to the facility still under construction behind him: the South Texas Family Residential Center. This center, located in Dilley, Texas, would become one of three family detention centers that existed at the time, along with the Karnes County Residential Center in Karnes City, Texas, and the Berks County Residential Center in Pennsylvania.

These facilities began detaining parents with children during the Obama administration as a response to a "surge" earlier in the year of thousands of asylum-seeking families, or "family units," as well as so-deemed unaccompanied children arriving at the Mexico–United States border, principally from the Northern Triangle countries of Honduras, El Salvador, and Guatemala (Chishti and Hipsman 2016; Department of

FIGURE 2 The entrance to the South Texas Family Residential Center, "Dilley." Credit Erin Routon.

Homeland Security Press Office 2015).[2] The vast majority of those arriving sought asylum in the United States because of extreme gang violence, police and government corruption and collusion with gangs, and/or an inability to receive local protection against domestic or intimate partner violence, among other things (Rosenblum and Ball 2016). While most asylum seekers originated in North or Central America, those detained at these facilities also derived from many other places, like Haiti, Romania, various MENA (Middle East and North Africa) and sub-Saharan African countries, and additional countries across Latin America.

---

2. I qualify the term "unaccompanied" because, as other researchers have shown (e.g., Schrag 2020), those children who are labeled thus by the government are not always without "accompaniment" when they are "apprehended" by authorities. Some are forcibly separated from family members not recognized by officials and are thus placed within what is objectively an improper category.

Although identified as "family" facilities, throughout most of their existence, they housed almost exclusively single mothers and their minor-age children. By historically excluding fathers and other family relations, these centers effectively engaged in family separation since they opened in 2014.[3] In this way, the notion of family separation, even as it relates specifically to the limited context of the detention of asylum seekers, preceded what the public came to associate with that term.[4] While the Trump administration instituted a wide range of new policies related to the administration's so-called zero-tolerance measures that indeed expanded the physical splitting of family members and familial relations through novel tactics, the government's practice of family separation itself is not new. Although not discussed in this book, these legal advocates also engaged in everyday work to reunite such separated family members with one another, prior to Trump's policy changes.

These facilities effectively functioned as punitive processing centers for asylum seekers placed into "expedited removal" legal proceedings. Created by the Illegal Immigration Reform and Immigrant Responsibility Act of 1996, expedited removal describes a truncated legal process in which immigration officers are given authority to make decisions on migrants' legal cases, potentially denying them the opportunity of having a regular immigration court hearing (American Immigration Council 2019). The mothers and children who ended up there after arriving at different U.S. border points—either at official ports of entry or at other locations at or near U.S. borders—and requested asylum were to all apparent accounts arbitrarily selected for placement in this legal category, which required them to undergo a part of the asylum process while in detention. This is known as the "credible fear" or "reasonable fear" interview.[5] Only by passing or receiving a positive decision in this interview—

3. This changed in practice over the years of this research. For a limited period, single fathers were detained with their children in the Berks and Karnes facilities.

4. The idea of government projects aimed at separating families, especially families of color, is threaded through U.S. history, in and through various spheres and mechanisms, from contemporary incarceration to residential schools that separated Indigenous children from their communities. For an extensive treatment of these exclusionary projects promoting settler colonialism, see Dunbar-Ortiz (2021).

5. While public discussions of these interviews often simply refer to them as "credible fear" interviews, there are actually two types. Those applicants deemed "subject to

one in which they must demonstrate both their credibility and how their experiences make them eligible for asylum—are they released into the interior United States, continuing the rest of the lengthy legal process outside of detention. Otherwise, they eventually faced deportation from the facility.

Although im/migrant detention in the United States has existed since the nineteenth century (Minian 2024) and massively expanded throughout the late twentieth and twenty-first centuries (Jones 2017), the practices and policies that have come to define contemporary family detention have a comparatively short history. In 2001, the facility now known as the Berks County Residential Center began incarcerating, on a limited scale, asylum-seeking families after detaining so-called unaccompanied migrant minor children for years. Following an influx of new asylum-seeking families at the border in 2005 and with the limited total capacity of the Berks facility to ninety-six "beds," the Bush administration, and Immigration and Customs Enforcement (ICE) specifically, began contracting with private corporations to detain these families. The T. Don Hutto Family Detention Center in Taylor, Texas, was the first facility specifically dedicated to the housing of migrant family units, limited again to only women with children of minor age. This facility, like many others to come, was privately owned and operated by CoreCivic, formerly Corrections Corporations of America. The facility's namesake—T. Don Hutto—was one of the founders of this company, which happens still to be the nation's largest and most lucrative private prison company.[6]

The facility began such operations in 2006, converted originally from an adult prison, and was closed shortly thereafter in 2009 as a family detention center as a result of strong litigation against its practices, which many characterized as abusive and intending to lead to greater deportations, rather than the fair adjudication of asylum claims (Sakuma 2015).

---

administrative removal" or who have had a "prior order of removal" from the United States must undergo a reasonable fear interview. Others who do not have this record will undergo a credible fear interview. Unfortunately and confoundingly, the burden of proof for passing the reasonable fear interview is much higher than for the credible fear interview, putting those who have previous records at an unfair disadvantage in their interview (USCIS 2019a, 2019b).

6. "CoreCivic Inc | AFSC Investigate," accessed May 21, 2024. https://investigate.afsc.org/company/corecivic.

Local and national legal advocates and activists played critical roles in both the aid and attention given to detainees in that facility as well as its closure. The ending of the Hutto facility's incarceration of families was the end of what was, at the time, "large-scale family detention."[7] Yet, the practice of incarcerating asylum-seeking families did not cease with its closure. Some of those held in Hutto during the process of its closure were then transferred to the much smaller family detention facility of Berks, which had continued to detain these groups throughout this brief history.

The Obama administration then expanded the use of family detention for asylum-seeking parents with minor-age children. The Artesia Family Residential Center, in Artesia, New Mexico, was the first "large-scale" family facility since the closure of the Hutto facility. This facility was opened on June 24, 2014, with a capacity for several hundred detainees, as officially the first facility created as a response to the increasing arrivals of asylum-seeking women and children. Legal advocates who volunteered their services to detainees at this center noted in a report they produced, following what would be the quick closure of this facility, that, like the infamous "deportation mill" of Hutto, the Obama administration's stated purpose with this facility was to serve as a sort of initial claim processing center which, officials believed, would lead to quicker deportations.[8] Several federal officials either implied or explicitly stated that they believed the majority of the claimants held in these facilities would eventually be deported, as they were unlikely to have "legitimate" asylum claims. In a press conference in June 2014, then–Vice President Joe Biden recognized both the vulnerability of recent migrant families, particularly from the Northern Triangle, and the dangerous realities that they were facing in their home countries that led them to seek asylum. Yet, he stated, "Once an individual's case is fully heard, and if he or she does not qualify for asylum, he or she will be removed from the United States and returned home. Everyone should know that. We expect many

7. "April Recess Family Detention Background and Talking Points," Detention Watch Network, accessed November 21, 2020. https://www.detentionwatchnetwork.org/sites/default/files/DWN%20Family%20Detention%20Backgrounder%20and%20Talking%20Points.pdf.

8. "The Artesia Report," accessed May 21, 2024, https://perma.cc/4CU6-WBWY.

of the recent immigrants—migrants I should say—to fall into this category. My guess is a vast majority, and they will be going home" (Office of the Vice President 2014). Data provided by one of the organizations—Innovation Law Lab—involved in legal advocacy at Artesia and then later facilities demonstrated the substantial drop in the credible fear passing rate during the exact time of the opening of this facility.[9] Coupled with administrative comments like those of former Vice President Biden, advocates believed that these facilities, like those that preceded them, functioned primarily as deportation centers and were not truly dedicated to the fair adjudication of detained applicants' claims. Rather than demonstrating the invalid nature of applicants' claims, advocates suggested, the drastic statistical drop in those passing fear interviews reflected the government's true aim of increasing deportations.

Claims of poor treatment and health services, excessive punishments, and abuse plagued the Artesia facility, and mere months after its opening, the government announced it would be closing (Del Bosque 2014). At the moment of the Artesia facility's closure in December 2014, however, Jeh Johnson stood in front of that sparse audience of reporters to usher in the opening of the South Texas Family Residential Center, what would become the largest migrant family detention center in U.S. history. Along with the South Texas facility, the Karnes County Residential Center and the Berks County Residential Center comprised the total landscape of family detention until the practice ended, albeit temporarily, in 2021. The practice of detaining families together has since returned at the outset of the second Trump administration, though reconfigured slightly; this will be discussed in the concluding chapter.[10]

As an anthropologist, I conducted my ethnographic field research on the facilities in Dilley and Karnes City. Still in operation, the South Texas Family Residential Center—known by legal advocates and activists as

9. "The Artesia Report," accessed May 21, 2024, https://perma.cc/4CU6-WBWY.

10. For the purposes of this book, I've included here only a brief account of the history of family detention and its associated facilities in the United States. Schrag (2020) offers an extremely thorough and helpful account of this history and the litigation surrounding these facilities and advocates' resistance to them. Harris (2018), cited in this text, also offers important contextualization of the return of family detention and legal advocates' responses to offer counsel and contest the practice.

FIGURE 3 The entrance to the Karnes County Residential Center. Credit Erin Routon.

simply "Dilley"—was at the time of my research the largest detention center in the country, located approximately an hour's drive south of San Antonio. With a capacity for 2,400 detainees, the facility rivals the population of the town in which it is situated and eclipses the capacity of the neighboring state prison, the Dolph Briscoe Unit of the Texas Department of Criminal Justice.[11] Dilley is contractually owned and managed by CoreCivic, the private prison corporation that once owned the Hutto facility. Also still a functioning migrant detention center, the Karnes County Residential Center has much in common with the Dilley facility, but it has a different history. "Karnes," as it is known by advocates, is located about an hour's drive east of Dilley. Karnes is owned and managed by the nation's second largest private prison corporation, the GEO Group Inc.[12] Prior to this modern instantiation of family detention, Karnes was

11. "Unit Directory," accessed April 21, 2020, https://www.tdcj.texas.gov/unit_directory/db.html.

12. "The GEO Group Inc | AFSC Investigate," accessed April 21, 2020, https://investigate.afsc.org/company/geo-group.

an adult-only migrant detention facility. Slightly ahead of the Dilley facility's opening, Karnes was converted to a family facility, though with a far smaller capacity of around five hundred beds.

These facilities on which I conducted my research and within which I worked as a volunteer legal advocate were institutionally complex spaces. Although they were officially ICE detention facilities, they were owned and managed by the aforementioned private prison corporations. Along with LaSalle Corrections and the Management and Training Corporation, these corporations own and operate most immigrant detention facilities in the United States (Cho 2021). The facility administrator, or "warden," as they were frequently referred to by detainees, staff, and legal advocates, is employed by the managing corporation. The various staff were also employed by these corporations. Additionally, because they functioned as spaces intended to initially adjudicate asylum claims, officers for U.S. Citizenship and Immigration Services and immigration judges had an important presence within them as well. The fact that these facilities were composed of many different federal and nonfederal entities had an important impact on not only the complex management of these spaces, among sometimes competing interests, but also the various roles that legal advocates came to play and the challenges they faced in doing their work.

THE ADVOCATES

This book portrays just one image of family detention, one that looks at these places and their concomitant issues through the lens of the legal advocates who migrated through them. They were the group of people I was meeting with that early evening for the first time in 2015, mere months after the opening of the South Texas Family Residential Center. Legal advocates, by which I mean mixed groups of volunteers and nonprofit staff, showed up daily to the Dilley and Karnes centers to provide free, universal legal aid to those detained. At the South Texas Family Residential Center, these advocates were part of a nonprofit project known, at the conclusion of my research, as the Dilley Pro Bono Project (DPBP), which had provided necessary legal services since the center's opening. This project was formerly named the CARA Pro Bono Project, CARA

FIGURE 4 Portrait of a legal advocate caring for detained child. Credit Molly McGowan.

being an acronym of the collective of associated nonprofits: the Catholic Legal Immigration Network, Inc. (CLINIC), the American Immigration Council (AIC), the Refugee and Immigrant Center for Education and Legal Services (RAICES), and the American Immigration Lawyers Association (AILA). At the Karnes facility, the Texas-based organization RAICES alone offered the same services and others as well. Whereas the DPBP focused its efforts on providing direct services to detainees while advocating for the closure of family detention facilities through remote litigation practices, RAICES, as a larger, local organization devoted to a number of different services for immigrants, provided direct services to detainees as well as various services beyond incarceration.

The DPBP was originally born out of a group of individuals, many of them attorneys, who volunteered their services to those incarcerated in the Artesia facility. Legal advocates began traveling to Artesia to aid detainees as a result, in part, of the exceptional dearth of legal resources available to detainees in the small, isolated town in New Mexico. Because detainees were limited in their ability to maintain contact with the world beyond the detention center, they were unprepared for asylum interviews and were, as documented by advocates, being denied necessary resources, like interpreters, to communicate their claims to asylum officers. Thus, denial rates in detainees' asylum interviews were remarkably, unusually high (Schrag 2020).

Legal advocates, at first, struggled to gain access to detainees to help them with their cases. Only one of the early ways in which this materialized was through keeping the identities of those detained unavailable to them; without this identifying information, they were unable to schedule visitations. Other barriers resulted from larger issues inherent to the rather ambiguous status of immigrant detention itself—as not a "criminal" but "civil" or administrative carceral space—as well as those affected by the lack of guaranteed access to legal counsel for "noncitizens," unlike that legally guaranteed to imprisoned U.S. citizens (Harris 2018). These barriers to ensuring immigrants, both in court processes and detention, have access to legal counsel, even when not afforded by the government, are not new but have a lengthy history in this country, with legal advocates having long fought to secure such necessary contact (National Immigration Law Center 2016). Many legal scholars have documented these barriers in terms of litigation and extensions of legal rights, though my research adds to other records that recognize how these barriers take shape in practical, everyday forms, regardless of legal conditions ("The Right to Be Heard" 2018). Such was the case with these projects, which were affected by both these institutional and structural forms of refusal through which advocates navigated.

Eventually, though, as these advocates began to routinize access, they were able to offer representative assistance, preparing them for interviews and in-detention courtroom defenses. Advocates' "on the ground," meaning in-person, work in and around these facilities was aided by remote volunteers and a complex cloud-based digital platform, created by lawyer Stephen Manning, through which cases could be documented and information could be shared with many individuals contributing to efforts. In this way, data on new "clients," as they referred to them, could be stored and passed along within communities of voluntary advocates, rather than a single individual needing to remain there, representing a single family.

Advocates with these groups contended that the practice of family detention constituted an unnecessary, cruel, and unusual form of treatment of asylum-seeking parents and children and, knowing the complexities inherent in navigating the asylum process, committed to a kind of universal representation of all detainees while simultaneously litigating for the closure of these facilities. Thus, unlike in most immigration defense settings, all detainees had the option of detailed, individual assistance regardless of the purported merits of their case or financial capabilities. This was critical for several reasons, not least because most applicants could not afford legal assistance with their cases. Without the help of volunteer legal advocates, those detainees would have had little hope of assistance with their cases while incarcerated in remote locations (Human Rights Watch 2009). The advocates' presence also proved critical because it was difficult to "pass" an asylum interview without prior legal advice, as Artesia advocates documented. Additionally, while the Trump administration effected numerous changes to asylum law that negatively impacted the likelihood of success for applicants, my observations of this process initially during the Obama administration also demonstrated this difficulty. The interview itself was and continues to be fraught with issues, from interpretation inadequacies to procedural failures to outright subversive, antagonistic behavior on the part of some asylum officials. It was clear that preparation and continued legal assistance were of vital importance.

Both these aid projects were composed of a small number of paid staff and temporary volunteers. Staff for the Dilley project were hired on a limited contractual basis, and during the period of my field research, they lived communally in the rented ranch home, mentioned earlier, near the facility where volunteer trainings and meetings took place. Temporary volunteers would travel to the area, residing in one of the few local motels, and offer their skills and services to the project. Notably, it was these nonlocal volunteers that did much of the daily work in detention. These migratory volunteers received training from project staff members on the ground, typically serving the projects for a week before being replaced with a new group. The volunteers ranged in associations and experience with the law and legal practice; some were lawyers or law students; others were doctors, social workers, or interpreters. Some had experience working or volunteering with asylum cases, while others had none. The organizations generally welcomed all who were interested in helping regardless of their expertise, but they emphasized the need for particular skills, primarily language or legal experience. The Karnes project functioned similarly to the Dilley project, but because RAICES provided many different services, as a large organization, there was a team specifically designated for work with family detainees. Staff members, who lived in and around San Antonio and commuted to Karnes City, would rotate their time at the facility along with volunteers.

Each week in these "baby jails" (as advocates called them), detainees' cases were passed along to a new group of advocates via the same vast online case management system previously used in Artesia.[13] These projects depended heavily on such forms of collective action: not only did advocates rely on the work of previous volunteers, but in daily practice, they also depended on one another to manage difficult cases and overcome myriad bureaucratic or legalistic roadblocks that arose, sharing different skills. The members' diverse backgrounds and expertise made the projects dependent on collective knowledges—for example, about asylum and immigration law, responses to trauma, and approaches in working with children. While advocates often worked individually with detainees, collaboration with others frequently unfolded in the background.

Although mostly beneficial to detainees, time limits in family detention significantly strained advocates' work, playing a major role in the frenetic, often crisis-like environment of the center. An important court decision known as the *Flores Settlement Agreement* made the case that children could be held in detention but only for brief periods. In 2015, in District Court Judge Dolly Gee's ruling on the agreement's terms, children were to be released "without necessary delay" (Preston 2015). This

---

13. I use both terms, "detainee" and "client," to refer to the women and children detained in these facilities. Even though "resident" was the term most often used by administrators in detention—and indeed is a characteristic term for facilities operated by some private prison organizations, like CoreCivic—I find this euphemistic term extremely misleading, so I only reproduce it in references to what I would deem propagandistic projects deployed by administrators and government officials. "Detainee" is an accurate term for these individuals, though client was the term used nearly universally by legal advocates, aside from the more personal language referring to the women and children.

came to be interpreted as no longer than twenty days.[14] While the government officially recognized this decision, often claiming they did not breach this deadline, many detained parents and children had been held beyond, some well beyond, twenty days. During fieldwork, I encountered some parents and children who had been held for months, while others were detained closer to a year. The Berks facility was known by many advocates to be where detainees were sent to be held for longer time than those in Texas, though the reasons for this were often unclear. Nonetheless, this seemingly arbitrary deadline made processes move quickly in detention, meaning that advocates had little time to prepare their clients for critical moments or to respond to deportation attempts. Thus, the "expedited" pace of the work environment typically resulted in fleeting encounters rather than prolonged care engagements.

Another challenge related to these time constraints had to do with the specific legal category for asylum under which most detainees' cases fell. There are different acceptable categories for asylum, though most applicants' cases there, during the period of my research, fell under the category determined by persecution based on "membership within a particular social group" (PSG).[15] The conceptual category was vague, but it was the category where the majority of victims of intimate partner or gang violence were placed. It was often more difficult for asylum seekers to prove their belonging in such "groups," so advocates spent more time discussing with clients many details of their pasts to build a stronger case for their membership, potentially locating aspects of their experiences that applicants might not have considered as playing an important role in their claim. The ill-defined boundaries of the PSG category were discussed and debated repeatedly between advocates as they worked with clients, trying to make sense of how their experiences could or could not fit within this category. Thus, just as detainees tried to make sense of complex asylum law and its limitations, so did advocates.

To clarify, these advocates did not seek to help detainees "win" an asylum case, an extremely long legal process that, even during my field

14. *Reno v. Flores*, 507 U.S. 292 (1993), United States Supreme Court, 23 March 1993, accessed April 21, 2020, https://www.refworld.org/cases,USSCT,4152e0ff24.html.

15. Legal Information Institute, "8 U.S. Code § 1158—Asylum," accessed April 21, 2020, https://www.law.cornell.edu/uscode/text/8/1158.

research, took on average multiple years (American Immigration Council 2024). Some volunteers who were professional lawyers could continue representation of clients after their release and elected to do so. These advocates primarily fought for the release of detainees so they could reunite with family, friends, and services, having the opportunity to properly prepare their asylum claim or pursue another form of relevant legal status. While advocates performed many different tasks in detention, arguably the most critical was to prepare clients for their interview so that they could secure the passing decision that would allow their release. Thus, most of the work revolved around preparing clients for this, with advocates repeatedly demonstrating the value of such forms of preparation.

Detainees did not have effective access to legal processual information from the government or facility contractors; few even understood where they were or how they had ended up there, much less what the asylum process entailed. Some did not encounter anyone who spoke their language until they met with these advocates, who frequently used their collective resources to locate remote interpreters. As suggested already, these should be considered part of the larger, ongoing landscape of issues related to the government's obstruction of legal counsel to specifically asylum seekers (National Immigration Justice Center 2023; Human Rights First 2022). As such, the effort of advocates' work derived primarily from a need to prepare families to achieve a sort of legal consciousness (Merry 1990) for their interviews in which they are required to articulate their case in terms meaningful to asylum officers, without the aid of legal translators (Cunningham 1992) or expert witnesses (Good 2006). While these legal projects collectively supported their detained clients, advocates could not officially speak on their behalf in interviews or in court proceedings taking place in the facility, thus necessitating quick work that helped clients understand the expectations set on them.

Back at the ranch house in 2015, I sat on a tired, torn couch, listening to a presentation. "This isn't a migrant crisis; it's a *refugee* crisis," Jason said firmly, standing at the front of the living room, his PowerPoint slides glowing behind him.[16] Jason was an immigration lawyer from Ohio, and

16. I use pseudonyms for all advocates in the following chapters, with the exception of one (the artist for one of the images). When detainees are mentioned "by name," I

FIGURE 5 Living room of the ranch. Credit Erin Routon.

in that moment, he was the managing attorney for the Dilley project, meaning that he was the official legal representative for those detained at the center, though the efforts of the project were done collectively. He wore a faded, wrinkled T-shirt and shorts, and although his eyes looked tired, he spoke and moved his hands about energetically. He gave his portion of the "orientation" training to us new volunteers, instructing us all on what we were about to be doing starting early tomorrow morning, when we'd enter the "legal visitation" building of the center.

When I sat down moments before, I couldn't take my eyes off Abe's shirt from across the room. It was tie-dyed, with a colorful butterfly and "Costa Rica" imprinted in the middle. Abe was an immigration lawyer from Tampa in the process of retiring, he told me, and he came with his close friend Lily, a psychotherapist, hoping that her Spanish-speaking skills would help him in working with primarily Spanish-speaking clients.

use a combination of pseudonyms and a mixing of personal or narrative details so as to obscure identification of any individual.

Lily wore a pair of rainbow-colored socks with strappy Velcro sandals and sat next to Abe. "I don't know how much help I'm going to be with everything. I don't have any legal experience," she said in the kitchen earlier as we scooped out our pasta generously made by the staff team onto paper plates.

I was seated between Millie and Darius. Millie was in her twenties, an immigration lawyer from Charlotte who came on her own to Dilley at her firm's suggestion. Darius also came on his own, arriving directly from a Peace Corps mission in Guatemala, where he had been living for nearly a year. He was also in his twenties and, like Lily, didn't have any previous legal experience but figured his language skills might prove helpful. Esther and Vera were seated across the room in front of a tall bookcase containing case law texts and various other books, like *The New Jim Crow* and *Wildflowers of Texas: A Field Guide.* They came together, both working for one of the project's nonprofit collaborators, CLINIC. Esther, a Nicaraguan American, had recently graduated from college, was in her early twenties, and came intending mostly to serve as an interpreter for Vera. Vera was an attorney, tall and thin with bright red hair, and an immigrant from Russia. Next to Esther and Vera was Madeleine, actually Sister Madeleine, a nun who lived in Albuquerque but drove out once a month to volunteer with the Dilley project. Sister Madeleine grew up in Queens and had short, graying hair and a surprisingly biting sense of humor.

Ryan, Denise, and Henry walked in late, as their flight was delayed. Ryan and Henry were immigration lawyers and Denise a paralegal, all working out of the same firm in Virginia. Ryan and Henry both wore full suits each day in detention, with the possibility that they might have to go to "court," or the courtroom constructed in the facility to display the remotely televised judge who adjudicated appeals. A group of project staff members and long-term volunteers were seated at the dining table set off to the side. Some of them watched the presentation but most faced their open, glowing laptop screens, continuing to work late into the evening on the legal cases of those detained. There was Amelia, a young Latine attorney staffed by the project; Abbas, a recent graduate who was volunteering through a fellowship with the national organization Immigrant Justice Corps; Alexa and Daniel, both long-term, nonattorney volunteers; and Mark, a nonattorney staff member who would end up being one of the longest-serving staff members in its history.

Jason continued, covering topics like the basics of asylum law and decision statistics of the facility's judges. Mark then took over, explaining how to use the online database of clients' cases and describing the ways that we were expected to behave and dress in the facility. Even though rules did exist, he noted, as administrators used them to bar entry to legal advocates, CoreCivic refused to give them any official, written guidance on such things. "Every week," he explained, "they put up new barriers, like this, to providing counsel to our clients." Abbas finished the presentation, emphasizing why we were there and the stakes of our efforts, as well as what sorts of conditions need to be observed and documented, like denial of medical care. This is what the project officially described as their "advocacy" work, that which the organizations could potentially use in antidetention litigation efforts. He told us that every child we'd meet would be sick, that we'd hear a lot of frustrating things about how women and children had been treated at the border and at these facilities, and that the two most common emotions we'd feel that week were anger and sadness. "When you meet these women and children, that will be the first time anyone in the U.S. has truly listened to them," he said seriously, continuing,

> ICE lies to these people, misleads them every day. It is our job to help them. It's our job to clarify this confusing stuff for them, to correct ICE's lies. And it's our job to treat them with respect, not like criminals. When you drive into the facility tomorrow, you'll notice that there's a big sign at the entrance with the closing stock price for CCA [CoreCivic] printed on it. This is a corporate internment camp. Our real goal is to shut this place down.

LEGAL CARE

In describing the collaborative history of the Dilley project's approach to such work, their now-defunct website once claimed, "This concept of what some called 'lawyer camp' captured the hearts and minds of willing volunteers. Rather than just taking over a paper file handed to them, they were taking over the legal care of a human being desperately needing their help."[17] The phrase "legal care" did not come into use on the ground.

17. Quoted from website, formerly caraprobono.org.

While I independently came to see the advocates' work as akin to care, after encountering this language on the site, I wondered what might in fact constitute legal care. My conceptual use of this phrase owes much intellectually to the anthropological and feminist theorizations of care cited further in this work. Legal care, in my use, draws attention to the ways that legal practitioners perform and share experiences as caregivers. In this formulation of care work, the law sits in a central position. It is the mechanism that brings about the need for care, as it is used to incarcerate and isolate those seeking a form of protected status in the United States. However, it also brings those needing care in detention into contact with those positioned in some way to assist with its provision. As this book will show, the law was simultaneously used as a tool for the provision and denial of care. In this setting, the law—as practiced and struggled with daily—becomes knowable (Mountz 2010) through its relationship to care.

Scholarship on care has a long, cross-disciplinary history, stirring important debates and new forms of social recognition. Marjorie Murray et al. (2017) contend that anthropological research on care, despite recently having expanded to studies of everyday encounters "beyond the clinical," has historically centered on the fields of health care. Care has long existed in the studies of feminist anthropologists and sociologists, science and technology researchers, and scholars broadly associated with the study of work, some of which have looked precisely at the clinical, others beyond it, examining the various forms of relationality and interaction that intimately involve care (e.g., Hochschild 1983; Tronto 1993; Boris and Parreñas 2010; Garcia 2010). Nevertheless, such research has rarely directly considered the relationship between care and the work of lawyers and other legal practitioners.

Care is analytically useful for understanding legal advocacy and the relationships in which legal advocates engage for several reasons. To start, legal assistance, in a general sense, is commonly interpreted as a unidirectional, often unsentimental encounter for those providing the assistance; scholars remind us of the many ways in which legal education itself often encourages a "casting aside" of personal emotions or empathy in favor of supposed neutrality and legal authority (Mertz 2007; Sarat and Scheingold 2004). Of course, legal anthropologists and migration scholars have demonstrated the extent to which legal encounters, especially those involving refugee or otherwise migratory groups, are fraught with emotions that engage all associated parties (e.g., Coutin 2000, 2016). My research affirms and builds on this insight. What I observed during fieldwork with legal advocates indicated an expansive form of assistance, attention, and relationality, far exceeding the limitations of aid or assistance and refuting a perception of their work as unidirectionally affective. What advocates did and how they articulated their roles led me, in a sense, to care. Advocates showed deep involvement in emotion work and emotional labor and experienced multidirectional affective exchanges that informed their own subjectivities and resulted, at times, in traumatic aftereffects. Care moved through the ways in which they practiced legal advocacy, tending to detainees and each other, and managing their conflicted relationships with administrators.

This book illustrates why care matters not only in how we understand these spaces and the work of legal advocates but also in how it brings into focus certain relational and institutional complexities. Taking a cue from the project's previous usage, I suggest a novel conceptual term—legal care—as a way to approach such forms of labor and relational encounters. Legal care offers a pathway to recognizing the work of legal advocates and aid workers as care work without disavowing the central role that the law plays within such contexts. It is, at its core, an extension of care into the legal practical terrain, and using such a concept effectively encourages a reconsideration of what constitutes vital, necessary forms of care, especially in immigrant detention.

María Puig de la Bellacasa (2017, 8) encourages becoming "involved with care as a living terrain that [needs] to be constantly reclaimed from idealized meanings, from the constructed evidence that, for instance, associates care with a form of unmediated work of love accomplished by idealized carers." Legal advocacy in family detention should by no means be interpreted as an "unmediated work of love," and legal practitioners are often far from the imagined ideal of a caregiving subjectivity. This is not to say that loving or deeply felt sentiments did not play a significant role in how these advocates interpreted their experiences; they often did. The intensity of what were fleeting encounters informed this. This is also not to say that legal practitioners did not possess or project idealized caregiving qualities. What this book asserts is a reclamation of care not delimited by either of these. In feeling terms, care was as much characterized by anger and sadness in this environment as it was by love or joy.

Similarly, caregivers negotiated conflicted interests and contradictory roles in their daily work, leading to more ambiguous feelings. The depiction of care that follows, then, represents ranging sentiments around care as well as the "compromised, shifting, and ambiguous dimensions of care practice" (Cook and Trundle 2020, 178).

The marginalization of care (Lawson 2007)—the unrecognition of the ways in which care is denied to some while affording others significant privileges—speaks to the need for greater attention to the subject in different environments and spheres of relationality. What motivates or influences the need for care to be given here, and what forms of recognition do caregivers receive? Victoria Lawson (2007, 7) suggests that individual relations of care involve "understanding how difference is socially constructed, and [thus] a critical ethic of care must be coupled with analysis of the structures and institutions that reproduce exclusion, oppression, [and] environmental degradation," among other things. This reminds us of the importance of analyzing why advocates are needed in such spaces in the first place. Although many advocates experienced what they characterized as transformative experiences in this work, most recognized that legal services should be guaranteed to detainees while also agreeing that asylum seekers should not be incarcerated.

Conceptually, legal care embodies significant potential for making sense of care practices in different sorts of social encounters. These advocates were typically not health-care professionals and thus not meant to offer aid in such ways, yet their work constituted a form of care labor, one that sometimes overlapped with bodily care.[18] There were significant stakes in the kinds of services they provided. As they helped asylum seekers navigate the legal processual complexities and the institutional ambiguities of incarceration, advocates tended to the many "wounds" created by such structures. My research thus necessarily engages with care as both an analytic device—useful not only for understanding the labor of advocates but also of these facilities' environments and own identifications with care—as well as an ethic. Ultimately, this book demonstrates the generativity and indeed the imperative of recognizing the contours

18. There were some medical professionals who volunteered with these organizations, but this was rare and not the primary function of these projects, which was to provide legal assistance.

of legal care work, affirming the claim that "if care practices are not carefully attended to, there is a risk that they will be eroded" (Mol, Moser, and Pols 2010b, 7). Especially in spaces where crucial services are more actively faced with erosion, sometimes through care-adjacent tactics, immediate attention and recognition are essential.

To properly treat advocates' work as care work, though, some conceptual outlines must first be sketched. While care often breaches categorical boundaries (Alber and Drotbohm 2015), it might be broadly understood as something involving both practical and sentimental, or affective elements. Care, in other words, is simultaneously done, thought, and felt. Starting with Joan C. Tronto and Berenice Fisher's broad definition of care as "everything that we do to maintain, continue, and repair 'our world' so that we can live in it as well as possible" (Tronto 1993, 103), my analysis also aligns with especially feminist scholarly views of care that emphasize its embodied, situated, and contingent qualities (e.g., Hamington 2004; Puig de la Bellacasa 2017) and caring practices as characterized, in part, by their relationality and interdependency (e.g., Kittay and Feder 2002; Cooper 2018) and fantastical or "imaginal" potentialities (Hunleth 2019). Annemarie Mol, Ingunn Moser, and Jeannette Pols's (2010a) articulation of care, which involves "tinkering" on uncertain grounds and living with "the erratic"—emphasizing unpredictability as well as a commitment to continuous engagement—is instructive for making sense of such emergent and urgent environs and legal advocates' necessarily experimental tinkerings. The inner world of family detention was truly an erratic one, and legal advocates' efforts to give care required constant flexibility and experimentation. Care does not take one solid shape in this book but rather shifts its form to suit the needs of different encounters and desires, often informed by fractious relations between advocates and administrators.

Care is also interpreted here as a form of resistance or counteractivity. The troubled or unsettled feelings of care (Murphy 2015) that advocates experienced in their daily work inside the facility—as they struggled against administrators, policies, and practices that did harm to detainees and themselves—demonstrates how care takes what appears as counterintuitive forms. In the illustrations that follow, what becomes apparent is the necessity of thinking of care not only as practice but also as something through which we think (Puig de la Bellacasa 2012, 2017). Facility administrators' repeatedly harmful yet carefully crafted actions align with what Miriam Ticktin (2011, 5) calls the "antipolitics" of care in which "brutal measures may accompany actions in the name of care and rescue . . . [and] ultimately work to reinforce an oppressive order." It's important to chart how violence may be evoked by acts intended as care, sometimes through expressions of indifference or "uncare" (Mulla 2014; Gupta 2012). Yet, it's also important to not draw simple boundaries around what constitutes care, denying its "messiness," as even within such objectively violent spaces, "compromised or wounding care still does the work of care" (Trundle 2020, 211). What these encounters will show is how, in situations with differently positioned participants, what counts as care or harm is constructed and contested through everyday practices. In each context, care is repeatedly understood as relative to the "ways in which someone comes to matter" (Stevenson 2014, 3), and this process of becoming is often a site of struggle.

In this way, care, especially in such an environment, cannot be fully understood without the kinds of frictions that shape it, both as an ethic or moral framework as well as a practical arrangement. Indeed, scholars have repeatedly shown how care does not "solely entail positive associations, sentimentality, or good intentions but rather involves tensions and frictions, including power asymmetries" (Coe 2019, 13; also citing Mol 2010 and Stevenson 2014). My analysis here is especially influenced by Anna Tsing's (2005, 4) use of friction, which itself is not meant to be equivalent to resistance but rather a way of describing the coproduction of cultures through the "awkward, unequal, unstable, and creative qualities of interconnection across difference" (also citing Clifford 1997b). Contrary to common usage, friction in this sense is understood as encouraging movement rather than only inhibiting it. The movement, or culture, of care in these spaces is defined by this sort of friction, in turn defining the contours of resistance. Further, as different actors and entities "grate" against one another in their work, there is an inevitable "wearing down," though not experienced evenly. These forms of erosion that unfold as a result inform our understanding of how care materializes amid conflict, which also help us make sense of future concerns around legal caregiving.

The research that this book presents is situated at a crossing point, an intersection of both ideas and spaces. This is in part a result of the complex nature of these facilities—as not only carceral spaces but also ones that function explicitly to adjudicate asylum cases—but also discursively, because it centers the work and experiences of a historically underresearched, though similarly complex, group. Much cross-disciplinary scholarship has explored legal work with asylum applicants and immigrants (e.g., James and Killick 2012; Eagly and Shafer 2015; Ryo 2018), with some giving necessary attention to lawyers and paralegals as ethnographic subjects (e.g., Henderson 1987; Pierce 1995, 1999). Others have focused on lawyers and legal practitioners as advocates and activists (e.g., Abel 1995; Sarat and Scheingold 2005; Merry 2006), but this type of representation demands more attention, particularly in today's political climate and related responses from advocacy communities. Ultimately, legal practitioners rarely receive consideration as caregivers, and yet as I illustrate, they often practice care. Interpretations of legal advocates' work and experiences, then, are understood through scholarly conversations on care beyond legal spheres.

This work also intersects with research on the constant manipulations of immigration, or "crimmigration" laws (e.g., Stumpf 2006; Hernández 2015; Dowling and Inda 2013), the use of incarceration and deportation as strategies to punish variously groups with various statuses (e.g., Boehm and Terrio 2019; DeGenova and Peutz 2010), and how those have affected migrant communities (e.g., Gonzales 2013) and those within their relational orbit, especially those "collaterally" impacted by such shifts. With the continuing rise in the global rate of incarceration, generally (Fassin 2017), and immigrant detention, specifically (Ryo and Peacock 2018b; Sampson and Mitchell 2013), more research on the lives and relations that circulate through these increasingly unexceptional spaces is needed. The ensuing chapters affirm the complicated relations between humanitarian actors and state entities that seek to exclude migrants, while also demonstrating the unique form of "penal humanitarianism" (Bosworth 2017) at work in family detention. In other contexts, administrative officials come to express their power through caring, moral, or explicitly humanitarian language and logics (Feldman and Ticktin 2010; Fassin 2012; Fassin and Brown 2015), particularly when deployed in relation to a real or imagined "emergency" (Calhoun 2010; Fassin and Pandolfi 2010); this is also evident here. Finally, although the work of these advocates must be understood within the context of existing critiques of humanitarian intervention in migration emergencies and collaborations with punitive or otherwise oppressive and exclusionary state entities (Rozakou 2012; Ticktin 2011; Tyler et al. 2014), my research focuses most greatly on those daily challenges faced by migrant advocates (Agustín 2007) and those diverse groups compelled to navigate restrictive asylum processes (Mountz 2010).

THE DIRT

Although social scientific research can provide essential insights into the lived experiences within the carceral space, it is important to recognize the challenges in even attempting to conduct such research. Lorna Rhodes (2001, 68) offers a clear consideration of the complicated ethical role engendered by this form of study, particularly with respect to work on prisons: "The academic study of prisons is enmeshed in [a] contradiction: On the one hand, the appearance of 'objectivity' contributes to the abstraction that protects these sites from view, while on the other, the intense engagement runs the danger of a compulsive intimacy with the terms provided by the prison itself." Yet despite its challenges, Rhodes still finds hope in our discipline's ability to illuminate such spaces, calling for anthropological engagement as the "carceral archipelago" (Foucault 1977) spreads.

Partially because of these problematic elements in conducting such research, there is still a limited amount of ethnographic engagements from within the carceral space. Researchers have noted this dearth, offering a variety of historical explanations for why it has occurred (Tonry and Petersilia 1999; Wacquant 2002) and calling attention to how qualitative investigation can be intimately constrained by political actors and policies. Alexandra Hall (2012, 4) adds to this discussion by specifically noting the lack of engagements with im/migrant detention facilities, through extensive "occlusion and securitization" of such facilities. This is deeply concerning, especially given that not only does the United States infamously incarcerate its population at a higher rate than any other country, but it also maintains the world's largest migrant detention system (Widra 2024; Young 2020). Despite these historic absences, social scientists (e.g., Comfort 2008; Hall 2012; Heidbrink 2014; Martin 2012a, 2012b; Reed

2003; Rhodes 2004; Gilmore 2007) have investigated these spaces in various ways, and although it is largely true that "research on carcerality remains undertaken primarily by disciplines other than anthropology" (Khan 2022, 60), anthropological and sociological scholars have meaningfully extended our ethnographic record (e.g., Speed 2019; Sykes 1958; Vélez Young-Alfaro 2017). I aim here to contribute to those efforts, demonstrating how different carceral spaces are similarly disguised and securitized as well as showing how administrative actors enact forms of domination on those nonprisoner others, like legal advocates, that move throughout them.[19]

Even in choosing to center the narratives of these spaces through legal advocates' experiences, the nature of the carceral environment elicited a certain level of wariness among my would-be interlocutors. I came to understand this hesitancy better as I observed the tenuous relationship between various administrators of the facility, including staff, asylum officers, and judges, and on-the-ground legal advocates, creating an often hostile and untrusting environment. The wariness that I experienced at different periods from my interlocutors correlates with a larger point in this book, which is that what might be described as a kind of observational anxiety pervaded this environment, affecting all sorts of encounters. Detainees expressed wariness for numerous reasons, from not being entirely sure who they could trust to help them to fearing that there would be repercussions for what they chose to talk about in their inter-

19. I also believe that it is important to offer an example of some of the potential difficulties faced by scholars conducting research in detention. My research itself was shaped by many challenges, including those mentioned by other scholars. Obtaining institutional review board permission from the university with which I was associated to conduct research on this topic entailed, not unexpectedly, a difficult process. Ultimately, however, this was managed through my commitment to work as a volunteer while inside these centers, conducting any official interviews with advocate interlocutors outside these spaces. Thus, while I aimed to conduct ethnographic research with legal advocates, on their work, I did not operate officially as a researcher within detention but rather as a volunteer with these organizations, with whom I gained permission to conduct my research. This was a commitment that was also similarly important for the organizations managing these projects, who repeatedly, extensively supported my project, so I was happy to approach my research in this alternative way.

views. As such, advocates worked diligently to establish trusting relationships with them. Because of these and other understandable concerns, repeatedly demonstrating my commitment and trustworthiness to other advocates played a crucial role in conducting my research.

Showing commitment to these organizations was also necessarily related to the fact of their humanitarian nature, which itself posed unique challenges for this research. Didier Fassin (2011) has described the relationship between anthropology and humanitarianism as "uncomfortably intimate" in that although they often share sympathetic perceptions of the "human condition," certain claims that serve to cohere humanitarian thoughts and actions tend to evoke discomfort within the discipline of anthropology. While, for instance, the values of empathy and compassion are key to both anthropology and humanitarian work, and while anthropologists draw on humanitarian tropes when making ethical or political claims, anthropologists tend to be uncomfortable with stances of endorsement, which are often fundamental to the organizing tactics of humanitarian actors. Anthropologists, he argues, are more comfortable with a critical stance. While still recognizing this "uncomfortable intimacy," I was and remain an advocate and engaged anthropologist, devoted to much of the work of legal advocacy projects with migrant and incarcerated communities. The critical stance that I brought to my fieldwork was not diminished by my participation in these aid projects but was shaped over the time of my participation. With this, I also mean to make clear that my goal was not to assess the organizations themselves but rather to chart the work of these projects' participants and the constraints under which they labored.

My field research spanned the years 2015–19. I began preliminary fieldwork in Dilley in August 2015 with another brief volunteer stint in February 2016. In July 2016, I moved from Ithaca, New York, where I was attending graduate school, to South Texas to begin a continuous year of fieldwork, which I completed in July 2017. I returned for follow-up field visits in 2018 and 2019. Throughout this period, I conducted over 150 formal interviews and had many informal conversations with advocates while also logging hundreds of hours working as an advocate inside. All interviews took place outside of detention, and because of the passing nature of advocates in this work (which I discuss further along), many of my interviews took place over the phone, after they had recently left.

It is important to clarify the different "types" of advocates that comprised these projects and thus my research. There were project staff, weekly volunteers, and long-term volunteers, unpaid and sometimes paid interns. Because each of these groups spent different lengths of time at work in the facilities, their experiences differed significantly, and my research reflects this. Each chapter will involve both the perspectives of those who spent little time passing through Dilley or Karnes as well as those who remained for extended periods. Most of my interlocutors in this research, and in truth, most volunteers and project staff, identified as women, and at least a few identified as transgender or nonbinary. While most advocates that identified as men were similarly supportive of my research, the significance of the apparent overrepresentation of individuals identifying as women—both in participation in these projects and in my research—should not be overlooked, particularly as it corresponds to the overrepresentation of women in caregiving roles. Although important to note, this is not a defining point of conversation here, though it is something I hope to reflect on further in future research. Even though I did not officially document their ages, my observations and anecdotal data suggested that volunteers and staff members ranged broadly in age, from those in their late teens to retirees in their sixties and seventies. I estimate that most volunteers were between twenty-five and fifty-five years of age, while most project staff were in their twenties and thirties.

Unsurprisingly, particular political positionalities marked the predispositions of these advocates, sketching the boundaries of what constituted a "like-minded" individual in this environment. However, I would argue that this work drew in actors through different impetuses. Some adamantly opposed the incarceration of refugees, while others were primarily motivated by the injustice of incarcerating refugee children specifically. Some identified as immigrant rights activists, while others expressed hesitancy with such labels. Project staff expressed unambiguously activist stances toward not only migrant incarceration but also immigrant rights more broadly. Awareness of these positionalities not only helped shape my participation as a volunteer but also my understanding of how these worlds of legal advocacy were constructed and bounded.

There were furthermore ways in which legal advocates were socialized to care for and about detainees, as well as for the aims of these projects. From the earliest trainings, staff members' use of language quickly reflected this socialization. For instance, they suggested that detainees be referred to as "clients" to express to detainees with whom they worked the seriousness and professionalism with which they regarded their cases. It was important to communicate to them that they were believed in the stories that they shared with advocates, and that it was not the advocates' place or responsibility to question the "credibility" of any client. This approach was meant as a kind of counter to how they were likely to be received by officials adjudicating their claims, which was often proven to be the case. In certain moments, this socialization involved reminding advocates of the delicate balance that must be maintained in administrative relationships; while not identified thus, this was another element of the care work in which advocates engaged. Volunteers were further encouraged to remain actively involved beyond their on-the-ground work, suggesting that care for detainees should be thought of as a continuous project, extending beyond "direct services" in these centers to political actions. The boundaries of legal advocates' care were thus also understood by the constructions of these formal and informal socializations that took shape in and out of these facilities.

"So, is it typical for anthropologists to get down in the dirt and do the same work as the people that you're studying?" Gabby, a young volunteer attorney, asked me as we sat working in a small office room in Dilley. I had been with the project for just over ten months at that point and had received some version of this question from fellow advocates several times, and yet, I still found myself unable to muster a terribly satisfying answer. Even now, I question the possibility of clear boundaries around ethnographic participation in engaged research that involves this sort of urgent humanitarian effort. Maintaining dual, though entwined, roles—as a researcher and advocate—was difficult to navigate, leading to ethical and practical quandaries that I explore in other writing, but it was important that the efforts of these projects effectively assumed primacy over my research interests. This was not just a result of my official commitments in research, but as an engaged anthropologist, I am both dedicated to the practical applications of the product of ethnographic research as well as in its thoughtful conduct. This meant playing a direct, though not authoritative or instructive, role in these advocacy communities. I take seriously various applied scholars' calls for researchers to "orient themselves not simply to the study of advocates as political actors but to work for them, exploring those questions that have not been answered and [aiding] in efforts to effect social change" (Slack et al. 2018, xv). What follows, then, is my attempt at a "caring ethnography" (Yarris and Duncan 2024b) and ultimately a consideration of ethnography-as-care.

As a final comment on the "strangeness" of this ethnographic endeavor, I return to the fact that the environment and labor that I studied was indeed one characterized by ephemerality, not unlike the "ephemeral state" of other facilities in which nonprofits come to play outsized roles in providing essential services (Greenberg 2019). In this way, my research and the data expressed appear differently from many other ethnographies. The people and interactions shift and rotate, while it is the space and work that remain the same. This was not without its practical challenges, as with research "in the temporary scene, limited time is available to secure relationships, establish trust, evaluate informants' utility, and, if necessary, distance oneself from unproductive relationships" (Paulsen 2009, 516). At the same time, this ephemerality defined this space and, as such, is a necessary element in telling this story. The story that unfolds here, then, is often tethered less to the rich, personal detail of specific individuals and more to the practice of care itself. This doesn't belie the depths of relations explored here; to the contrary, my research demonstrates care's relational possibilities even in passing.

CHAPTERS

Each chapter draws out the many ways that care took shape inside these facilities, taking into account the constraints that affected care practices. I begin with a proper introduction to these facilities and the work done by legal advocates therein through an important concept to advocates' work as well as the experiences of detainees: orientation. Detainees and advocates alike underwent separate but overlapping orientations in preparation for what they would experience inside these centers. In chapter 1, I discuss this and deploy the concept of orientation further to orient the reader, focusing heavily on the important affective and emotional elements that defined these spaces and advocates' work, including the various sorts of "social whiplash" (Greenberg 2019) that accompanied such contrasting, ephemeral environments. Introducing these surroundings through the concept of "embodied space" (Low 2009) initiates an investigation into caregiving practices and experiences in which material conditions and sensations played a significant role. I also introduce the legal and institutional processes that detainees underwent in family detention that guided the services provided by advocates as they worked to create "spaces of care" (Conradson 2003).

One of the most critical functions of advocates' work involved preparing detainees for their asylum interview. This involved at least one private conversation ahead of the interview with an asylum officer where advocates discussed the details of an individual's asylum claim, helping to shape and narrate their cases on their own, as legal advocates were not allowed to "represent" or speak for detainees at this stage. Chapter 2 explores this encounter, considering how advocates expressed resistance through kinds of counternarratives and counterstorytelling (Delgado 1989). This challenged exclusionary mechanisms in this process, which inherently functions to differentiate "worthy" asylum seekers from those deemed "unworthy" or "bogus" (Nayak 2015). While the chapter attends largely to this preparatory conversation, it also addresses other ways that narratives and practices of counterstorytelling functioned in subtler forms in their work. I argue that in this kind of narrative care work, new stories and alternative realities were forged amid the "imaginative practices" (Malkki 2015) of advocates.

Chapter 3 demonstrates how advocates experienced frictions (Tsing 2005) in their care work through the unpredictable and frequently hostile environment in which they labored. In this environment, care work also entailed tending to other relationships, those with nondetainee actors and administrators. Exploring this side of their work shows the interdependency at play in the fractious everyday encounters between different actors. This sometimes arose from a kind of "friction of utility" that resulted in "competing expectations and practices of care" (Backe 2018, 464). This chapter shows how this was due, in part, to the exceptional and indeed "unstable" (Greenhouse, Mertz, and Warren 2002) nature of these centers, as spaces intentionally yet awkwardly identifying with care. Situating this next to the previous discussion further demonstrates the kind of emotional whiplash advocates often experienced in their diverse efforts, as expressions of power and forms of resistance necessarily fluctuated and shifted.

In chapter 4, I examine advocates' care work in two other spaces: the asylum interview and subsequent in-detention court proceedings. Legal advocates variously accompanied detainees to their interview and court, where those who received negative interview decisions sought to overturn the decision by having their case reviewed by an immigration judge. In both spaces, advocates were denied the ability to speak on behalf of their detained clients unless given permission by authorities in limited moments. Acting almost solely as observers or minor participants, then, advocates' care was necessarily reconfigured. Their care in these settings could be understood as falling within broad practical configurations: presence or accompaniment, witnessing, and documentation. These acts—of accompaniment or "being-with" (Horton 2024; Yarris and Duncan 2024b), bearing witness (Farmer 2005), and documentation as "countersurveillance"—are different but no less significant kinds of care "tactics." Their roles in these spaces, as more akin to friends or allies, extended the possibilities of how we might draw the boundaries around legal care in more muted encounters.

Chapter 5 explores the crossing of literal and symbolic boundaries. As detainees crossed beyond the carceral border, advocates crossed the threshold of the facility as their work came to an end. Whereas earlier chapters focus only on advocates' labor with and for detainees, here I look at how advocates themselves were accompanied by disturbing or unsettling experiences inherent to this work, which I characterize as a kind of "haunting." I continue an existing argument around consideration of how legal caregivers were similarly and uniquely impacted by the "continuum of violence" (Scheper-Hughes and Bourgois 2004, 1) that informs asylum and carceral norms, and how they were exposed to consequences of the "structural shrapnel" of destructive immigration processes (Caswell and Ruehs-Navarro 2023). Rather than making a sort of "clean break" with that violent continuum, advocates' experiences of leaving make further evident how such collateral effects of migrant incarceration and related punitive processes inflict harm on communities that surround those most directly impacted.

In chapter 6, I consider how those ambiguities, inadequacies, and even impurities in legal advocates' care were informed by the broader implications of their presence in these spaces. I engage more directly with the question of how "care proceeds amid uncertainty in contexts of relative scarcity" (Livingston 2012, 6). I explore how their labors were co-opted—principally by facility administrators—for aims that ran counter to theirs and how this affected their sense of their own contributions, responsibilities, and impact on those they hoped they helped. In another part, I look at how a form of hope played an important if paradoxical role among advocates, especially those familiar with the challenges beyond detention that lie ahead. I consider what a continuous presence in such spaces meant for the achievement of specifically abolitionist goals, and how the desire and commitment to care appeared to leave them, for good or bad, caught in an unjust system seemingly without end. Drawing on claims about movement as a political act (Jones 2017) and the significance of the figure of the "nomad" for our current and future times (Hamilakis 2018), I suggest a kind of "nomadic hope" as a way of approaching both unsettling uncertainties and painful continuities as we seek, through care, to "maintain, continue, and repair 'our world'" (Tronto 1993, 103).

The final chapter explores related policy and practical changes that have occurred since the conclusion of my field research, while also looking at probable shifts to come. I offer a reflection on my role and responsibilities as an engaged anthropologist, examining my own experience of traumatic "wounds" from research. Drawing from that, I consider the kinds of care that specifically ethnographers can provide their interlocutors, pointing to a need for greater awareness of such possibilities as well as unintended impacts. On the conceptual subject at the heart of this book, the conclusion responds to two principal questions: how does this story demonstrate both the significance and salience of the idea of "legal care," and how might it be usefully deployed beyond this context, across other instances of similar legal mobilizations? Taking seriously those appeals of care scholars for greater recognition and further critical reflections on the subject, the concluding chapter aims to consider the present and future potential for care in legal exchanges, while also thinking "beyond care, beyond help" (Ticktin 2011). I argue that engaging with and beyond legal care is simultaneously complicated and vital; this is especially relevant as we continue in an era fraught with material and symbolic violence toward migrant communities facing strained caregiving resources. Movement forward must involve a full accounting of the collateral consequences of institutional and structural harm, including those affective, experiential dimensions and impacts on those unexpected others who struggle to tend those wounds.

Last, a necessary clarification on the critical period in which this research took place. The ethnographic detail presented in this book largely covers the period from when the Obama administration had reinstituted the incarceration of asylum-seeking families to approximately halfway into the first Trump administration. Thus, while documenting the rebirth of family detention, I also witnessed administrative changes in legal policies and practices that dramatically impacted the constitution of family detention. What this book does not focus on—as this was beyond the scope of my research at the time—are the many other changes the Trump administration made that inflicted violence on asylum seekers attempting to seek safety in the United States, like the institution of new forms of detention and exclusion (Flagg and Calderón 2020). This is important to note for a few reasons, one being that it both draws attention to the harm these administrations have inflicted on asylum-seeking families but also because it highlights the adaptability of legal advocates engaged in forms of caring resistance as they navigate a rapidly shifting asylum landscape. The degree of violence imposed on refugees by solely the Trump administration far exceeded that of the preceding one; I certainly would not dispute this fact. This research is, nonetheless, a demonstration of how such violence and resistance persisted before and will continue long after.

BEGINNINGS

Back in Dilley in July 2016, a different group of strangers sat in the ranch house's mismatched couches and wooden chairs on a Sunday evening, eating messy tacos and sipping beer, before their first day in the facility next door. After introducing ourselves to one another, Allie stood up and began the evening's training presentation. Allie was a young lawyer originally from South Texas, then named as the new managing attorney of the DPBP project, moving from her home in New York City back to Texas for the role. "Our job," she said with a gentle seriousness,

> is to help these women and kids be their own advocates. They are strong, and they've gone through hell to get here. We're just going to help them

> continue to be that strong in this next step they've got to go through. This step is very complicated, and there's info that they need in order to get through this that they just don't have. There are some things that we can do on their behalf in this fight, but the most important thing we can do is to help them advocate for themselves, fight for themselves. This is about *them*, not us.

I heard this often during fieldwork. What advocates did and what they went through in their work was for them, those detained families, what *they* needed and deserved. And yet, telling the story of contemporary family detention would not be complete without a serious consideration of the role of those legal advocates. As long as Dilley, Karnes, and the Berks facilities operated as such, legal advocates had been present within, providing consistent, pro bono aid to those detained. As the Dilley and Karnes facilities replaced the center in Artesia, those same advocates began strategizing and organizing to prepare for a committed ongoing effort. As some who were the original volunteers in those spaces recounted to me, when they first started arriving at Dilley, they would be forced to wait for hours, sometimes the entire day, to even attempt to visit with detainees. Some days, they were simply turned away after waiting, denying detainees' rights to legal counsel. They persistently returned day after day, eventually being allowed inside. Each morning, they would cart in boxes of files, printers, intake documents and computers, and each evening, as visitation ended, they would pack it all up. They continued that cycle for weeks until eventually being allowed to establish a space within to meet with potential clients (which turned out to be nearly all of those detained). At Karnes, legal advocates continued throughout to cart their materials—printers, documents, and all—in and out of their meeting spaces daily, and on days where their access was challenged, they would sit and wait until they were allowed in. That waiting, I would learn, was itself an expression of care. Because these centers had but for only brief periods of time existed without their presence, legal advocates' efforts were integral parts of their processes.

What this book aims to do is recognize advocates' presence in these spaces as significant, and often critical, and complicate assumed borders separating care from something else. In helping detainees advocate for themselves, as they are forced to do for much of this stage, legal advocates became entangled in the complex, multidirectional circulations of care in these environments. They gave care, they received care, and they fought over care. They attempted to soothe the diverse pains of detention and asylum while also experiencing, or being reminded of, wounds of their own. While their liminal status left them struggling to navigate the frictions and ambiguities of caregiving, their relationships with detained families often, ironically, reached significant depths of familiarity. The story this book tells of family detention, then, serves as a kind of rejoinder to Allie's motivating claim. Understanding these spaces and institutional processes in yet-untold ways—how they felt and functioned from the perspective of legal actors that made them, in part, what they were—as well as making sense of how their collateral impacts reached far beyond those most directly affected, requires a reconsideration of how a story of *them* crosses paths with one of *us*.

CHAPTER 1

ORIENTATION

"What's your name? Who are you with?" The guard working the front desk stares at me blankly, like she's never seen me before in her life. We have, in fact, seen each other repeatedly over the past several months, but whereas I remember her face, she never seems to register mine. One or two of the other guards do, but most don't. I explain who I am and what organization I'm with, exchange my ID for a temporary badge, and sign in. After walking through a beeping metal detector, I have my computer bag and items scanned through the machine while another guard stops me, holding up their hand. "Ma'am, you need to take off your sweater before you go through the detector," he says curtly. I sigh and turn back, toss it in a bin to be passed through the scanner, and walk back through. It still beeps, but he waves me on. I won't point this out because I know that it doesn't matter; next time, the procedure will be different. I gather my things and pass through to the space, known as "visitation," where I'll spend the next approximately ten hours.

Within two hours, the space is filled with a flurry of energy and activity. I'm sitting with a mother, trying to help her fill out legal paperwork, and as she talks about her experiences, she begins to cry. I listen and try to console her while her child, a four-year-old boy, gets up from our desk and walks over to the guard's desk stationed in another part of the room. He's crying himself now, I don't know why, and decided to crawl under the guard's desk. I pause assisting the mom and start walking over to check on him when the guard angrily yells over toward us, "Make him get out of there! Tell him to go back to his mother." I don't say anything, but I kneel and try to coax him out. He didn't seem interested in budging, and I wasn't going to make him move, so I walk back to help his mom as another few women and their children arrive to the space, ready to fill out paperwork.

A few hours later, I'm talking with another mother about her case, and she's sobbing. At the same time, a baby is loudly crying in another area of the room, her mother trying to soothe her to sleep in one arm as she fills out forms. As we finish our discussion, I notice the mother I was supposed to meet next isn't in the waiting area. I ask the guard if she knows where she might be since I have no way to reach any detainee directly. "I don't know where she is," she replies. "We can't find her." I sigh and go back to one of the tables, typing up notes from previous meetings while I wait for my client for the next couple of hours. One of the kids waiting on his mom—who's speaking with another advocate—wanders over to the small play area and starts pushing buttons on a little toy plane. The plane starts a loud song on a loop, to the familiar tune from the show *Barney & Friends*, but with different lyrics. In the next minute, the guard's loud walkie-talkie bleeps: "Oak to elm, oak to elm," and the conversation cuts out. Then, over the room's intercom, a man's voice: "Vilma Garza, reporte a visita. Vilma Garza, reporte a visita." It's noisy, freezing cold, and I'm exhausted, but there's a lot more work to do as families continuously cycle in and out.

I begin this chapter with this frenetic composite of field notes as a brief "orientation" to help situate the subjects and concomitant sensations that follow. "Orientation" was a term meaningful for both advocates and detainees, and conceptually, it plays a central role in telling the story of this group of legal actors. Before they entered the facility, volunteer advocates were given an orientation training. For volunteers with the Dilley project, this comprised two parts: a group phone call done a week before volunteers arrived and an in-person training on Sunday evenings, the night before the first day of work (referenced in the introductory chapter). For those volunteering at Karnes, this preparation was less extensive. For asylum-seeking families arriving at these centers, "orientation" amounted to the showing of a relatively brief, looped video that explained limited aspects of their detention and legal processes for asylum.[1] As I came to view this recording myself, it was, in the most generous reading, a minimally informative video about the asylum process. The effective failure of immigration authorities and facility administrators to properly inform detained parents and their children of the meaning of their detention and legal rights—merely beginning with this orientation—speaks to geographer Lauren Martin's (2015, 231) well-supported claim that "detention is more than a fixing of bodies in space; it is a process of isolation, criminalization, and marginalization."

However, this chapter examines other ways that specifically advocates were oriented to the space of the detention centers and the work they did within. I will explore this through different avenues—place, sense, time, and disorientation—considering the varied ways that advocates came to adjust to this, at times, surreal environment, including how these centers *felt*. Setha Low (2009, 10) suggests that researchers need "theoretical formulations that provide an everyday, material grounding and an experiential, cognitive, and/or emotional understanding of the intersection and interpenetration of body, space, and culture," which she terms "embodied spaces." An engagement with affective experience through the conceptual lens of embodied space is critical to a richer understanding not only of those spaces but of the broader phenomena that have produced them. Indeed, migration itself is an "affective, embodied, and sensorial experience of becoming, a process of place making, self making, and world making, which cannot be understood by statistics alone" (Hamilakis 2018, xiii). Sensorial qualities of family detention spaces have a way of demonstrating the diverse pathways through which the daily exclusionary practices related to migration control unfold. The apparent arbitrary, contradictory, and especially ephemeral nature of these spaces and the processes within play an important role in understanding them, drawing out the frictions that exist between the

1. At the time of my research, it was effectively unclear if those applicants who spoke languages other than Spanish were shown a version of this in their own language. Although the facility incarcerated many Spanish speakers, this ultimately excluded those others who spoke other languages or those who were challenged to hear or read; it was unclear to advocates whether these many individuals were ever given this or other critical information in other formats.

legal function of migrant detention and experiential realities, often as punishment (Hiemstra 2019; Golash-Boza 2010). This is experienced by advocates in their work as well as detainees, though in different ways. This chapter only begins to talk about the role of emotion and affect in advocates' work, considering how these affected the initial, as well as the lingering, experiences they had. Through an early attention to these sensory qualities, the complex care realized by these advocates begins to take shape. Understanding these sorts of strange, liminal spaces through their affects will start to situate my contention that although these were ultimately harmful spaces—contributing to the both symbolic and physical violence inflicted on migrants (Jones 2017) and their caregivers—advocates participated in creating, within them, spaces of care (Conradson 2003).

PLACE

To start, the towns in which these detention centers resided—Dilley and Karnes City—share broad commonalities. They have roughly the same population size of only a few thousand and are surrounded by miles upon miles of farmland and oil fields. Although it was unclear if this was also the case in Karnes City, it had long been rumored that the water in Dilley had been poisoned by local fracking practices. During my field research, volunteers were cautioned by fellow advocates not to drink the tap water. Most often, advocates at both centers drank only bottled water, while detainees did not have that option; we often heard complaints from detainees that it made them sick (Schrag 2020). The Dilley facility sat adjacent to a large state prison and off a narrow farm-to-market road. The facility itself was not visible at all from the road, unlike its prison neighbor, which struck an imposing image. In driving past the prison to get to the center, advocates often witnessed a scene that some likened to a different era: large groups of jumpsuit-clad prisoners, nearly all Black and Brown, tilling the fields or harvesting the crops on the property of the prison, surrounded by cowboy-hatted, rifle-toting officers astride horses. As disturbing as the visual was, this is not particularly anachronistic, especially for Texas, in part given the historical lineage between American prisons and Texas slave plantations (Perkinson 2010). The crop harvested by the

FIGURE 6 On the outskirts of Dilley's downtown. Credit Erin Routon.

prisoners—watermelons—stood as a source of identity for the town of Dilley, which deemed itself the "watermelon capital of the world."

The road that led to the detention center itself was unmarked, thus proving challenging for some first-time visitors to find. This confusion led the project team to create a makeshift map for new volunteers, recalling Alison Mountz's (2012) reflection on how advocates actively contest the isolations of detention through oppositional cartographic efforts. She argued that such revelatory work, which involves actions like locating relatives as they have been clandestinely moved from one detention facility to another, counters the concealing work of the state, which often places immigrant detention facilities in remote locales. Legal advocates in Dilley practiced this by not only helping to locate families separated, ironically, by the practice of family detention, but also in quite literally mapping the location of the facility in order for incoming volunteers and new staff members of the project to find their way to it.[2] In contrast,

2. These facilities were already engaging in the practice of "family separation" prior to when it became most publicly discussed during the Trump administrative era, by only allowing a single parent to be detained with their children of minor age. All other forms of relation were denied the possibility to be detained together.

although the Karnes County Residential Center was also remotely located, it was much easier for new visitors to find. The center itself, while similarly located on a country road off a main highway in Karnes City, did have a locational marker. Its large blue-and-white facade also sat clearly on a barren hill, making it quite visible to passersby.

Even though serving the same function, the Dilley and Karnes detention centers struck quite different visual impressions. These differences were shaped both by their divergent histories and managing organizations, CoreCivic and GEO Group. The structural appearance of the Dilley facility reflected its existence as a response to a perceived crisis; the center was marked by a sense of impermanence, composed of a collection of mobile trailers and temporary edifices. As one advocate, Juana, described after her time in Dilley, "What was weird was that it felt like and looked more like a refugee camp. Everything was temporary, just thrown together like a FEMA [Federal Emergency Management Agency] camp. It felt very surreal." The Karnes center, in contrast, existed long before the Dilley center and was simply converted from an adult detention center to one for families. As a result, the Karnes facility projected a more ordinary, permanent image, composed of buildings that resembled an American elementary school.

Mary, an immigration lawyer from Colorado who visited Dilley around the time of the 2016 presidential election, said she often found herself at a "loss for words" when trying to explain the facility to those back home. "It's really hard to describe," she said, "and that's the reason why all of this is such a challenge to begin with. I mean, it's in the middle of Texas, in the middle of nowhere, and it's there for a reason. It's because people can't see it and can't understand the problem." Mary's comments reflect the need, and yet also a kind of inability, to think about these centers' physical locations in space. Scholars of migrant detention have repeatedly reflected on these interrelated issues, frequently referring to both these spaces and their concomitant histories as "invisible" (e.g., Danze, Torres, and Faria 2021; Minian 2024). Although journalist Mark Dow (2005) reported on how some detention facilities in the United States remain less publicly visible despite being located within cities, deploying Aleksandr Solzhenitsyn's (1974) influential concept of the "gulag archipelago," many of these centers today are located in rural communities, far from even the urban periphery, adding to the layers of invisibility (Noguchi 2019). At the time, some, like students in the University of Texas at Austin's Architecture Department, drew important attention to this connection between Texas detention centers' locations and barriers to necessary legal resources.[3] Many detainees, then, are consequently consigned to "legal deserts" (Burridge and Gill 2016), denied the availability of assistance with claims more readily afforded to those within or around urban areas (Libal, Martín, and Porter 2012). In more than one respect, this recalls historian and architect Dolores Hayden's (1995) assessment that cities have a "hinterland" of dependent places and vice versa.[4]

Within the walls of the facility, legal advocates were allowed to enter only a few spaces: the area where they met with clients, areas where facility staff allowed advocates to lead legal presentations on certain occasions, the courtroom, and the asylum office where fear interviews took place. They were not allowed beyond these areas, and their knowledge of the rest of the center often rested on the ability of others who could traverse these spaces to share this information. This greater freedom of movement, though through official escorts, was at times offered to those like nongovernmental organizations (NGOs), journalists, ambassadors, and few others who visited the centers. Yet, despite repeated requests to "tour" other parts of the center, this was almost never afforded to legal advocates.

There was a similar barrier with respect to image-taking in and around these facilities. While some had been allowed to capture images within these centers, like journalists or representatives of the managing private prison companies, legal advocates were denied this right and had been

3. "Spatial Stories of Migration and Detention | Texas Architecture | UTSOA," accessed April 21, 2020, https://soa.utexas.edu/work/spatial-stories-migration-and-detention.

4. I would also note the scholarship that draws attention to constructions of "remoteness" (e.g., Loyd and Mountz 2018; Bonds 2009) that disavow complex dependencies between rural and urban spaces. "Narratives of remoteness," Loyd and Mountz (2018, 11) contend, "often rely on geographical imaginaries that associate isolation with rurality, provincialism, conservatism, and racism (Bonds 2009). Remoteness, thus, is discursively constructed and materially built in opposition to cosmopolitanism, connection, community, rights, and freedom." We can see such discursive reproductions and misleading associations in certain comments from legal advocates throughout these chapters.

threatened with severe punitive repercussions, like permanent banning, if they were to do so.[5] In response, advocates used other forms of representation, such as maps and drawings, to visually depict these centers from the inside. Throughout the book, I deploy admittedly crude graphic renderings of my own, often using the most convenient media available—legal pads and pens—as well as those of others. Additionally, I have included photographs of the spaces around the work of these advocates, from those in which they lived, like the ranch, to the towns in which they resided. Visual representations are important for mapping facilities like these, which are hidden in many ways from public scrutiny, contesting that which is "purposefully made invisible" (Kohn 2016, 4). This I consider to be a kind of "visual disobedience" (Cornejo 2024) allowing for visual representation in ways not officially sanctioned by administrative authorities, in some cases directly challenging those representations and in others simply extending the visual record of these spaces.

Advocates spent most of their time at the facility within one area known as the legal visitation area or simply visitation (as it doubled as a space for the rare family or friend visit). The setup of these spaces at Dilley and Karnes differed significantly; at Dilley, the visitation area was in a raised mobile trailer connected to the security office and main entrance by a grated metal walkway. This area was one large, rectangular room, with individual private rooms, including a designated office space for advocates, lining the longest walls. At each end of the building, flanking the entrances, were desks staffed by facility guards. At the back of the trailer was a play area for children who arrived with their mothers. In this unsupervised room were a few coloring books with broken pieces of crayons, plastic toys and blocks scattered about the carpeted floor and low tables, and a TV that played one or two movies on a loop, sometimes dubbed in Spanish. Within the large room were several round desks and plastic chairs that were rearranged all day to fit the needs of each group gathering. For instance, when a group of clients arrived for the initial

5. For instance, DVIDS, "Photos of South Texas Family Residential Center," accessed April 22, 2020, https://www.dvidshub.net/image/1919810/photos-south-texas-family-residential-center. It is unclear how different private and public entities have been allowed to take photos within these centers. Legal advocates were not only denied access to other areas but also this ability to collect photographic documentation.

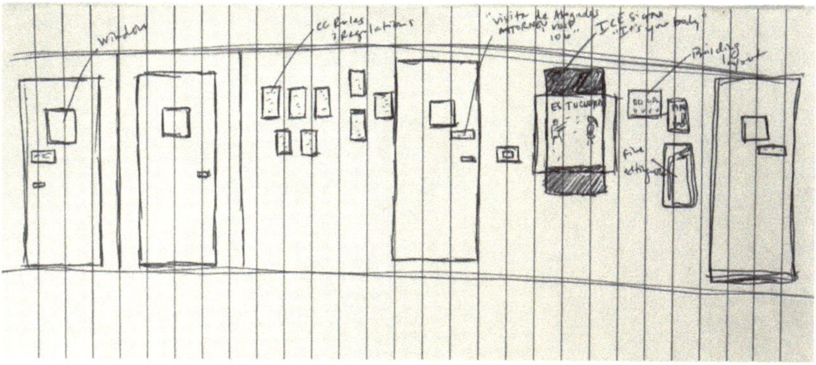

FIGURE 7 Rendering of entrance to private meeting rooms at Dilley facility. Text denotes the following: windows, "CC" or CoreCivic Rules and Regulations signage, attorney visitation signage, Spanish-language ICE signage, building layout map, and a fire extinguisher. Credit Erin Routon.

"intake" session, chairs were arranged in a small circle within which an advocate would lead an information session first, then tables and chairs would be rearranged for clients to fill out paperwork. Covering the walls were various signs and legal notices, some that outlined the dressing and behavioral rules of the facility, offered information for clients about using phone services and hair salon hours, or displayed childlike posters meant to warn young children to report "inappropriate touching." Around American holidays, these walls were covered in simple festive decor, from construction paper hearts and fat turkey legs to Mother's Day streamers and plastic Uncle Sam hats.

The visitation area of the Karnes center was located near the end of a long hall within the facility's main entrance building and was smaller than the space at Dilley. The area had one desk at which a GEO guard always sat, situated directly in front of a door through which detainees entered. Unlike Dilley, clients at Karnes had to wait in a smaller, enclosed waiting area before being allowed to meet with advocates. The configuration of space in this way created certain barriers to providing legal care to clients that did not exist in the same way in Dilley. Once the guard had properly "vetted" the detainee waiting in this area, they allowed them entry to the meeting space. At times, if they did not have a scheduled appointment with advocates—meaning that guards were made aware ahead of said meeting—guards would turn them away. Sometimes they would do

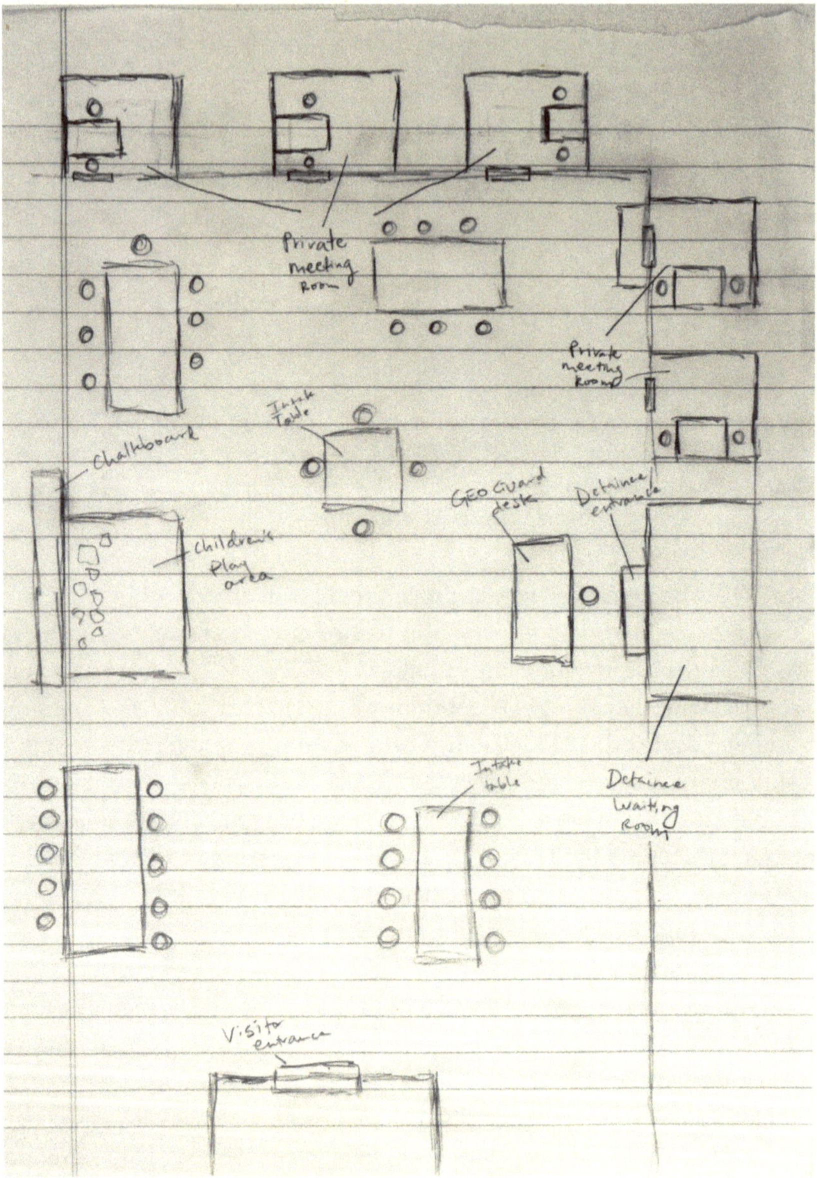

FIGURE 8 Elevated rendering of Karnes visitation area layout. Meeting rooms line the farthest walls from the visitor entrance, while intake tables and chairs fill the center, along with the children's play area and guard's desk. Entrances are at lower and right center. Text denotes the following: the visitation entrance, private meeting rooms, chalkboard and children's play area, intake tables, GEO guard desk, and detainee entrance and waiting area. Credit Erin Routon.

this without alerting advocates, so advocates weren't necessarily aware of why a client might have failed to come to visitation to meet with them. Guards' rules and everyday practices around this changed frequently, often negatively impacting the ability of advocates to meet and work with their clients.

The space itself was, like Dilley, entirely cut off from the rest of the facility. Unlike Dilley, though, the visitation space at Karnes had only one small window, which at times could make the workdays feel nebulous, leading one project staff member to remark, "Time flies when you can't see the sun." Within the space, there were five private meeting rooms, each of which were less private than those in Dilley, as they had large glass windows on the inward-facing walls, allowing those passing by or standing outside to easily look inside. Although seemingly a small difference, this did affect advocates' work with clients, as it served to create an atmosphere more replete with disruptions to the exceedingly intimate conversations that took place between advocates and clients within. Across from the guard's desk was a rectangular cut of green carpet on which sat a collection of children's toys: plastic trucks, a wooden bead maze, a miniature toy oven with a grocery basket of plastic foods. The concrete walls were also sparsely decorated with a few informative documents about legal rights and blocky, childish artwork.

SENSE

Alexandra Hall's (2012) work shows us how a focus on affect and emotion can extend our understanding of the physical environments of migrant detention. She advocates for the use of these as analytical tools for such spaces, noting how they "supplement abstract accounts" of the infamously exclusionary Agambenian "camp" (17). Only through "moving inside" the detention center are we truly able to make sense of its realities: "While the secure detention [center] brings to mind the rationalized, ordered regimes of the disciplinary spaces described by Foucault . . . the mechanisms of secure detention are always shot through with affective, emotional and symbolic concerns" (21). Emotion and affect, then, are already understood to be integral to the workings of the detention facility, thus readily available for analysis. Hall argues that an attention to such things "offers a way of going beyond the abject space"; while giving visibility to the ways that the carceral space is imagined by publics, an attention to affect and emotion can also reform those images (31). My conversations with advocates reflected these spatial reimaginings, often interpreted through sensorial experience.

Patricia was a retired commercial lawyer living in Evanston, Illinois, when we met during her volunteer stint in Dilley. I asked her to describe what it felt like to be at the center. "So, I went on a business trip to India a couple of years ago," she replied,

> and before I went, a cousin of mine, whose husband is Indian, tried to prepare me for the trip, telling me that going there is like a full-on, 24/7 assault on your senses. It's the best of what you can imagine and the worst of what you can imagine. It's the most colorful, the kindest, it smells the best, it's the most beautiful, and it's also the meanest, and the poorest . . . it's just all there in the same moment. I feel like Dilley is a little like that. It's like these awesomely wonderful things are happening, and at the same time, it's kind of a nightmare. You see children that can still laugh, which makes your heart sing, but they're consoling their mothers who are crying, telling you their story. It's just the juxtaposition of everything, in this very intense encapsulated environment.

Patricia's illustrative comparison, as simultaneously meaningful and simplistic as it was, initially offered contrast to the ways that many advocates immediately responded to this question. Indeed, advocates often hesitated, offering first a familiar, vague refrain: "I don't know what I expected, but it wasn't that." Eventually, however, they, like Patricia, would come to describe the *senses* that shaped their experiences and perceptions of the place: the sights, sounds, bodily affects, and even smells that formed some of the most lasting impressions.

Advocates' feelings about the material qualities of the center reflected opposing attitudes: there were those that perceived the center to be "nicer" than they expected, and those who were disturbed by this same environment. In later reflections, most shared some element of both. Advocates arrived, surprised that the center was not more "jail-like"—meaning it differed from either their imagined perceptions or actual experience of other carceral spaces—but then came to perceive it as more punitive, recognizing the harmful connection one might make between these and other carceral spaces. Some were, in fact, unsettled by the fact that the center had this sort of inoffensive or even ordinary appearance. This never led to advocates opining that they felt the facility wasn't harmful to their clients, just that it consistently confounded their expectations. "I wasn't expecting it to look like an elementary school annex," Samantha, an undergraduate from Maryland, told me. "In terms of [visitation], I definitely expected it to look worse. But standing outside, watching the buses [that brought new detainees] go in and out, seeing the surveillance cameras, it just hit me: this is a jail." Other advocates compared the appearance of the facilities to schools, particularly those who spent time at the Karnes center. In truth, there were other strange qualities of the material environment, beyond the building structures, that were reminiscent of child-adjacent spaces. Sleeping quarters were separated into "neighborhoods," as they were called, which in both Dilley and Karnes were designated by childlike names. At Dilley, these neighborhoods were named by a color-animal combination, like "blue butterfly" and "brown bear." This, along with the childish imagery to accompany, were noted on map signage within the facility. At Karnes, quarters were also given similar designations, like "oak" or "elm." Additionally, both mothers and children were required to wear the same sort of plain clothes, childlike uniform: blue jeans and a bright, primary-colored T-shirt.

Such material qualities shaped advocates' responses but in widely varying ways. Laura, a legal intern for the project at Karnes, shared Samantha's sentiment in certain respects: "It was a lot better than I expected," she said with a small laugh.

> With the way that you get prepped to go in, talking about walking through metal detectors and everything, I had this crazy idea of what it was. I honestly thought it would be more chaotic than it was; that it would be this madhouse with everyone running around, you know? But you go in there, and it's not a madhouse. There's a play area for the kids. Maybe it's because GEO prides itself on being so clean. Plus, I don't really see the rest of the facility. You go there and go into one room and stay there all day. I don't really even know what [the rest of the facility] is like.

Laura's reference to the significance of "cleanliness" for GEO Group, the corporation that managed the Karnes facility, is an important topic that will be discussed again. Her comment about the apparent order within the center is also quite important for a couple of reasons. Advocates, in their work, played a role in the construction of "order" at these centers, placing themselves in complex positions. Although Laura herself did not imply that this order, or her sense of a lack of chaos, was attributable to the advocates and their work, they participated in this. Over time, the projects that organized this type of aid work built and rebuilt relationships with facility administrators while also refining their processes around helping their clients. In this way, through the work they did to create productive relationships and functional structures, the environment became less chaotic than it initially was at its start.

Those who served these projects over the years reflected on what legal advocacy in family detention previously looked like and how it felt, especially those who worked in the detention center in Artesia. They spoke clearly of a chaotic and an even more deeply unwelcoming environment, both for legal advocates and detainees. They told stories of having to sneak in phones to make legally necessary outside calls because the centers did not allow detainees to make such calls. They talked about how they had to get names and identification numbers of detainees clandestinely from other clients that they met with in order to continue providing services, simply because administrators would not allow them to meet with potential clients without identifying information (an impossibility, as they could not access that). For these and other reasons, the Artesia family detention center carried with it a sort of mythic quality among those involved in family detention advocacy; its very name was carried on by the massive listserv through which all those who had volunteered with those projects communicated about family detention–related issues.[6] As mentioned in the introduction, those who volunteered in the early days at Dilley lamented the fact that they would have to simply show up at the center and wait in the lobby of the security trailer, day

6. None of the chapters of this book address one important element of the work of these advocates, and that is the role of digital communication among current and former advocates on family detention issues. The functioning of the listserv is complex, and I hope to discuss it at greater length in another forum.

after day, until they were finally allowed inside. Over time, in part due to the persistence of their physical presence, the relationship between legal advocates and facility administrators shifted, and they were allowed continued access, relatively unabated.

While it was common to hear this refrain about the "niceness" of the facilities, some advocates immediately focused on the exclusionary and controlling qualities of the atmosphere. Angela, an advocate from Juarez who had spent time volunteering in border safehouses, was one of the rare few who expected the opposite: an environment that was more like the safehouses in which she had spent so much time. She, like others, arrived at similar conclusions: "This is the only detention center I've ever been to, and I had this completely different idea before of what it was," she explained.

> The safehouses are nothing like this. I thought this would be a more relaxed environment than it is, like I thought we were going to have *real access* to them. I didn't know we were going to be stuck in this trailer, that we couldn't interact with them normally. That's what killed me the most: how much of a prison it is. It's not a detention center; it's just a jail. It's just a nice name for a jail.

Angela's expectations regarding having "real access" to her clients referred to the constraints placed on the relations between clients and advocates and their strictly controlled movement inside. These forms of control were what quickly differentiated this space from others explicitly intending to shelter migrants.

Still others struggled to make this connection between prisons or jails and the centers. Some had worked in other carceral spaces previously and were quick to remark on how those differed significantly, particularly in the relative freedom detainees had to move throughout them. Rebecca, an immigration attorney who had a wealth of experience in detention, characterized Dilley as "less than a prison" but that there were certain "prison conditions that served as reminders that you're still in a detention center, like that they're not free to go." Like other advocates, she affirmed that while it was indeed a sort of carceral facility, it was still "a lot better" than many other detention centers she'd visited. Those, she explained, functioned more like jails.

Mia, a young journalist from New York who volunteered in Dilley before traveling to Mexico for research, found this apparent liminal status to be what made the place so unsettling. "I think the conditions in Dilley are shocking," she said,

> not because it's like a jail, but because it's really in between. It's a little bit too much like an office, at least in the part that we were in, to seem like a jail, and yet people are stuck inside. It doesn't look as hideous as a jail, but it has that sort of monotony that I think comes with jails. The fact that guards are kind of lounging around with their matching red collared shirts is what makes it just tolerable enough for the general public. It's still very horrible, but it's not as visibly detestable as the inside of a prison in a way that would shut it down automatically.

Mia importantly recognized, as some did, that these facilities were situated in a strange position; they were not quite prisons or jails, but they did share qualities with other carceral spaces. They resided somewhere amid, as not but also *not not* prisons (Castañeda and Crabapple 2023). Dow (2005, 17) examined this conflicted characterization of immigrant detention when he reflected on how such liminal positioning affects the experiences of those held within, questioning, "What must it mean to be held in a prison for weeks or months, even for a decade or more, and to be told by the administrative agency renting bed space for you that you are not a prisoner?" In fact, given shared lineages and realities, Dow (2007) and others (Longazel, Berman, and Fleury-Steiner 2016) have chosen to use the term "immigration prisons" to describe such spaces.

Recognizing the significance of Dow's question, I consider how this ambiguous identity—which often and in various ways attempted to align itself with care—in fact challenged the work of legal advocates inside. Indeed, on CoreCivic's website, specifically, the Dilley facility was described thus: "Employing several hundred individuals, this center's mission is to provide an open, safe environment with residential housing as well as educational opportunities for women and children who are awaiting their due process before immigration courts."[7] This broader alignment with care was not unintentional; indeed, the historical promotion

7. http://www.correctionscorp.com/facilities/south-texas-family-residential-center.

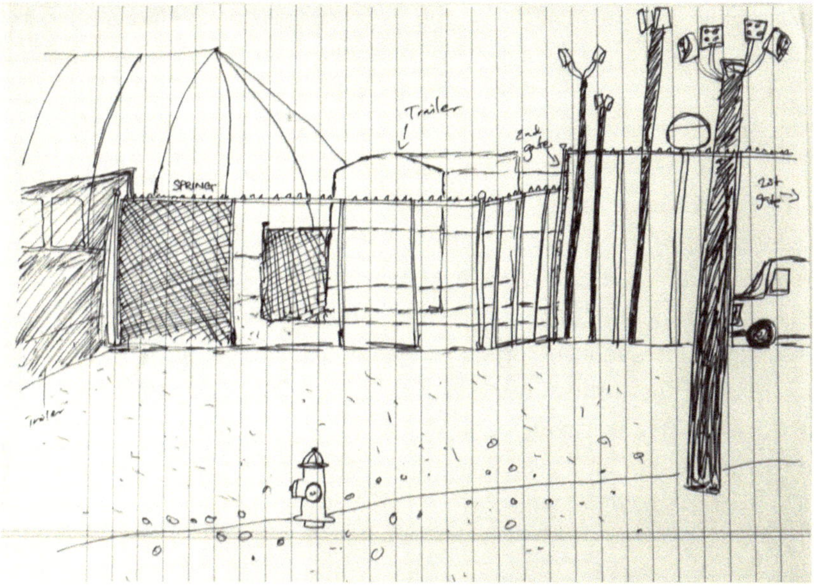

FIGURE 9 Rendering of the inside of the Dilley facility, from the perspective of one of the private rooms in the visitation trailer. Text denotes the following: mobile trailer buildings and entrance/exit gates. Credit Erin Routon.

of these so-deemed residential facilities—as "better" than jails or other detention centers and not to be associated with punitive measures—aimed to further promote "civil detention" in immigrant enforcement measures. In a more extensive historical discussion of abolitionist work around ending family detention practices, Silky Shah (2024) shows how some of these markers indicative of this approach that struck advocates were familiar, even characteristic. These material qualities noticed by advocates reflected this precedented, intentional distancing from incarceration in sometimes obvious, other times subtler, ways. And yet, Mia's comments additionally reflected how the facility staff, whom advocates referred to as guards, came to serve as representative figures of the facility's carceral identity as a result of their practices and behaviors despite these attempted material signifiers, like more casual uniforms.[8] She also further drew important attention to this relationship between a visual public

8. I use the language of "guards" to refer to CoreCivic and GEO Group staff, in keeping with the language of my interlocutors.

palatability and the facilities', and thus family detention's, continued existence. This is crucial, as it helps to set the stage for an understanding of the competing conceptions of care that defined both everyday and exceptional frictions between advocates and facility administrators.

Speaking to advocates about their experiences of the detention center either directly or indirectly involved talk of the body, including both their own and the bodies of others. Advocates experienced a kind of reorientation of their bodies in different ways, including adjusting to the different sort of soundscape they would be exposed to, that which frequently included the sometimes-cacophonous sounds of babies crying. One of the earliest bodily reorientations took place in the security processing area of the centers, where advocates learned how to comport themselves and pass through without difficulty. When entering this area, one would also notice posted signs warning of exposure to illnesses inside the center, like chickenpox.[9] All children at the centers were given multiple vaccinations when they arrived, at times without clear, express permission from their parents, with many children and even babies being given several shots all at once, sometimes causing them pain. Young children who would accompany their mothers to visitation would sometimes cry out from the discomfort, while their mothers gently lifted their tiny folds of clothing to show advocates the multiple shot sites along their little legs. Even with these excessive precautions against transmitting illnesses, children and their mothers were frequently sick and the severity of these sicknesses ranged. Many, we believed, became ill at least in part due to the conditions they experienced at *las hieleras/perreras*. The *hieleras* ("ice boxes," named so for their cold temperatures) and *perreras* ("dog pounds," for their gated holding areas) were the temporary ICE holding facilities where asylum seekers were held for briefer periods before being transferred to longer-term facilities, like Dilley and Karnes. These facilities were known to have extremely harsh conditions, even potentially leading to deaths of those detained (Gómez 2018). Many mothers and children we met in Dilley and Karnes had been traumatized after even only a couple of days there. At the mere mention of them during intake, some women would start to

9. As noted in the introduction, this research took place before the COVID-19 pandemic, so this refers to other vaccines.

cry, while some would sigh and toss their hands up in the air, beginning long diatribes about the awful treatment they endured there. Medical professionals employed by the facility, as we were told every day by clients, repeatedly dismissed their health concerns and often suggested that mothers simply feed their sick children honey and water (Costantini 2015), stating that their bodies only needed to "adjust to American foods." These inadequacies in medical care—forms of "structural violence" (Farmer 2005) reflective of larger trends in the substandard medical care of detainees in the United States (Human Rights Watch 2017)—will be shown again, as it impacted the work of the advocates and their relationships with facility administrators.

In turn, many advocates also became ill while working in the centers. Their illnesses ranged in severity as well, with some having to visit hospitals for treatment. I became ill on numerous occasions. As a result of the constant need for help at the facility, illness was rarely something that deterred advocates from showing up for work (and unfortunately, negatively impacted the ongoing cycle of illness). Because of its ubiquity in both the experiences of detainees and advocates, sickness was an omnipresent topic of conversation. Often, my recorded interviews included the sounds of coughing, sneezing, and sniffling. Constant illness was just one manifestation of how experiences of detainees were, at times, shared with the legal advocates, due in no small part to the intimacy of their work together. The multisensory experiences of these facilities—which have been only introduced here—reflect some of the different ways that these spaces were interpreted and felt through embodiment.

TIME

Fassin (2016, 108) reminds us that "the world of prison is a space-time existence—a confined space for a specified length of time. It is this dual dimension that demarcates the inmates' world. This is what defines the concrete sense of the punishment. Being a prisoner boils down to this: being confined in a space and being constrained in time." Much of this book is meant to show how the experiences of these legal advocates, while notably different, at times ran parallel with the experiences of the detainees. While advocates' perceptions and feelings of time could reflect this shared experience, this section, more so than others, will showcase the disparity. While for a detained family, time might feel as if passing slowly, for the legal advocate, it could often feel the opposite. In this somewhat counterintuitive way, however, their experience still ran parallel to those of their clients in that they are also, as Fassin says, "confined in a space and . . . constrained in time."

As mentioned previously, one of the reasons time was such a complicated concept with respect to family detention had to with a legal agreement that made the case that children could be held in detention for only brief periods. Throughout my research, the average length of stay for detainees was a month, not including the time they spent detained in ICE facilities at the border. This is in sharp contrast with the sort of "slow violence" (Saunders and Al-Om 2022) effected by asylum legal proceedings beyond these contexts that families would be subject to once they left. In turn, this legal decision, intended to lessen the negative effects of detention on those most likely to be harmed by it, also shaped how legal advocacy operated. There were many steps to the process of helping clients prepare their cases, and there were often hundreds of clients to be served weekly. In contrast, each week rarely had more than twenty advocates working inside the center, serving all clients. At the Karnes facility, this was usually far fewer, both in terms of clients and advocates. Because nearly all clients' cases moved quickly through the processes at the center, advocates needed to work hastily to make sure that they were properly prepared and knowledgeable about their rights. Being attentive in this way to individual clients was especially challenging when the number of advocates was outweighed by the need.

Because of this, time in the facility could feel to advocates as if moving at light speed. Carolyn, a lawyer from Colorado, connected this with her experience working on the then-recent Clinton presidential campaign. It was like that experience, she explained, in that it

> parallels the constant need for work and the constant need for volunteers. I mean literally, there wasn't a moment where you're like oh, I'm just going to check my email or update my status on Facebook, that's ridiculous. You're just like no, no, I've got to get this noted as quickly as possible because someone else is waiting to talk to me. You're moving constantly.

Every minute of the day saw crowds of women and children waiting in visitation to speak with an advocate individually or to sit in on a *charla* (or chat)—an information sharing session directed by an advocate to a group of clients—or to do paperwork. For those advocates who were skilled in language abilities or had an immigration legal background, time moved even faster, as they were in constant demand. Some would even forget to do necessary things, like eat or take bathroom breaks, preoccupied with the needs of their clients and the tasks that need to be accomplished within a short window. Some would find themselves running to catch up with their clients at court or in their interviews, hurriedly grabbing laptops or legal pads, while others might sit at a desk for a full day speaking to client after client, hearing story after story, until required to leave by administrators. The fluctuation between such experiences of time in the center took their toll, and this would be something that wasn't registered by some advocates until after their experience ended.

It is important to note the ways that temporary volunteers' experiences of time differed from those of project staff. Because staff remained in their roles for months or even years and because they were ultimately responsible for all aspects of the project's daily work, time was perceived at different scales. Project staff typically worked on more labor-intensive cases and appeals for negative interview decisions, and their work involved constant communication with facility administrators and off-the-ground members of the project. They documented issues at the center to share with other project members involved in legal advocacy outside of detention, serving the project's other goals of bringing about the abolition of family detention and making sure those who needed immediate release (for medical necessities, for instance) could get out more quickly.

For both volunteers and project staff, the work evoked a sense of urgency. This is in keeping with norms of an "ephemeral state," one in which, as Max Greenberg (2019, 6) describes it, "the state acts through a multiplied field of fleeting interventions into institutions and daily life that encourage rapid transformation." This contrasts with the "slow state," which in one sense might be a productive way to describe the lengthy, years-long asylum process; it's also, surprisingly, a way to understand the everyday of the detention facility itself. It was an ephemeral space, construed through urgent, fleeting encounters, but it was also defined by its waiting, its slowness. The paradoxical coexistence of these qualities led to a sense of "social whiplash" (Greenberg 2019) for advocates. "It seems to me that the whole system in which [the advocates] operate is like a triage system," George reflected. "It's like an emergency room. Just constantly running from one potential disaster or real disaster to the next." George, a nonimmigration lawyer from New York, was far from the only person to characterize the work and space in this way. This sense of emergency was represented in both time and space; while time collapsed, as if in an emergency, there were also material, sensorial elements that reflected this, from the crowd of people consistently filling up the room, waiting to be helped, to the constant sounds of crying babies.

Scholars have noted how work of both humanitarian and carceral entities tend to cohere around crises, or a shared sense of emergency provoking their involvement in "managing" such issues. Such perceptions are in fact central to the instigation and continuation of humanitarian and carceral work; not only do these two forms of labor effectively operate as responses to perceived emergencies—at times simultaneously to the same crises, such as with refugee migration—but they also both serve to imagine an event as a crisis. It is helpful to think about these events through the framework of "social imaginaries" which, as Charles Taylor (2002, 106) offers, concern "the ways in which people imagine their social existence, how they fit together with others, how things go on between them and their fellows, the expectations that are normally met, and the deeper normative notions and images that underlie these expectations." Craig Calhoun (2010) demonstrates how specific events become constructed as humanitarian emergencies, calling out for humanitarian responses. For Calhoun (2010, 3), the core features of humanitarian emergencies are that they are sudden, unpredictable, and urgent exceptions to the normal order and that they are constituted by a sense of neutrality; such action in response to these emergencies is based on a perception of an "ethical obligation to a common humanity." This is certainly representative of family detention and the responding legal advocacy documented here.

More recently, scholars have also shown how humanitarian entities often play a role in managing the various crises involving refugee or asylum-seeking groups, indeed demonstrating how state-manufactured crises can be reified by the involvement of such entities (e.g., Agier and Fernbach 2011). Comments like George's liken this situation to an emergency, while also reflecting a more layered understanding of the production of that emergency. Although most affirmed the idea that there were crises being produced by gang, intimate partner, and political violence that had resulted in large numbers of particularly women and children fleeing various countries, the environment of emergency that so many advocates reflected on was that which was made by the government through processes of detention. To start, the large influx of asylum-seeking families arriving at the Mexico-U.S. border in 2014, being subsequently deemed a crisis, allowed for the creation of these facilities. Scholars note that framing this event as such "proved a reliable fuel to bolster enforcement-oriented responses in the forms of detention and the off-shoring of asylum" (Loyd and Mountz 2018, 220; Mountz and Hiemstra 2013). Furthermore, the way detained individuals were treated, uninformed about their rights or why they were incarcerated, and the unpredictable nature of processes at the facility produced this chaotic environment, in keeping with the manufactured chaos of detention more broadly (Hiemstra 2019). Those advocates attempting to provide aid were effectively forced to navigate, and in a way manage, that crisis.

Geographers studying detention have noted how such spaces are simultaneously and paradoxically marked by their relationships with both mobility and a sense of "stillness" (Gill 2009; Mountz et al. 2012). This was evident in family detention, where advocates and detainees experienced differing material forms of the "violence of waiting" in relation to asylum processes (Haas 2023). At both facilities, there were no opportunities for advocates to directly reach clients without the aid of facility staff. This formed a significant barrier between advocates and clients, leaving advocates sometimes waiting for clients for hours at a time. In checking in on their whereabouts, advocates would hear the familiar refrain from my opening anecdote: "We don't know where they are," or "We're looking, but we can't find them." The irony of a deeply securitized space being unable to maintain knowledge of the location of their inmates might have been comical for advocates had it not so negatively impacted their ability to give necessary legal aid to their clients. Invariably, and in the view of some suspiciously, clients would often be located by facility staff near the end of the workday, when advocates were required to exit the center. This interfered with their everyday workflow as well as with assisting many clients who needed immediate attention. Some clients would have same-day interviews or court hearings scheduled, and instead of, per their requests, "calling up" these clients to meet with advocates prior to these appointments, facility staff would only locate them after their appointment time had passed.

Regardless of intentions, these repetitive issues played a substantive role in the emotion work of advocates, frequently frustrated by affecting circumstances that felt punitive but around which they were unable to truly express that anger (a problem that will be unpacked later). The ways that advocates perceived this all-too-common behavior, often by guards—forcing both advocates and detainees to wait for services—as an intentional act to delay or disturb encounters between them corresponds with what sociologist Javier Auyero (2012) refers to as "daily lessons of political subordination." While Auyero focuses on the way marginalized communities experience this waiting, we can see how in the context of family detention this apparent punishment spread to those who aided or associated themselves with those individuals as well. The consistency of the failure to locate individuals for critical meetings with legal advocates implied an intentionality rather than mere ineptitude. This specific type of encounter between guards and advocates exposed a fraught relationship between different "managers" of crises in detention.

Care, Jessica Cooper (2018, 126) notes, is "intimately bound to temporality"; time, she suggests, is "needed to watch relationships unfold." Time is also a mechanism for control and punishment (Munn 1992); this is especially evident in and around carceral spaces. Caring relationships between advocates and detainees in detention were not denied by the severe limits placed on their time together, but their relationships, as well as the relationships advocates had with administrative actors, were shaped by paradoxical temporal constraints. Thus, understanding how advocates' care was construed and moved throughout these facilities requires a temporal reorientation.

DISORIENTATION

"Welcome to baby jail!" Mark exclaimed loudly, his arms outstretched to showcase the wide room before us. I was sitting at a round table in the open area of the visitation trailer, waiting to be told what to do. It was my first week volunteering in 2015, and despite our trainings, I truly had little awareness of what I should be doing from minute to minute as I arrived on Monday morning. Mark, the member of the advocacy project staff mentioned previously who had been there for nearly a year, had walked into the trailer after being held up by security. He was noticeably exasperated by this, dropping the large boxes he was carrying at his feet and immediately telling us that he was stopped by the guards for an extra ten minutes while they inspected his boxes of printer ink cartridges. They finally allowed him to pass through, but not until after they perused the contents of each box.

I came to hear Mark's sarcastic remark often, though when I first heard it, I naively assumed he was simply welcoming us as volunteers to our new "workspace." I later understood that such phrases were not only meant as introductions to the facility but also as a sort of commentary on the normalized unpredictability or misanthropy that permeated the space. When a new advocate witnessed upsetting events, the sort that regularly occurred in the center, this was a common response from project staff. These apparent asides served as kinds of orienting comments that corresponded with both the space and what happened there. In certain respects, orienting oneself to these spaces was impossible; while there were consistencies to the work and environment, there was much inconsistency as well, like a sudden, unexpected package inspection. This was the sort of thing that having spent an extended period there made clearer, and it helped explain the deep frustration exhibited by Mark for having to spend a "mere" extra ten minutes going through security. For most voluntary advocates, this inconsistency was not particularly obvious; because most spent only a week working at the center on a given visit, all qualities of the environment were new and any changes they observed throughout that week were not necessarily placed in contrast to anything else. For those who spent extended time at the center, like long-term volunteers or project staff, these inconsistencies became a given part of the daily landscape. Orienting oneself to this environment, then, necessarily involved expecting a dynamic atmosphere, becoming accustomed to and quickly cope with disorientation. In this way, in such unpredictably fragile yet also urgent environments, advocates faced the imperative of learning to improvise their care (Livingston 2012).

Like detainees, advocates' bodies, as they move through the detention center, were made "docile" in particular ways and were always subject to disciplinary maneuvers (Foucault 1977). This first occurred in the security trailer, where they and their belongings were examined before being allowed entry. This involved unpredictable encounters with facility staff, and the rules that allowed or denied entry played a significant role in this unpredictability, as they constantly shifted. Such rules determined what constituted appropriate dress and proper documentation for visitors, and whether an advocate had been included on a weekly visitor list required to be given to the facility staff ahead of any visit, among other things. Advocates' frustrations from the constant sense of novelty in navigating these spaces characterized many experiences in the center; they were rarely informed of changes to policies or practices in a manner that would allow them appropriate time to prepare for those adjustments. Sometimes, such changes took forms that, because of this gap in understanding between the actions of facility administrators and the information given to advocates, appeared abstract and potentially ominous. An example of this occurred when one day, after receiving news from clients, the Dilley team learned that one of the quarters or "residential wings" of the facility was being "cleared out," rather that those who had been living in that area had suddenly been informed by staff that they would move to another, with the result being that an entire area was unexpectedly removed of all its inhabitants. This provoked questions and concerns in families and advocates, leaving advocates especially concerned that this could mean a major shift was about to occur, whether that was a population increase or decrease (both could potentially be concerning). In similar moments, advocates were left to try to reassure worried clients while they themselves still wondered, disconcertedly, about the meaning behind such actions.

Even though such bewildering events occurred frequently, they did not simply inspire concerned rumblings among the advocates; sometimes, they directly impeded their work. In keeping with the pace of the center, these changes would sometimes leave advocates to adjust unreasonably quickly. For instance, the same week that all clients in one wing were moved into another, large groups of new clients started arriving at visitation not with documents explaining the date and time of their interview, per usual, but with documents known as Notice(s) to Appear (NTAs). These were the documents clients received at the final stage of the process in their detention, effectively informing detainees that they were to appear in immigration court outside of detention to continue their legal case. This was strange and confusing to advocates because it meant that they would not be interviewed in detention, negating the entire supposed purpose of their detention. The team was effectively at a loss to explain this. *Why was this happening, and what did it mean for these families? Why was this happening for just some families but not others?* Although it was important for these questions to be asked—questions that ultimately went unanswered—the more pressing concern was then how to attend to those families' needs. Because much of the work was structured around preparing clients for interviews, such changes created an even more chaotic environment. With little time to process this shift, one of the staff attorneys for the project was forced to immediately stop the critical and time-sensitive work she was already doing on other precarious client cases to create a new plan of care. Within a few hours, she had devised a plan to reorganize the labor for the volunteer advocates, and collectively, the staff reoriented the efforts toward preparing those families for legal processes beyond detention.

Throughout fieldwork, such shifts occurred repeatedly, rarely accompanied by administrative explanation, and advocates were left to cope with these sudden changes, finding avenues to continue to help those who were most greatly affected by them. Considering these actions by administrators, as many advocates did, as intentionally disruptive or punitive, however, calls into question the intended target of such actions. They implied that through constant "rearrangements," literal bodies and metaphorical boundaries were being collected and circumscribed. Facility staff used the medium of both detainees' and advocates' bodies (Douglas 1971) to exercise authority through practices of spatial and procedural control. These sorts of expressions of power demonstrated the variability and resonance of the harm committed inside these centers. Thinking about them as forms of spatial disorientations meant to disrupt care draws out how advocates had to navigate around them rather than simply reject them.

DAY'S END

"Do any of you have kids?" Tara asked those of us encircled around her, her eyes searching the room. It was around eight in the evening, and our group of ten or so volunteers and a few project staff were sitting in a small, dimly lit communal area of the Days Inn Dilley. There were maroon couches that lined the walls and large plush chairs pushed together to create a circle in that corner for our twice-weekly "Big Table" meetings, where volunteers reflected on their experiences and addressed remaining questions. That night, project attorney Allie had asked us if there was anything that they, as staff, could have done to better prepare us for what to expect at the center, both in terms of the work itself and to sort of cushion the shock of being within the space. In response, Tara, an immigration lawyer from Colorado who had six years of experience with asylum work, asked her own question. After a couple of women raised their hands, she continued. "Well, I feel like this reminds me of childbirth," she said.

> You know, when you have kids, nobody can prepare you for what childbirth is like. You [the staff] gave us this mountain of paperwork before with lots of info about the work, which was helpful, but there's nothing you could've done to prepare me for this. Doing preps back-to-back, the chaos of the place . . . nobody can prep you for that. I don't mean that this is a failure [on the part of the staff], and I don't mean that it's painful like childbirth, but more that it's like childbirth in that it's just something you have to experience yourself. No one can prepare you.

The women who had raised their hands quietly nodded. The preps Tara referenced, as noted already, were one of the most difficult aspects of the work.

Each Big Table meeting occurred directly after the end of the workday and lasted for around two to three hours. Some ate their dinners—which they might get from the few local restaurants or gas stations—while reflecting on what transpired throughout the day. Despite everyone's exhaustion, most volunteers had a lot to say, especially after that first day. These meetings tended to exhibit the full range of emotions people felt; they laughed as they talked about funny things children did, cried when recounting clients' stories, and raged about the harm they witnessed unfolding inside. People expressed their immense surprise at the pace of the work and the amount of people constantly moving throughout the trailer. While feelings and topics often shifted as the week moved along, certain sentiments punctuated all meetings: sadness, frustration, joy, confusion.

FIGURE 10 The Days Inn Dilley, where volunteer advocates stayed during their visit. Credit Erin Routon.

Tara later told me that she had actually done a lot to prepare before coming. As she sat on the plane from Colorado, she pored over the many pages of reading material the project had provided to help prepare advocates for the various responsibilities of the work they would be doing. She even spoke with a former project staff member before leaving home to help prep herself for what to expect. Her comments at that Big Table meeting reflected a recurrent theme in advocates' reflections: that to understand family detention and the work they did, one needed to *be there*. This emphasis on "presence," or being there as a way of being-with (Horton 2024), is something that deeply informed the kind of care that these advocates practiced.

While advocates expressed desires to influence publics unfamiliar with these spaces to care about the injustices embedded within family detention, in their commentaries there was an inherent intimacy and collection of sensations that cohered their own experiences which, for many advocates, was somewhat untranslatable. As an anthropologist, this reminded me of both the significance of the "being there" of material experience (Richardson 1982), so necessary for ethnographic exposition, but also of the difficulty in translating experiences, especially when embodiment played such a prominent role. Low (2009, 15) contends, however, that this sort of conflict, or rather "this tension between 'language' and 'experience,'" is resolved, to an extent, by the fact that "language not only represents or refers but 'discloses' our being-in-the-world." And yet, this common sense of untranslatability or an unbridgeable gap between description and sensation was one of the initial intrigues motivating my research. I, like other advocates, endeavored to translate those complex experiences and feelings into a more nuanced story of what something like family detention did to those various bodies ensnared within its web, just as other scholars have shown how the "doing time" of incarceration isn't simply limited to those who are themselves imprisoned (Comfort 2008).

Attention to affect, especially in these sorts of highly affective, ephemeral spaces, is necessary. Feminist scholar Ann Cvetkovich (2012) notes how a focus on affective experience contributes much to discussions of the real effects of often destructive global phenomena, such as war or the spread of neoliberalism. The sensational effects of these things have the potential to challenge "master narratives"; this can be reached through an attention to affect. As she argues, "talk of permanent war, states of exception, and new security states, important and useful as it might be, frequently operates at such a high level of abstraction that it fails to address the lived experiences of these systemic transformations" (12). Affect can move us toward bridging the experiences of the individual with broader social movements and complicate narratives about social life that dismiss the ways that these phenomena are felt, which, of course, matter.

This chapter has begun its examination of family detention through the conceptual lens of embodied space, charting their material and sensorial qualities as experienced by legal advocates at work inside. The carceral environment "is also a sensorial experience. . . . It is made of both lack and excess" (Fassin 2016, 113). While the work here has moved the discussion inside, looking often at the "excess" of sensorial matter there, the entire book will only ever be able to provide a partial view of these centers. These facilities, in their entirety, remained veiled to those, like myself, who were neither center staff nor prisoners. Partiality and exclusion were thus characteristic markers of these places, and this "lack" will travel throughout all spaces advocates were allowed to traverse.

With that, then, a kind of orienting caveat should be offered before concluding this chapter and moving forward: Although various administrative others—facility guards, asylum officers, and immigration judges, principally—appear throughout the following chapters, their presence is undeniably lacking in the same sort of dimensionality given to advocates. This should not be construed as a refusal of similar depth or complexity in those actors, or a denial of important constraints under which they operated, but rather as a simple fact of the nature of this particular research project and its own limitations. As noted, this book examines family detention from the perspectives of the legal advocates who navigated those spaces, and administrators played deeply significant roles in the kinds of experiences advocates reflected on. As such, it is impossible to tell this story of legal advocacy without those others, even in serious recognition of the fact that they are depicted in an incomplete way.

With this chapter, I've begun an exploration of the ways that spaces, specifically those of care, are produced or created within these facilities. David Conradson (2003, 508) notes that a "space of care" might be understood as a "socio-spatial field disclosed through the practices of care that take place between individuals" and that "the emergence and endurance of such spaces depends both upon the willingness of some individuals to move towards others and, among those being engaged in this way, upon a receptivity to such initiatives. Spaces of care are shared accomplishments and, in reflection of this, may at times be socially fragile." The following chapters will further examine how advocates created spaces of care within the areas in which they were allowed to inhabit, and that in doing so, they resisted the centers' more constraining effects. Advocates, with the willing and at times collaborative participation of detained clients, worked together to make these areas into spaces intended to evoke a greater sense of care and security for those families.

CHAPTER 2

COUNTERSTORY

The private rooms of the visitation space were always very cold. So much so that whenever I could, I immediately pulled up the blinds on the window and propped it open to let that predictably warm breeze pass through. Xiomara, along with her ten-year-old son Martín, sat down on one side of the bare, maroon desk, and I sat at the other.[1] They were from El Salvador and, despite the age difference, were roughly the same size as each other. Xiomara had her long, black hair pulled neatly back into a low ponytail, and they both wore the standard issue brightly colored T-shirt and blue jeans. I introduced myself, explaining my role as a non-lawyer legal advocate and the work of the organization. After asking a few basic biographical questions and the date of her upcoming interview, I reminded her of the confidentiality of our conversation before asking her to explain why she left her home to seek asylum in the United States.

Xiomara was the kind of client a legal advocate in these spaces might hope to work with. "Do you want me to explain why I left, starting from the beginning and then explain what happened later on, to get to the point where I fled [my country]?" she asked me at the outset of our conversation. The palms of her small hands faced each other, mimicking the

1. As noted earlier, all names are pseudonyms and personal details about specific clients/detainees have been mixed to further obscure identification.

movement through time by waving her right hand farther away, increasing the gap between. As an advocate, hearing something like this from a client effected an immediate sense of relief. This came from the fact that one of the greatest challenges for advocates in these conversations—those in which they intended to help applicants shape their asylum claim ahead of their fear interview—involved establishing a clear "timeline," one that might help them explain to an officer how their circumstances led to them to seek asylum. Understandably, many didn't think of their life decision-making in terms of a clear, progressive timeline, so in these sorts of conversations, part of the work involved helping clients to both perceive their experiences in this strange way as well as to come to articulate it thus for their interview. Hence, moments like this, with Xiomara's comment, felt slightly relieving.

Xiomara was a skilled storyteller. She spoke slowly, deliberately, and with great clarity, expressing a clear timeline of events that led to their departure. She repeated significant elements that impacted this decision and provided extensive detail, something legal advocates encouraged with clients. Her's was primarily a case of intimate partner violence. "When I first met my husband," she told me, "things were good. Everything was fun. And then things began to change." He became increasingly abusive with her and her children, even while she was pregnant. On multiple occasions, she sought protection from the police but to no avail. Eventually, Xiomara and her four children fled, first moving in with her sister, then traveling to the United States. Unfortunately, she was forced to leave three of her children behind with family, in part because she could afford the transit for only one; as her story came to demonstrate, she needed to take Martín. This was illustrated clearly for her after a particularly upsetting moment in which her young son had protected her from the physical violence of her husband, an incident that left Martín with scars that left noticeable ridges along the frame of his tiny body. Through tears and a tired gaze, Xiomara explained that she had left primarily to protect him, as he had protected her. As I regularly came to do, I quietly listened, trying to focus on how best to help while also keeping myself from crying. As our conversation came to a close, we talked about what parts of her experiences she shared should be emphasized in her interview, and I answered several questions she had about the process after, to the best of my knowledge. I thanked her for sharing her story with me and asked if she had any other questions before we parted. She asked if I could accompany her to her interview the following day, for support, and I agreed. The three of us walked out of the room together, passing a seated group of five or so women, all waiting to speak with the next free advocate about their cases in those same little rooms.

The conversation that took place between Xiomara, Martín, and me was known among legal advocates as the prep. The prep was a private conversation between advocates and clients meant to prepare them for their interview (CFI/RFI) with an asylum officer. Looking at the prep offers an opportunity to see how legal care work is complicated both by detention and asylum law. How it was approached by advocates—and, importantly, how that differed from the interview—was just one expression of the ways exclusionary legal norms were contested, to some extent, in their work. To unpack how this exchange might meaningfully differ from those others in family detention—rather, how their efforts to construct a legal claim might differ from those encountered in official processes—it's necessary to first recognize the inherently compulsory manner in which asylum stories are shared. As Michelle McKinley (1997, 70) puts it, such "life story elicitation is ineluctably coercive in the legal context—it is neither intimate nor dialogic." McKinley referred to legal encounters in which refugees are required to identify their claim through personal "narratives," stories intended to support their legal case (Vogl 2013). Without disavowing the coercive nature of asylum legal processes, I contend that advocate-client encounters could be understood as intimate, caring, even at times dialogic. These could also lead to cocreated stories that go beyond those typically expected of legal encounters with refugees (Smith-Khan 2017). These sorts of moments unfolded in the prep.

I consider here how this narrative cocreation might represent a kind of care work. As will be illustrated in chapter 4, observations of the fear interview or court, wherein applicants meet decision-makers that make judgments on their "credibility" and eligibility for asylum, indeed affirm claims about how refugee stories are perceived as "messy" or "unmanageable" (Malkki 1996, 385). This could be understood, in part, as a result of the expectation for people "especially in Western countries . . . to create a 'coherent, acceptable and constantly revised' (3) life story that they can tell" (Götsch and Palmberger 2022, 12, citing Linde 1993). When asylum applicants, or others, cannot do this in expected ways, this can lead to suspicion and dismissal of their stories and, consequently, legal claims. While it needn't be this way, my own and others' observations in those spaces confirm the kind of "reductive narrative parameters" (Woolley 2017) of the interview process, one that relies on a "rigid, interrogative, closed question and direct answer format" (Baillot, Cowan, and Munro 2009, 209), a format that few of us are capable of navigating with ease. Thus, by approaching the creation of a personal asylum narrative in a different way, legal advocates are engaged in a kind of narrative care, one that aimed to make situated, contextualized, legal "legibility" of the "messiness" of individual life experiences. The way that this was practiced by advocates was itself messy, complicated; the environment and constraints around caregiving in such a way shaped this. Although the chapter attends largely to the way this occurred in the prep, it also addresses how other narratives and practices of "counterstorytelling" materialized. This demonstrates the importance of recognizing forms of what have been deemed "implicit activisms" (Horton and Kraftl 2009) or "quiet activism," those "small, everyday, embodied acts . . . that can be either implicitly or explicitly political in nature" (Pottinger 2017, 215). In this exceptional liminal space, the stories of strangers—advocate and detainee—transected, sticking together in different ways; new and sometimes alternative narratives were allowed to take hold in these encounters between the two. Even within the constraining and often misleading narrative parameters of asylum processes in detention, legal advocates located various opportunities for smaller forms of resistance, through practices of counterstorytelling or counternarration.

THE GAME

First, a clarifying point: I shared the opening composite story not because it corresponds with the work I or other legal advocates did in the prep meeting to help shape an "asylum story" out of any individual applicant's experiences. Indeed, in that sense, I did very little work, as Xiomara already understood what was expected of her in this process, and she was able to clearly show how their experiences supported a strong case for asylum, without any significant aid from me. Rather, I offer this story to illustrate other things: first, the kinds of common experiences that

FIGURE 11 Rendering of a meeting between an advocate and client with her child. Credit Erin Routon.

characterized much of what legal advocates heard from clients. What Xiomara and Martín experienced—the intimate abuse, the inability to seek safety, the extremely difficult circumstances that led a parent to have to choose to bring only one child on their journey—were commonplace experiences for those detained families. Much contemporary research on particularly gender-based violence experienced by Central American asylum seekers reflects this (López Ricoy, Andrews, and Medina 2022). It stands as a representation of the kinds of stories legal advocates encountered every day, particularly in this prep encounter. I share this story also to demonstrate how legal advocates commonly approached the prep, which was in intentional contrast to the way in which the asylum interview would be conducted. The interview is in many ways a continuation of the violences, though more symbolic, experienced by asylum seekers (Menjívar and Walsh 2019).

The prep conversation directly followed the second of the *charlas* known as the "CFI/RFI *charla*." This *charla* focused on the interview itself: what it's meant to accomplish, what constitutes asylum, how the interview would take place, and how it fit into a larger picture of the asylum process. Clients would learn of the "five protected grounds" of asylum law—race, religion, nationality, membership in a particular social group, and political opinion. These inherently limited, categorical "boxes" are those in which applicants' experiences and thus their cases need to fit to receive a passing decision, allowing them to continue in this process. Clients were told about the significance of establishing the "nexus" in their interview, or rather the meeting point between their reasons for having left and the inability to obtain protection from that harm. Along with this, they were told about important questions that would be asked by the asylum officer to get to the heart of these concerns. Afterward, clients waited to meet with advocates individually in the private rooms that lined the walls of the visitation area.

The conversation generally proceeded in a more open-ended fashion, with advocates guiding it into areas that were considered important. The advocate would ask follow-up questions and take notes throughout the conversation, recording pertinent details for later stages of the process. Each prep varied in its qualities, though there were consistencies: they were emotionally challenging moments, for both advocates and clients; intimate and traumatic stories were shared; and clients and advocates alike worked together to establish a reasonable legal claim and a sense of preparedness for the interview. While the *charla* served to inform clients about the asylum process, fully comprehending the complex, convoluted categories of asylum law could be challenging for those who were unfamiliar, including advocates. The prep, then, was crucial work because it helped to connect personal experiences with legal categories relevant to asylum.

Applicants almost solely rely on their ability to communicate their claim through their own narration. For this interview, "a refugee applicant is expected to present largely unchanging autobiographical testimony, where the relationships between events are clear, causative and able to be placed within [the] finite narrative arcs" that might define a "successful narrative" (Vogl 2013, 83, also citing Ewick and Sibley 1995). This is despite the fact that their lives, like all others, do not neatly fit such "narrative conventions" and that, what's more, the expectations in a single interview are neither predictable nor static but are rather context dependent, relying on an individual "decision-maker's multiple, deeply embedded and implicit narrative-based understandings of the world" (Vogl 2013, 83) and subjective assessments of vague concepts like "credibility" (Millbank 2009). Even though certain forms of nonnarrative evidence could be presented—such as documents, like police reports, or bodily "evidence," like scars—the asylum officer's decision truly depends on an applicant's responses to questions and presentation of their credibility. Bodily suffering is still a prominent subject within the asylum process—a point that has been critiqued at length (e.g., Fassin 2005, 2007; Fassin and D'Halluin 2007; Fassin and Rechtman 2009; Ticktin 2011)—though such suffering is often spoken about rather than displayed. This helps explain the emphasis legal advocates placed on prepping clients beforehand. Joe, a former attorney from Austin and long-term volunteer with the project at Karnes, described the importance of the prep to me over our lunch one day in the small breakroom connected to the visitation area. "The interview is like a basketball game," he told me through a mouthful of cookies he scarfed down before his next meeting. "The preps are like practice. You can't go out onto the court without knowing the rules of the game first, right?"

Joe's use of the analogy of a basketball game, with the prep being practice, recalls Granfield's (1992) "game orientation," or the adversarial ideology that partly informs law students' training. This orientation clearly affected how some advocates, particularly lawyers or law students, imagined the problem they faced in this context and how to respond to it, so the analogy, from that perspective, seemed well suited. However, what some, especially experienced attorneys, found frustrating about what they witnessed in Dilley and Karnes concerned the fact that this stage of the asylum process is not meant to be adversarial (Augustine-Adams and Núñez 2021). As volunteer attorney Rebecca remarked, asylum is supposed to be different from other forms of immigration proceedings:

> Removal proceedings and bond hearings, those are supposed to be adversarial. Think more like criminal court, where you're on the defense, there's hardly any room for dissent, and there's no real room for a defense. But with asylum, technically it's supposed to be helpful. They're supposed to find a reason [for why the seeker deserves asylum]. They're supposed to be on your side.

Indeed, as training documentation for asylum officers shows, processes like the fear interview are specifically intended, through official policy, to be nonadversarial (USCIS 2019b). But as Rebecca and other advocates recognized, that was not what often emerged in practice, highlighting the importance of the prep. The interview was frequently committed in an adversarial manner, regardless of any undisclosed intentionality of the officer (to which my research cannot speak). This counterintuitive nature might, then, be better navigated through a kind of game orientation. Asylum is a kind of complex, dynamic game involving things like misdirections and secretly meaningful key words or phrases. Some experienced legal advocates used that orientation to the advantage of those ill-prepared to play it.

Anthony Good (2006) deploys Conley and O'Barr's (1990) "rule versus relational" frame to make sense of important differences between asylum seekers (relational) and their lawyer's (rule) orientations to their cases. He claims that this orientational approach offers a better way of understanding how asylum seekers' cases unfold, as the personal narratives of these "users" of the law are suppressed by the necessity for "translators" of various sorts. He addresses the ways that such processes reproduce power inequalities within the asylum process by noting that the asylum seeker is inherently dependent on these others to navigate them. Although Good's assessment is instructive, in this context—wherein detained applicants can rarely have lawyers or other representatives speak on their behalf—they must come to inhabit this rule orientation themselves. If not, their ability to pass this stage becomes more like a game of chance. An individual asylum seeker might elect to articulate their case and prior experiences in terms expected and desired by the officer. As many advocates here and elsewhere have argued, however, because of the extremely complex nature of asylum law—which confounds even experienced immigration attorneys—they are unlikely to do so. Not only this, but detained applicants were both frequently and profoundly unaware of their rights as well as unable to properly defend those rights (for a range of reasons, including language barriers, disabilities, health issues, etc.).

While temporary volunteers were advised by staff on how to approach the prep, the work was done privately and thus was committed with relatively no immediate supervision. Advocates approached this task in their own way, though they often constructed their approach through collaborative efforts with other volunteers and project staff. While conducting the prep, they took notes on a client's case, later uploading this information to the online data management system used by the team in tracking the information and processual steps of each of the clients they served. As clients explained why they sought asylum, their reasons

FIGURE 12 Notepads from interview preps. Credit Erin Routon.

understandably did not always align with the expectations set for a so-called legitimate asylum claim. While many advocates saw their role in their prep differently, all attempted to draw out personal experiences that served an asylum claim while, without invalidating other reasons or details, trying to shift the client's gaze toward those experiences that would be meaningful to the officer's determination. As they listened to what the client had to say about why they came to the United States and requested asylum, they searched for the legal claim among the details shared with them while also testing the strength—or likelihood of obtaining a positive response—of that claim.

Sally Engle Merry (1990) attends to this sight, or the ways that ordinary laypeople come to understand and use the law, achieving a sort of "legal consciousness." Legal advocates perform as kinds of "legal brokers," rather those who "carry out a 'legal translation role' by reducing gaps in meaning between the institutions of the receiving country and newly arrived immigrants, who have little or no knowledge of complex immigration laws and bureaucracies" (Galli 2023, 12, referencing Coutin 2000 and Lakhani 2013, 2014). The work committed in the prep also corresponds with how such actors participate in determining an asylum applicant's "humanitarian capital," which Chiara Galli (2023, 14, referencing Bourdieu 1986) defines as a "form of 'symbolic capital' that legal brokers activate relationally as they interview their clients by recognizing specific instances of suffering in their lived experiences and attributing differential value to each." The translational work advocates performed aimed to assist their clients in reaching this sort of consciousness, deemed necessary for proper self-representation. As Galli notes, legal brokers operate as both agents and critics of the law, and the ensuing sections will demonstrate this uneasy navigation within and beyond the prep. Their narrative work served to contest things like the euphemizing language of those employed within the facility as well as affirm certain experiences of injustice, either at the center or prior.

CHALLENGES

Noe, a volunteer immigration attorney, explained what it was like for someone with her professional background to do a prep:

> CFI preps are hard. Our minds keep running past [the story] to get to the merits of the claim. We're thinking ahead, after all of [this stage]. . . . Even though this is a humanitarian emergency, you're forcing this person to get the facts out in a certain amount of time; it's really hard. They could've repressed it. It's hard to fish for that. It's painful and traumatic. I focused on making them comfortable with me at first to get them to open up. If I didn't feel that person trusted me, I would take 10–15 minutes at the beginning to communicate that I was on their side, what happens after, that we will work together on this. Some wanted to know what happens later. It's really about adjusting to different needs.

There were many challenges inherent in doing this part of the work, from remaining focused on the singular stage at hand to establishing trust in a brief period to language barriers, among other things. Such challenges tested the abilities of advocates. Noe's comments here touch on some of those challenges, such as building trust and potentially pressuring the client to dredge up painful memories for the purposes of building a strong asylum claim. "It's a crazy thing to ask of a stranger," Molly, an immigration lawyer from Colorado, explained. "Like, hey, tell me about the terrible things that happened to you 'cause I'm helping you to practice to tell it to somebody else, who has the power to open the door to asylum or slam it in your face. That's a bizarro thing. . . . It just doesn't happen in real life very often." In fact, many advocates shared this sense of the strangeness of specifically the prep. This sort of discomfort resulting from the fact that advocates often had to take up unexpected roles—at times feeling more akin to counseling—is something that speaks to larger issues surrounding manufactured crises like these and the capacities of humanitarian action.

Building trust with clients was of paramount concern in this exchange. Establishing a dynamic of trust allowed for a more productive and honest conversation that could lead to a claim. Advocates had different approaches to establishing trust in the prep, though there were specific ways that were encouraged by the project staff, such as reminding the client of the confidentiality of the conversation. This proved to be immensely important. Some clients expressed concern that their abusers or gang members would somehow be able to find out where they were, at the center; they were also afraid that things that they might say against such persons would somehow find their way back to those individuals, possibly incurring further harm. Some clients even expressed fear of using the telephones to speak with family or friends, afraid that such calls would be surveilled or recorded. Some advocates argued that the nature of the environment in which both detainees and advocates were observed at nearly all times encouraged this sense of unease, creating barriers to establishing trust with clients. Molly agreed: "You can be so good at [building trust] and then be in this weird, artificial prison scenario. . . . I mean, I think it would be my natural instinct not to trust anybody in this environment." In response to this, one of the project staff attorneys described how to approach resolving a problem with a client that was reticent or unclear in what they shared with the advocate. "If you have the sense that a client is lying or withholding info," she suggested,

> maybe it would be better to remind her who isn't going to hear the story that she's telling. Start from the place of believing her and building up her confidence in the confidentiality of your conversation and see if that gets you anywhere, rather than starting from a place of trying to pick apart the

> inconsistencies in somebody's story and point out how they're lying to you. Starting from a place of trust helps you build more trust rather than the other way around.

The "other way around" referred to the way in which the actual interview took place, wherein, as previous advocates' comments have noted, the seemingly adversarial and untrusting approach to locating an asylum applicant's claim was common.

One of the challenges for advocates in these preps involved struggling against and eventually coping with the reality of the inflexible asylum law with which their clients would be faced to contend. When an advocate worked with a client in a prep who had, as many would describe, a "complicated" claim—meaning the details of her claim didn't fit neatly into a particular asylum category—the ensuing struggle inevitably involved both parties. The client struggled to prove both the validity of her claims as well as her deservingness of refuge in the United States, while the advocate struggled to help the client shape varied experiences into a claim while also coping with the emotional toll that accompanied that labor. In truth, the work of the prep was almost inevitably an emotionally challenging endeavor. When a client either struggled to understand the allowances and barriers to asylum or was challenged to identify details from their past that would fit the limited legal boundaries, the work was doubly stressful for both.

This issue could take many different forms. In the prep, a client could, for instance, either imply or state explicitly that they were not "afraid" of anything, rather that they did not flee their country out of fear of something but that they were leaving out of a lack of economic opportunity. Fear, of course, was central to articulating a claim, as it is implicated in the central question involved in seeking asylum. This involves what is known as "claiming fear"—a fear of returning to one's home country—upon crossing the border and thus "triggering" the official asylum legal process for an individual.[2] Additionally, some clients would enter the prep claiming what advocates called a "generalized fear," meaning that

2. This process was impacted by the legal and procedural changes to asylum that occurred during the Trump administration (and continued during the Biden administration). At the time of this research, however, this was still the norm.

they described their reasons for leaving in more depersonalized terms. When a client entered a prep making such statements, advocates would likely then have to spend a longer amount of time working with them on helping them to articulate an individual, though contextually situated, claim. Sometimes this required multiple preps, hours of time (in certain instances, stretching out over days), multi-advocate brainstorming, and increased stress. For some advocates, this could make them feel an additional degree of discomfort with the prep, as if they were "pulling out" past experiences from a client rather than helping a client hone their case. This could make an advocate feel as though, even if attempting to help them, they were harming them.

Some clients, even after spending a great deal of time working with advocates, simply did not seem to have reasonable asylum claims. This was quite rare, with some chalking it up to factors like the carceral environment, the limited amount of time following a traumatic journey, or the stress induced by those combined conditions. The existence of such cases placed undue stress on both client and advocate in the prep, with advocates searching frantically to identify a client's claim. During immigration lawyer Tara's week in Dilley, she performed an unusually large number of such complicated preps. "Honestly, the thing that was the hardest for me out of the whole time," she explained,

> which I was not expecting at all, was meeting with the women who didn't seem to qualify for asylum. If they came to me in Denver, I would say, I'm not going to file this claim. I think I have a different view of it [now], for sure, of the importance of getting through the CFI process to be able to get out of jail, and of course, I wanted to help them through it and get a positive. It wasn't like I was like "Oh you don't qualify; you should be sent back," but it was very exhausting for me to try to pull out what felt like pulling out something from nothing, you know? Or something from very little. Or something just to fit into that asylum box when really it seemed more like a TPS [Temporary Protected Status claim].

Like Tara, Andy, an undergraduate student volunteering with the group through a Jesuit missionary project, also spent a great deal of time working with mothers who had such complicated cases. Because of his characteristic ability to connect with clients in ways that would lead to a stronger sense of trust and comfort, and thus a more fruitful conversation with reticent clients, he was often asked for help with these cases. For him, however, these were hard to stop worrying about. "When I'm in a prep," Andy tells me,

> and the woman just explains what happened and you can easily identify why she'll get a positive, those almost just go out of my head pretty quickly. Like OK, she's good to go; I can go on and start thinking about the next one. But the women who have these stories that are very complicated, or the women who just don't necessarily have the strongest fear stories . . . I don't want to leave them behind, and I don't think anyone at the project wants to leave them behind, but it's almost like we're fighting a battle that's not going to be successful in the end. We know that, but we still have to [do it].

Andy and Tara expressed important common sentiments in having to do these sorts of preps, that there is an inherent responsibility for the advocate to locate the claim and that the burden of the complicated case rested on them as it did on the clients themselves.

Molly described this in terms of conflicting agendas: "You, as the person doing the prep, have an agenda, and that makes it hard too. It's a hard thing to balance, my agenda versus their need to tell their story, in their words." For many advocates with whom I worked, a sense of these agendas as incommensurate was clear. Many expressed that one of the more important roles they served involved the positioning of their work, distinguishing it from that of the asylum officer. Yet some advocates saw what they did as forcing clients to divulge traumatic experiences in ways that led them to question their aims. These advocates felt a more significant discomfort with their role as legal actors who, despite their deep interest in the welfare of detained families, were situated in a position of authority over the client, even if they were not, in fact, legal professionals or authorities on the subject of asylum (as was the case for a significant number of volunteer advocates). Although detainees were in no way required to meet with advocates, to share any information with them or receive assistance with their cases, they were effectively left without options. Mia, the student journalist, eloquently expressed this layered sense of unease:

> It's very intense to sit through a CFI prep because people bare their souls to you very quickly, not necessarily out of trust but out of necessity. They feel obliged to. It's very one-sided. . . . It's incredible to hear really difficult stories, to sit through those for hours and piece them together. There's a certain part of your brain that shuts off so that you don't try to compute everything that they're saying. . . . [And] it's more like confessional. . . . [I felt] like I was in a position of power over them, but I essentially got a PowerPoint and was telling people what to say about their life. It's like puzzle-solving. When you recognize that, that's a very scary thing; that's bad that you feel pleased that you structured somebody else's difficult, painful story. So that was very confusing to me to think through.

Mia's candor reflects a valid though rarely articulated sentiment, in certain respects. Although many advocates shared this attitude that they, as nonimmigration attorneys or even immigration attorneys who were not experienced with this stage of asylum, were ill-equipped to be helping women prepare for such a critical interview, few expressed their discomfort in relation to this disparity and indeed precarity in power.

Both Mia and Molly, though articulating distinct reasons for discomfort relative to the prep, together demonstrate another necessary point: that the questioning and challenging of the legal advocacy work itself had a constant presence. Project staff routinely expressed sincere receptiveness to feedback from temporary volunteers and were also themselves often critical of elements of the work, expressing frustration at how they felt hamstrung by larger organizational and administrative constraints. These sentiments, indeed even debates, reflected a kind of challenge to what has been called the "unquestioned logics" of "humanitarian reason" and related efforts (Fassin 2012). Although not many expressed the sort of deeper critique or concern that Mia offered, advocates and project staff frequently debated the functions of their work and the roles they potentially played in facilitating the very things they contested.

Richard Delgado (1989, 2440) argues that stories are powerful tools "because they invite the listener to suspend judgment, listen for the story's point, and test it against his or her own version of reality." For some, one of the difficult elements of this work was not having to test clients' stories against their own reality but having to consider it within the limits of asylum law. This was painful for advocates who recognized both the value of stories that didn't fit neatly within asylum, in those challenging preps, and the responsibility to work within those constraints, searching for a legally acceptable experience of fear. This was exacerbated by a recognition of the potentially harmful power imbalances between advocates and detained clients as well as the unpredictable nature of work dependent on volunteer, often nonexpert legal care.

The challenging preps did also help prove arguments about the necessity of advocacy, of a different kind of legal attention or care—one that, especially given the constraints, called for a degree of creative or imaginative problem-solving. The prep should not be understood simply as translational work but also as a form of encounter that was deeply imaginative. Liisa Malkki (2015, 13) reminds us that "humanitarianism is an object of imagination, and aid projects engage in many imaginative practices." Amid conversation, advocates worked to imagine a client's asylum claim: to listen to the complex, multifaceted details of a person's experiences and through that, build a case that fit within the narrow boundaries of the law. This was fraught work for a number of reasons already discussed. But such imaginative work was not limited to prep; they also worked to create alternative narratives, some of which were indirectly related to their legal efforts.

COUNTERS AND CORRECTIONS

One concern tied to this specific sort of narrative legal work involves "the institutional co-opting and subsequent translation of asylum seekers' stories into legalese or into psychological categories [which] risks alienating asylum seekers from their own experiences" (Haas 2023, 29). In response, Haas encourages "listening differently" to asylum seekers' self-narrations, especially attending to their own "counterstories," those that "challenge dominant public and even scholarly representations of them as either passive victims or potential threats and expose the asylum system as a site of political and social injustice" (29). Thinking about the concern in broader terms, the crucial work of critical race theorists has demonstrated the multitude of ways that power is asserted and contested through language. Delgado (1989) explores this in acts of counterstorytelling. Looking at how legal counterstorytelling acts were used to reform racist policies, Delgado shows how such contestations of power challenge dominant discursive constructions of reality, those that are otherwise expressed, through law, as natural (which of course they are not). Beyond the work of the prep, advocates engaged in other narrative contestations, acting as counterstorytellers. For some advocates, this meant emphasizing clients' undue victimization through punitive incarceration. For others, emphasis on the opposite, in a sense, mattered more, as they instead hoped to reiterate and affirm the personal power and fortitude of detained clients.

Carolina, an undergraduate student volunteer, was seated on the couch at the Big Table meeting one early evening. She had come to Dilley intending only to serve as an interpreter for the several non-Spanish-speaking law students with whom she traveled from New York. She was excited about the opportunity, as the law school paid her way, though she didn't imagine that she would end up doing legal work on her own. This was a common preconception among folks volunteering explicitly as interpreters, though it was rare that such a volunteer would perform only that task.

That evening, she shared an encounter with a mother she'd prepped for her interview. The details of her case, Carolina explained, were extremely upsetting, as another case involving serious domestic trauma. "After a while, I told her I needed to go talk to a lawyer [to get feedback on helping her shape her case], but in my head I was thinking, I need to get out of here, I'm going to cry, I need to get out of here," she explained. Streaks of tears began to shine down her cheeks, the streams running parallel to her long, dark curls. "I was saying to myself, 'Don't cry, Carolina. You have to be strong. You're not supposed to cry; you're here to help her.'" Carolina was openly crying during her retelling to all of us encircled around her, though she continued. "I told this mom, who was very young," she said,

> "You know that you're strong, right?" I mean, this mom was a DV [domestic violence] victim and had been told these awful things about herself, and so I told her, "You know whatever [your abusers] said isn't true, right? You are a brave, good person. You're a strong, independent woman. You know that, right?" And she said to me, "Well, that's what my mom always tells

> me . . ." and I said, "Well, it's true." And that, to me, doesn't have anything to do with legal help, but it's really important.

What was meaningful to Carolina in this exchange, a story that left most of us in tears, was her attempt to reframe a kind of narrative in this client's "story." Although Carolina characterized this as not having "anything to do with legal help"—an opinion shared by several of my interlocutors around related exchanges—what she did unexpectedly reflected impulses and accompanying acts that played a significant role in these advocates' work. This form of cocreated, almost micro-counterstorytelling took many forms, but it always took aim at what were perceived by advocates to be destructive or disempowering narratives. These were narratives that clients alluded to in conversation as a result of previous trauma or more current conditions; they were also harmful narratives that circulated, in varied formulations, inside the facility itself. For some, like Carolina, such comments were intended to respond to the manifold injustices experienced by clients; not only had many experienced significant trauma prior to leaving, but they continued to suffer, in detention and through asylum processes.

In another week in Dilley, after working with a Haitian client extensively on her complex asylum claim, Jack, a volunteer attorney, felt at a loss. Always sharply dressed in a full suit, Jack was an experienced attorney in his seventies with a friendly, warm demeanor. Despite this, he struggled to get his client to speak openly with him. As this client had received a negative decision on her interview, she needed to enter into additional processes to maintain her case, meaning she would have to see an immigration judge, appearing remotely via the facility's courtroom, to decide on her case's future. Jack had done additional work to prepare her for this appointment, and before their third meeting together, he had sought advice from a fellow volunteer about how to bolster a sense of comfort between them. Jane, a volunteer from Chicago experienced with working with assault victims, advised him on how to approach their next meeting. "'Affirm her,' she told me, 'affirm her,'" he said.

> "Tell her she's strong, tell her she's a good mother, tell her what she's done is amazing." As soon as Jane tells me that, I think, of course that's what I have to do! So I had this realization and was using a Creole interpreter for

> that third meeting. I told the interpreter, "Will you please tell her that I think she is an incredibly strong person, and that I admire and respect her." And I waited for the interpreter to say those words, and the client lost it, and I lost it, and I saw that she understood what I was saying to her: that I respected and admired her.

He felt as if even by uttering those simple words to her, the dynamic of their relationship had changed. She appeared to relax around him, and after she returned to the visitation trailer from court, having received a positive decision on her appeal, she ran to embrace Jack. Both Carolina and Jack expressed how affirming the strength or "goodness" of their clients was meaningful for each client involved. Even though, of course, this research cannot definitively speak to a sense of meaningfulness of these narrative exchanges from the perspective of clients themselves, it was evident that for those advocates, an impact was felt or observed.

Project staff also expressed an impelling desire to counter, or rather "correct," particular narratives. Carlos, a kind, energetic person with what seemed to be immeasurable patience, was a project staff member who wore many hats, from organizing volunteer work to prepping clients and leading *charlas*. By the time we sat down to talk one Friday night at the ranch, it was pitch-black outside, and he was exhausted from a long, hard week at the center. His voice was hoarse from speaking with clients and volunteers for the typical ten- to twelve-hour staff workday. When I asked about how it felt for him to do the preps, he spoke frankly:

> It's not so much that this is like affecting me; it's more like, "This is what you need to know for your CFI because it's so important that you do a good job." They need to understand that they are the victim here. They aren't the ones that have broken a law; these people are fucking them over. They should not have gone through any of this experience. So that's the thing; my mind isn't in like this mode where I'm listening to her story and thinking, "Oh my God, this is insane"; it's more like, "Fuck everyone else." It's like, "This is what you need to know, do a good job, and I'm so sorry this happened to you."

Carlos's comments reflected the conflicted emotions advocates frequently expressed feeling within even a single encounter, but they also reflected a common desire to correct ideas implicit in their clients' detention. This kind of contestation or counternarrative recalls a familiar trope in humanitarian engagements with refugees, particularly in the ways that narratives are used for political or social justice ends and especially those that center stories of suffering (Kisiara 2015): "NGOs and other organisations supporting refugees can also perpetuate stereotypes by choosing to tell certain kinds of stories—victim/hero/survivor—in order to elicit sympathy and influence public opinion," among other purposes (Sheringham and Taylor 2022, 289). Deploying the language of "victim" here also harkens to the binary so often used to differentiate refugees—between victim and threat—to determine "worthiness" of sympathy, empathy, or protection (Nayak 2015; Polychroniou 2021).

The usage in this context, however, complicates such an interpretation, as advocates found themselves in an active struggle against administrative authorities who either explicitly or implicitly communicated to asylum seekers that they were in detention as punishment for some legal infraction. This was not the case, and Carlos, like other advocates, found himself amid an immediate need to correct this incorrect narrative, one perpetuated by administrative officials of various sorts. Additionally, this strong desire to correct such misinformation ostensibly operated as a kind of distraction from the primary goal of preparing clients for their interviews, as the emotions tied to such an injustice took hold. Clients frequently shared the many forms of misinformation disseminated to them by officials, often in their encounters that occurred with border patrol officers or ICE officials at the border. They would mention these comments to confirm their accuracy, as these lies were often of the sort that caused serious concern. Some were told that they would not be able to receive asylum without physical proof of their claims (which many did not have), again like police reports or death certificates. Others were informed that because of their nationality or age, they would not be given asylum (Routon 2024). These sorts of experiences, while deeply disturbing, are not uncharacteristic of the practices of ICE or U.S. Customs and Border Patrol, especially in their entanglements with migrant detention (Detention Watch Network and Heartland Alliance's National Immigrant Justice Center 2018). It was important for many advocates to immediately refute these claims, as they were not only harmful to clients' ability to defend themselves in the face of such misinformation, but they were also harmful in that they served to normalize punishment through incarceration, as a necessary response to those seeking asylum.

Delgado (1989, 2412) reminds us that the "dominant group creates its own stories," and that the "stories or narratives told by the ingroup remind it of its identity in relation to outgroups, and provide it with a form of shared reality in which its own superior position is seen as natural." The ways that the qualities of the space itself were discussed daily, even in casual, passing moments, lie on deeply contested grounds. Facility staff repeatedly worked to affirm the space's identity as a noncarceral facility and their own roles within it as noncarceral as well. Their intention was to project a "caring" image of the center, and they did this not only through the material designs of the facility but also in the language used in everyday encounters. Advocates contested these caring ideologies that were embedded within this obfuscating everyday language.

"We can't make her come here. It's not like this is a prison," a male facility guard said to a group of advocates one day in Dilley. On that frantic afternoon, he said this as he looked off in the distance, leaning back in his desk chair. He was visibly annoyed at our request for his assistance in "locating" a client with whom advocates needed to speak on an urgent matter related to her case. Legal advocates were incapable of notifying clients directly, so the advocacy team relied heavily on the guards' cooperation in this effort to find and notify clients. His response—which implied that he or other guards had notified the client of our interest in speaking with her but she was intentionally choosing not to come to where we were located to meet with us—was a common refrain from guards. Such comments, concerning the nature of the facility, were not infrequently made without prompting, and their constant, unprovoked presence hinted at a specific intention: to affirm the identity of these facilities as noncarceral.

Such narrative conflicts between facility staff and advocates were common. Norah, another project staff member, shared a story of how in one of what was the project's weekly meetings with ICE officials, in part to discuss important concerns legal advocates had about clients and their treatment, she had apparently and unintentionally offended one official by referring to those in his profession as *la migra*. He angrily scolded her for using the term, telling her that she could not use this word because it was a derogatory slur for officials. Norah's encounter in this instance, which was repeated in different forms between advocates and guards, ICE officials, and judges, reflected an additional point about counterstorytelling in this context. Facility officials often rejected the language that was in circulation not only with advocates but also with detainees, and several advocates experienced encounters with those officials in which they forcefully sought to deny such terms. This extended even beyond advocates themselves. In another instance, an interpreter in the courtroom with a client, advocate, and judge had deployed the almost universally applied term *grillete* to refer to the ankle monitoring device after the judge had wanted this device explained to the client. When the televised judge then asked the interpreter what *grillete* translated to—to which she replied, "a shackle"—he flew into a rage, telling the interpreter that she should have used the language used by officials: ankle bracelet. The interpreter challenged this, arguing that by using the term for a bracelet, the client would be confused, as *grillete* was the term in use by detainees. The device about which they were speaking was not a bracelet to them, she explained. Many instances like this occurred in different forms, often creating conflict between advocates and officials, particularly those who sought to use euphemized terminologies around care.

Power can be seen as exerted or contested through language in daily, grounded invocations such as these. The sorts of oppressive, controlling linguistic tactics practiced by guards and other administrators here is, in fact, not uncommon in private immigrant detention settings (Bailey-Hall and Estrada 2022), though they are not exclusive to those spaces and entities. Richland (2008), in his ethnographic work on Hopi tribal courts, describes these invocations as the "discursive microdetails" of legal practice. His and other related work show how contests over power, authority, and adjudicatory legitimacy can only be understood through an attention to the microdetails of discourse in courtroom interactions. While this will be explored more deeply in chapter 4, it is important to think about how the discursive microdetails of legal practice function beyond the courtroom or asylum office. Immigration officials and administrative staff, in these instances, exerted their considerable power through attempts to control narratives that impacted legal aid and rights. When legal advocates insisted on referring to the setting in which they met with clients as a baby jail, prison, or detention center, they were using language to contest both the legal and ethical legitimacy of the place. They were challenging the discursive reality through these kinds of "corrections."

Advocates, in the language they chose to use with or around clients, were staking claims on numerous aspects of the "legal reality" of the context through, sometimes, their own manipulations of the space's varied "microlinguistic dimensions" (Matoesian 2001). By repeatedly affirming the carceral and punitive nature of the facility, and consequently rejecting the sanitized, caring language in use by the administrators of the center, they were constructing an alternative story. This may have been a less comforting narrative than that provided by the facility's administrators, but from the perspective of advocates, it was important that this reality be affirmed. As Delgado (1989, 2438) notes in relation to legal storytelling for racial progress, "complacency—born of comforting stories—is a major stumbling block. . . . Counterstories can attack that complacency." In addition to a kind of narrative complacency, a lack of recognition of the reality of these spaces could inflict material and symbolic harm, not just on detained families but advocates as well. In the following final section, though, I think about counterstorytelling between advocates and their clients in a different way. Up to this point, I've considered narrative work in more intentional terms, with advocates engaging practices to shape narratives in facility encounters. Counterstories circulated in another form, albeit one that was less expected by advocates; at least for some, these significantly impacted their own stories.

STICKY STORIES

In returning to that other crucial part of storytelling—listening—Maria Tamboukou (2021, 149) reminds us that "in the same way that we are situated speakers, we are also always, already situated listeners: we always listen from somewhere, no matter how open or willing we are to move from our position." In my conversations with interlocutors, one question I always asked was if there were encounters with the mothers or children or stories they heard in their work that "stuck with them." Some would initially reply that none came to mind, but then, eventually, as the conversation progressed, there was always at least one that rose to the top. Many would identify it quickly, and we'd talk through why. I came to think of these as "sticky stories," inspired by Sara Ahmed's (2014) conceptual use of "stickiness." Ahmed discusses the circulatory "economies" of emotions and how emotions are used to "stick" certain persons together with figurative others. In her work, she specifically notes the way that fear is used to cohere the figure of "the asylum seeker" with that of "the terrorist," while also showing how hatred is economically galvanized in relation to the figure of the bad or bogus asylum seeker. This, in turn, affects how aid workers might shape their contrasting narratives about migrants seeking asylum. While the actual effects of their renarrations—as not inherently threatening or dangerous persons—may not quite meet the intended effects, it's important, following Ahmed and others (e.g., Laliberté and Schurr 2015), to chart the variety of emotional entanglements circulating throughout, as this leads to a better understanding of advocates' experiences and contestations. For my work, I was interested in exploring the sticky stories of labor and emotions in client encounters.

"Narrative helps explain the world, but it also helps imagine other possible worlds" (Götsch and Palmberger 2022, 8–9). This sort of narrative affect was evident in some advocates' sticky stories, like Paula's. Paula was a paralegal for an office in San Francisco that mostly worked on business immigration cases. She had had experience with pro bono asylum work before and had volunteered with some legal clinics, most often as a Spanish interpreter. When she was asked to accompany a partner in her firm to Dilley, as their interpreter, she did not even know these facilities existed. And yet, Paula's personal connection to what she encountered in Dilley was profound. She herself had migrated to the United States without legal documents with her mother when she was nine. "When they were telling me their stories, I knew what they had gone through," she said.

> Crossing is hard. I was lucky enough that I had an uncle in Mexico, and we were able to stay with him during the process. Some of these women don't have support like that, so in that way their experience is really different. They would come from Central America just on their own. But I could still put myself in their shoes. I said to myself, that could be me, or that could be my mom or my brother. A lot of the women I worked with were from El Salvador, which is where I'm from. I remember the whole experience well. There are certain things, certain details that never leave you.

While Paula connected with the women she worked with over their shared experiences of crossing, the more meaningful connection she found between them had to do with a common experience across many clients' lives: having to leave children behind. Many detained mothers, particularly those who had asylum claims related to the children that they had brought with them on the journey, were capable of bringing only one or some of their children. This was often a painful point of discussion, both in preparations for and during their interviews. In working with clients who had effectively been forced to leave children, Paula felt that pain, albeit from a different perspective. "I cried a lot with the women that I worked with, but that last day that I was there in Dilley, one story from one of the women just hit me kind of hard," she told me.

> I thought about when I left El Salvador. You see, I grew up with my grandmother there because my mom was here, in the U.S. I understand that when mothers leave their kids behind, they make a decision to do that, come here either on their own or with just one child. So my mother left me and my brother, and we grew up with our grandmother. She became the only mom I knew. I called her mom. So when my mom would come to visit, I didn't even know her because I didn't grow up with her. She would say to me, "I'm your mom," but to me, she was a stranger, you know? I didn't feel that she was my mom. So when she came back to take us to the U.S., it was like I was coming to a new country, with a new everything else, and with a stranger. They were our parents, but they were strangers. I left my grandmother behind, and I never saw her again because she passed away. So one of the women I was working with that last day, she told me that she had to leave her *viejitos*, and it just reminded me of that. She said that they were crying and told her not to leave, and it just reminded me of my grandmother, my *viejita*, saying the same thing. Probably because she knew we were never going to see her again. So that was really hard for me.

Paula not only understood what it felt like to have to leave, possibly never seeing family members again, but also how it felt to be the one that was left. She was deeply empathetic toward her client's position, while at the same time reflecting on this intimate pain.

> I would ask the women how many kids they had, and they would say three or four, but they could only bring one because of the costs, or could only bring the youngest because they were breastfeeding, or whatever. I didn't really press them on that. I'd say to them, you know, "You're really strong, that's a really hard thing to do, as a mother, leave someone behind." But I

> think, from the perspective of the child that's left, it's hard to understand any of that. Does that make sense? Because when you're a kid, you just feel like you're being abandoned. I was a baby when my mom left, so I don't really remember it happening, but as I grew up, learning that my parents just weren't there, it affected me. You think, they just decided to leave. You don't know all the reasons why it happened, and you can't really even comprehend them when you're a child. So I understand that it was hard for them, but I'm also looking at it from the perspective of the child left. I really don't know which is harder: having been left as a baby, when you don't understand, or being older and understanding. When you become a parent, you come to understand the kind of decisions parents have to make, but it still doesn't take away the things you experience when you're a kid. I look at other people now, people who got to grow up with their parents, and I think they're very lucky. I didn't get to have that.

Paula eloquently demonstrates how "intimacy forges distances and proximities as well as bonds and attachments and creates new meanings" (Sehlikoglu and Zengin 2015, 20; also Stoler 2008). In working with mothers who had left children behind, she was reminded of those feelings of abandonment, confusion, and pain, both from being left and having to leave behind others whom she cared for. The exclusionary realities of immigration law and enforcement in the United States served, in part, to create the kinds of situations that shaped Paula and her family's entire lives. Although Paula understood, then as a parent, the difficult decisions parents faced, she also actively engaged with what those feelings meant for her as a child who only understood that her parents weren't there and that when they were there, they were essentially strangers taking her away from her only home. Doing this work, then, gazing directly at the effects of structural violence from the other point of view, offered a kind of situational opportunity to confront those narratives and their associated feelings, even if in the end they remained unresolved.

Betty, an undergraduate student also from San Francisco, was not meant to be in Dilley at all. What became a deeply meaningful experience volunteering with the project began with a sudden change of plans. Shortly after finishing her first year at college, she began a summer volunteership with a migrant shelter in Mexico, which ended abruptly after she had started to be followed by local gang members. People in her volunteer community were concerned that she had been "targeted" by these men and that she could potentially be kidnapped. This was believed to be due to her physical appearance. Betty was biracial, with one Mexican parent, and appeared light-skinned. As she described it, she had often struggled with these dual identities, white and Mexican. "I've always felt like I never fit into either category," she explained.

> My white friends think that being Mexican is just a perk that I use to get scholarships, while all my Mexican friends say that I don't know what it's like to be Mexican because I don't look the part. . . . I had this huge doubt about going to Mexico for this project, and then when I had to leave it, partially because I was singled out because I looked white, it was hard. I thought, wow, I really don't belong here either. I felt really shitty coming out of that. I just didn't fit in there. I didn't blend in enough.

After leaving Mexico dejected and pessimistic, someone helped set her up as a long-term volunteer with the project in Dilley. "When I got to Dilley, I thought, well, here we go again. All these women are going to think I'm just another white face telling them what to do. Maybe they won't understand me, or I won't understand them. By the end of the very first day, though, I realized that it was just way too busy and there was too much to do to worry about stuff like that. I realized that really all any of us had were the words shared between us and that was enough." There were moments that reframed her own sense of identity and belonging, and one of those came at the end of her time there. She was serving as an interpreter with a new volunteer, a white lawyer whom Betty described, frankly, as being a "pain in the ass" to work with. While Betty could do this work alone, she instead offered to interpret for the lawyer, who then directed the flow of the conversation. Advocates who were fluent in another language spoke of how they sometimes preferred this interpretive role, as it allowed them to simply talk with the client rather than simultaneously process the details of their asylum claim. "So I was working with one of the oldest women I had ever worked with there," she said.

> She was like fifty or maybe even sixty. She was kind of a baller. She would answer every question I asked with a question for me. So I asked where she was from, and I was expecting some normal response like, "Oh, I'm from

> Guatemala or El Salvador," and that's it, but she responded with "Well, I'm from El Salvador, and you? Are you white too? *Y tu eres gringita también?*" She was referring to the white lawyer there with us, asking if I was also white. So I explained to her, "Yes, I'm white, but I'm also Mexican." And she replied, "Ahhhhh, *eso explica todo*."

Betty laughed in the retelling and continued,

> I thought to myself, this is so sweet. Within just a few seconds of meeting me, this woman understands where I'm coming from, when I feel like I've been so misunderstood for such a long time. This place, it's an easy place to belong to, in this prison of outcasts where everyone feels like they don't belong. You find a sense of belonging to a group of people that feel like they don't belong. I wasn't expecting to have that. Working with the women really taught me a lot about my identity in a way that I could've really only learned from them.

Betty's interpretations of this and other related encounters speak to how new stories can take hold in these unexpected moments, involving, like Paula, narratives of the self. In her study of Finnish humanitarian aid workers, Malkki (2015) considers the following pertinent questions: What kinds of self-to-self relations did they form through their work? How did the self, engaged in work that is often characterized as "selfless," undergo certain transformations? She contends that this has to do "with the imagination in terms of which this humanitarian subject, or self, framed both the world and her place in it" (3). As she described it, Betty felt seen in a new and deeply meaningful way, even in such brief encounters, and this, as it did with Paula, made imaginative space for their own, arguably necessary, counterstories. These sorts of "sticky engagements" (Tsing 2005), those that come out of a recognition of frictions, helped make sense of both larger and more personally-felt processes. However, sometimes those same experiences led advocates down more ambivalent paths, demonstrating that even amid clear efforts at "making life more bearable" (Mol 2008) for clients, those "unsolved tensions" (Puig de la Bellacasa 2017) of care practice remained.

Project staff, particularly in Dilley, often reminded new volunteers that they would likely be the "first people to welcome" the families with whom they worked. Given the sorts of experiences most clients described upon encountering officers and other officials at the border or the detention center, even well before the Trump administration, this seemed to be unfortunately true. This comment also made quite an impact on advocates, as they reflected on it in my conversations with them. Alicia, an immigration attorney from Detroit, volunteered with the project after her firm decided to go as a group. As a preteenager, she also came to the United States with her family as a refugee. As she aged and began working herself in immigration law, she watched as the sort of "welcoming" reception she believed she had received when she came to the country disappeared. She said that before she came to Dilley, she knew how refugees were being treated, how the United States rarely welcomed any immigrants, and that she wasn't expecting the work to be "all warm and fuzzy." She told a story of a young mother she prepped who was, incidentally, around the same age as her own children. After the woman's interview, she came right back to see Alicia. "She was so traumatized [by her past and the interview] that she wanted to just come back and talk to us some more, just to kind of decompress. And I felt like, hopefully, for an hour or so, I could be a friend to her. I could even be a mom to her." While Alicia reflected positively on her role in being able to give this attention to her client, she, like many advocates, struggled to cope with the fact that caregiving within these confines was inherently messy. "You know, I've had no, like, training in psychology or counseling or anything like that," she said, "and I wish I had training for how to deal with people who've experienced trauma beforehand. Because it's fine to just be kind, but I felt like I don't have the words. I mean, I can tell her that she's brave and strong, I can tell her that I'm proud of her . . . but is that enough? I don't know."

CONCLUSION

The discursive work of these advocates was laden with an unresolvable tension: the legal need to engage in difficult conversations often revolving around trauma. Sheringham and Taylor (2022, 289) recall for us that ideally "there is a balance to be achieved between creating safe spaces within which stories can be told and falling into the trap of soliciting traumatic narratives." Family detention and the immediacy effected by "expedited removal" asylum processes made striking this kind of balance incredibly difficult for voluntary legal advocates. How does one make a transitory, inherently punitive space safe enough to share intimate personal experiences with effective strangers? As the deadline to be interrogated by an unknown decision-maker rapidly grew near, how could advocates engage in preparatory work that hinges on explication of trauma that wouldn't cause further harm or rely on methods that delimit important human experiences?

Woolley (2017, 392) discusses how "in a context in which asylum stories may not even be heard by those institutions able to apportion rights, creating spaces for nuanced narratives of refugee experience has never been more important." This is true not just for those experiences pertinent to their legal cases—prior to arriving in the country in which they sought asylum—but also those experiences afterward. My research shows, in part, how nuanced stories were informed by the work of legal advocates in family detention, mapping onto scholarship that considers the involvement of others, including legal actors, in the construction of an individual applicant's asylum "story" (Smith-Khan 2017). I've suggested that rather than reducing—or worse, muting—experiences of asylum applicants in detention, legal advocates made space for nuance and complexity, even for apparent contradictions. While unable to undo the narrative constraints to come in the interview, these everyday practices were expressions of care that worked as a kind of counter, a denial of the primacy of "fact-finding" or determination of "credibility."

The harm that asylum law inflicts on applicants, through its myriad exclusions and varied invocations of trauma, is repeatedly made evident. This chapter has introduced some of the ways that the violences of family detention extended beyond the physical to include "assaults on personhood, dignity and the sense of worth and value of a person" (Merry 2007, 42; Scheper-Hughes and Bourgois 2004). What was less visible, though, was how legal advocates contended with this harm, thus effecting, both intentionally and unintentionally, an unavoidable form of friction. I've shown how this was approached through the prep encounter, how care was deployed to not only mitigate further harm but also to allow for different kinds of storied relations. Beyond the prep, advocates challenged dominant narratives that served to either dehumanize detainees or mischaracterize, even deny, their experiences. Legal advocates did much more than simply keep clients from being "ground up in the gears of the machinery" of the asylum process, as project attorney Allie once put it. Through caring stances in strangely intimate conversations, they offered value to experiences dismissed by the law's limited range of interest, and they helped to affirm lived realities that were experienced by clients and yet seemingly denied by officials. Their work involved changing conversations, both with and about asylum seekers, as well as scripting new stories together. In this and other ways demonstrated in the ensuing chapters, their efforts reinforced Tsing's (2005, 6) claim that "friction refuses the lie that . . . power operates as a well-oiled machine."

Scholars and activists draw our attention to the immense, even healing, power of storytelling; indeed, creating and sharing stories can be a form of care (Vargas Reyes, Lopez, and Duncan 2024). While the interview is a kind of storytelling space, even in the lead-up, it is far from careful. The way a particular officer approaches the exchange has meaningful impact, yet the nature of the process is coercive and exclusionary. In this way, the interview disallows any degree of healing through the kinds of "storytelling" it compels in asylum seekers. What I emphasize here is that in that space, the experience of creating and sharing stories could not be understood monolithically, as determined only by the requirements or limitations of the legal process. Other forms of storytelling took place in those spaces, in encounters between advocates and detained families. Some of those counternarratives occurred incidentally to advocates' legal work, impacting some in unexpected though deeply meaningful ways. In this sense, the practice of storytelling involved both expressions and experiences of care.

From the vantage point of his work with "at-risk" youth in an interpersonal violence prevention program, Greenberg (2019, 16) reminds us that "stories are social objects. Making order from chaos, they unfold action over time as a series of events or scenes, which individuals use to make sense of the past, present, and future, and the links between them. Certain details are privileged and others omitted. . . . That is, stories have power: they do things." Advocates' narrative work with detained clients demonstrated this in various ways, for various purposes. This kind of work was messy for a number of reasons that I've only begun to elucidate here; thus, this is not meant to offer a romanticized portrayal of narrative counterstorytelling in family detention. In an albeit different way, legal advocates themselves were trapped, constrained by the nature of the environment, requirements of legal processes, and unpredictable limitations placed on the kinds of care they could practice, an argument that will continue to unfold. What is evident, though, in looking at how varied stories were constructed and challenged, advocates practiced their care also in those narrative forms. Those counterstories did things, making different sense of an often chaotic, seemingly senseless landscape.

CHAPTER 3

FRICTION

On a chilly December day close to Christmas, a child collapsed on the floor of the visitation trailer and stopped breathing. Chase, the advocate who was with the girl when it happened, recalls the scenario for me. He and another advocate were in one of the small, private offices where he was playing with children while their mothers worked on their cases with other advocates. "I had to pick her up, and I ran into the main area and said to the guards, 'This child is not breathing. You need to call 911.'" They told him that neither they nor he would be making that call.

> I was like, "What are you talking about? This child is not breathing." One guard said to me, "We don't make 911 calls here." It seemed like they were trying to imply that it was related to some marketing or publicity issue. One of the project staff, one of the lawyers, ended up trying to make the call to 911 herself, but the guards didn't let her. Luckily, there was a doctor volunteering with us that week, and she was able to sort of revive the girl.

This was an extremely jarring incident, especially for someone like Chase, who had volunteered with the project for the first time that visit. He was a law student from Oregon, with a future career interest in human rights work, and would volunteer repeatedly with this project. Prior to this event, he had spent the day mostly playing with the children, sitting for them while their mothers worked on their cases. He didn't speak Spanish and wasn't experienced with immigration law, so when he looked for other ways to be helpful to the project, he found it in spending time with the children. Project staff began to playfully refer to him as the "child whisperer" for his ability to connect with many of the children, especially those who were particularly shy. They would later regale new volunteers with stories of how he would place the smaller children in the plastic bins used for document collection and push them across the floor while they squealed gleefully. "That first trip," he tells me, "I was going to the local dollar store and getting all these stickers for the kids. In the facility, we made up one of the private rooms into like a kid playroom. We had all these notepads and pens, and the kids would go around asking each other questions as if they were doing intakes. It was the most adorable thing I've ever seen." His perception of the facility, and the roles of advocates, changed after this incident. The moment in which this young girl suddenly stopped breathing, collapsed on the tile floor in front of him in the mock playroom, with him virtually helpless, was a disturbing reminder of the threatening environment in which they labored.

Moments like this, experienced in different forms by many advocates, demonstrate both the potential for extreme harm embedded in these spaces as well as how the provision of care could crash into the seemingly immovable object of the administration. The administrative response in this case, which seemed to extend beyond a sort of expression of disregard or abandonment (Biehl 2005, 2012) and instead appeared to advocates as a strategic denial of care, was directly tied to the public image of these facilities. As demonstrated by Chase's encounter, while officials were interested in projecting a caring image of the center, their practical care often remained superficial at best or as a kind of mirage at worst. From the advocates' interpretations, caring interests expressed by administrators revolved around the care of the facility rather than its prisoners.

While the explicit reason for the legal advocates' existence at these facilities was to assist detainees with their asylum claims, what they did extended far beyond the concept of legal aid. This chapter delves more deeply into how care took shape beyond explicit legal work, with particular attention to the relationship between care and conflict. How do these two conceptual objects—which seem to be at odds—inform or feed off each other in these contexts? Michelle Murphy (2015, 719) recalls for us the idea that "the exercise of power operates through care in many divergent ways," which is made evident in events like those witnessed by Chase. In the prep exchange, power operated through care via narrative contestation or counterstorytelling, as a kind of narrative care. Here, I look at the relationship between apparent expressions of power through more explicit conflicts around care.

In simple terms, this chapter considers how conflict appeared in the everyday life of these unique facilities. I show that it was commonly found in contentious encounters between advocates and administrative actors, particularly facility guards. This was due in part to the fact that guards were the administrative group with whom advocates shared space and certain work responsibilities daily; it's also due to the inherent conflict between those tasked with the microdetails of daily control and management of a carceral space and the resistance naturally effected by "free" or nonincarcerated persons traversing this same terrain (Comfort 2008). Whereas correctional officers' work is shaped through core principles and responsibilities defined, albeit ambiguously, by the triangulation of "care, custody, and control" (Peak 2023), advocates aimed to effect their own practices of care.

What I characterize as frictions between these two groups took multiple forms, while also expressing certain shared qualities wherein beliefs about what was good, necessary, or harmful for detainees and their advocates were contested. This sort of "friction of utility" of care (Backe 2018) defined the contours of these conflicts, and it played a substantive role in advocates' perceptions of and feelings about the environment. Simultaneously, the practical movement of advocates' work with detainees was determined by administrators themselves and the kinds of relationships maintained between the two groups. To give care to detainees, in other words, advocates depended on a certain level of "collaboration" with administrators. I look not only at the tensions between advocates and administrators but also at the distinct care that was given to the maintenance of those relationships. Last, I begin to examine elements of the frictions that reside within the advocacy group itself, considering how these related to the movement of their work and the ways they managed relationships with one another.

Theoretical work on care that emphasizes its "contested terrains," its interdependency (Puig de la Bellacasa 2017), as well as how practicing care involves continuous "tinkering" on uncertain grounds (Mol, Moser, and Pols 2010a), offers a window to the multilayered and complicated landscape of legal advocacy in this context, one in which the administration's implicit and explicit identification with care paradoxically delimited much care practice. Again, my work is deeply influenced by Tsing's (2005) use of friction, which is a particularly suitable concept for understanding the sorts of encounters and relationships that are borne out of legal care work in this environment. How advocates and their work grated against administrative processes and actors in these facilities was palpable every day, and the use of punishment as an expression of power (Foucault 1977) and control was not simply limited to incarcerated persons but was seen to extend to those who cared for them. Following Tsing, I consider how the boundaries of care within this space must be reimagined and reconstituted in light of these momentous and mundane frictions.

Each chapter in this book, in its own way, touches on the various frictions that existed in these facilities. This is inevitable, as I argue it was a defining quality of both daily existence within and the experiences of advocates. This work engages with only some of the ways that ideas and practices of care are made evident through frictions. What care became, from one moment to the next, was necessarily shaped by both resistance and compromise, deriving from those frictions. The scenarios presented here demonstrate that indeed frictions often revolved around questions of care: In any given encounter, who is giving care, and who is denying it? How is good (or bad) care perceived? How can care be practiced considering severe constraints? Focusing on the qualities of these boundary-defining inquiries exposes the conceptual and practical fluidity of care as well as how necessarily interdependent relationships were continuously reshaped through tinkering with care.

In making sense of these frictions, it is crucial to remember that the encounters between advocates and others in family detention were fleeting. Although this care has potentially important implications for legal encounters beyond this context, this transitory quality of the relationships defined the kind of care possible in detention. As the fleeting nature of these encounters simultaneously shaped the care given, it also informed the conflicts with which legal advocates contended. Thus, legal care in family detention was necessarily also construed through these conflicts that emerged from frictions. "Friction reminds us," Tsing (2005,

5) claims, "that heterogeneous and unequal encounters can lead to new arrangements of culture and power." Using legal care, I identify the kinds of configurations of power, relationality, and resistance that issue especially from the sorts of everyday frictions that define spaces such as these.

INTERFERENCE

Legal advocates in family detention were child caregivers. Figure 13 depicts gifts, remnants of encounters between child detainees and an advocate, after she sat with them at tables and desks or sprawled out on tile floors. Together, they colored and waited for the children's mothers to finish discussing their cases with advocates in private rooms. While mothers wiped away tears with the edge of their government-issued T-shirts, talking about *la violación,* the unreasonable *impuesto de guerra* they owed "MS" (MS-13), or even the lies *la migra* told them, their babies would sit at a table, talking about their pets from home, asking which colors they should use for the Hulk's pants, and wondering if the advocate could draw them a cat (and subsequently name it). Far from

FIGURE 13 Drawings made by anonymous child detainees and legal advocates at Dilley and Karnes. Photo credit Erin Routon.

simple colored drawings made to pass the time, the children's images were tangible expressions of quiet distraction, of attention to something at least remotely pleasurable in places that are objectively not, and of care in contested terrain.

Young children in these centers needed sources of entertainment and distraction while their mothers worked on their cases—sometimes for hours—discussing intimate details many did not want their children to hear. These conversations took place in private rooms, primarily for purposes of confidentiality and comfort. Both inside and out of these private rooms, in the open area of the visitation buildings, crayons and paper became critical tools. If children resisted separation from their mothers, they could be given these to play with in the room so that they wouldn't be listening in or distracting her from speaking. If the mother needed them to be outside of the room, other advocates could sit with them while they colored. Crayons and coloring books provided an excellent option for work with children due to their mobility in the space and the attentiveness involved in playing with them.

From the facilities' earliest days, administrators had instituted various rules about crayons and coloring books. The outlines of these rules changed frequently, and understanding the greater importance of the crayons, advocates consistently pushed back against them. In November 2016, administrative officials banned crayons at the Karnes facility, at least within the facility's visitation area (Laughland 2016), where legal advocates met with mothers and young children. It was not the first time that such items had been prohibited at a family detention center. In 2014, an incident known as "crayon-gate" had occurred at the temporary family detention facility in Artesia, New Mexico. Advocates at Dilley were also often met with barriers in attempting to bring in crayons or coloring books. At Karnes, ICE claimed that the ban had resulted from "an action resulting from crayons which RAICES staff/volunteers [had] given children which [had] caused property damage to the contractor." In other words, a child had colored on a table in the open space of the legal visitation area. Advocates of both projects responded quickly, releasing statements to the media about the ban, posting on social media, forming petitions, and tweeting about the incident to Crayola, cheekily asking for instructions on how to clean crayon marks. In a release, advocates argued not only that "such markings are a cost that comes with the detention of children" but also that "it is extremely disturbing that ICE's concern for GEO's property takes precedence over the well-being of the children and their mothers' rights to legal advice" (RAICES T. n.d.). As this statement illustrates, the uproar from advocates did not simply result from the apparent absurdity of the ban. The latter also impacted advocates' abilities to give care and mothers' abilities to obtain legal assistance because it took away options that allowed mothers to speak comfortably about their cases and thus receive the sort of attention they needed.

In this incident, advocates were the intended recipients of punishment. By explicitly naming RAICES as the instigator of the event that "destroyed" property, administrators laid bare their intentions: Children coloring on tables did not cause damaged property; advocates giving them crayons did. This incident, and the language used to describe it, demonstrates a critical argument in my research. Administrators deployed punitive strategies against advocates in both overt and covert ways, and the friction between these groups inspired different responses to what was an irreparable conflict, as their distinct efforts appeared to exist at counterpurposes. Yet despite this conflict, both administrators and advocates deployed care as a central force in their strategies and tactics.

Mere weeks after the crayon ban, I walked into the legal visitation area to find a large chalkboard installed, an apparent response to advocates' fierce and viral pushback. Many advocates wondered how facility administrators had still missed the point behind their frustration. The chalkboard, like the facility's toys, remained firmly outside of the private spaces in which parents met with advocates, where things like crayons proved the most useful. Months after the installation of this large chalkboard, I passed with a client into one of the private rooms and saw newly mounted miniature chalkboards. None of these chalkboards ever had chalk at them; that was kept at the guard's station. Children were usually too anxious around the guards to ask for the chalk themselves, and thus the boards remained perpetually blank.

Superficially, the addition of chalkboards was a material expression of care by facility administrators. This act, though, did not resolve the problem that the ban had created, and it did not assuage the friction between advocates and administrators. The chalkboards were not an equal replacement for crayons and coloring books; they did not meet the needs of the children. As a result, advocates believed, as they did in many other scenarios of conflict, that administrative responses after the fact were committed in the interest of maintaining a positive self-image rather than in the interest of actual care for the well-being of their detainees. Clients' well-being was connected to their ability to receive legal assistance, functionally impeded by not being able to separate children from their parents for brief periods.

This broad point of conflict, in which material objects meant to benefit the work of advocates became "contraband," manifested itself at various times throughout my research. It is possible to interpret these refusals as forms of punishment for advocates, as many did, as well as an expression of the state's power and authority to control and police the activities of both detained children and their parents. These often overlapped in detention. In other scenarios, administrative punitive measures appeared to more overtly correspond with efforts to interfere with the work of advocates, sometimes painfully so.

PROXIMITY

Contrary to Michel Foucault's (1977) broad assessment of the historical trajectory of the prison as by and large a shift away from bodily punishment, scholars of incarceration (e.g., Fassin 2016) show that significant degrees of punitive work on bodies have not left carceral spaces. While not often explicitly considered official elements of punishment, persistently poor health care and unmitigated sexual assault are just a couple of the ways that prisoners are subjected to forms of this body-work. With each of these examples, a disregarded care for the body is bound up with the status of imprisonment. Because care work requires bodily as well as emotional proximity (Alber and Drotbohm 2015), giving care to incarcerated individuals becomes complicated by these normative punitive strategies, especially in places like the family detention facility, which, while reproducing punishment familiar to other carceral environments, nonetheless attempt to maintain a caring identity. In the cases studied here, legal advocates became entwined in these processes; they were not only involved in counteracting detainee mistreatment, but they could also be unwittingly subjected to punitive strategies themselves.

One day in Dilley, Maria, a mother from Haiti, was on the verge of a panic attack. Sitting in the plastic chair in the empty room, she began hyperventilating. The stress of recent developments with her case seemed too overwhelming, and her future appeared ever more hopeless. She had received a negative decision from her interview, meaning that the officer did not find her claim credible. In subsequent appeals, the judge had affirmed the officer's decision; Maria was therefore left with few options before the initiation of deportation proceedings. Alejandro, a staff member of the legal project at Dilley, was seated on the opposite side of the table, watching her anxiety swirl like a dust storm. He then did what he felt she needed: He swiftly walked to her side of the table, sat next to her, and placed his hand on her shoulder while speaking softly to calm her.

After a brief period, the dust cleared just enough, and they carried on talking about the next steps for her case. Not many days after that, Alejandro walked in as usual on a Monday morning to start work with a group of new volunteers and was casually handed a piece of paper by facility staff in the security building. The letter communicated that he had been banned from the facility. Unlike the many volunteers and staff that passed through the facility, he would never enter that space again. All this because he had touched the client he was working with, and an employee of the facility saw it happen. Facility administrators decided that this gesture constituted a threat to detainees and banned him, apparently in the interest of their care.

Alejandro's experience demonstrates the unpredictable practical applications of security in detention (Hall 2012). The event was followed by intense litigation on behalf of the legal project attempting to reverse the decision to revoke Alejandro's access permissions. The experience proved incredibly difficult for him to process. Simultaneously abrupt and drawn out, he had to wait for at least a month in relative silence from administrators and his own project team to learn that the legal challenges would remain unsuccessful. He felt hurt, angry, and guilty for leaving the few remaining staff members to manage the immense workload inside without him. He was sad that he did not get to say goodbye to his clients and that he would not get to meet and help the new clients arriving every day. When we met up at a taco shop in San Antonio months later, he said he was still trying to reckon with the fact that he would not be coming back. It turned out that this ban had been expanded to prohibit him from entering all other detention spaces operated by CoreCivic—the private prison corporation that operated the Dilley center—which meant that what he had hoped would become a career of helping detainees with the language and legal skills he had built would be seriously limited. As noted previously, most migrant detention facilities are owned and operated by CoreCivic and the GEO Group, with CoreCivic currently operating over seventy facilities across the country (Bauer 2018; CoreCivic Inc. 2024).

This incident between Alejandro and Maria led to what advocates came to call the ban on hugging. This forced change in behavior proved difficult for many to accept, as the development of kinds of "intimate" relationships were a constant in advocate-client interactions. Clients often reached out to hug advocates, typically in gratitude, forcing advocates to move their own bodies away. Some advocates considered this practice a hurtful gesture, difficult to explain to clients and denying them their right to a typical yet meaningful human exchange. Some would speak about how they would quickly jerk backward if they saw a client reaching out to hug them within view of security cameras and guards. Others chose to reject the rule and embraced clients in those moments of closeness that called for it, awaiting potential repercussions that inexplicably never seemed to arrive. Still others would argue that it happened too quickly, that they did not have time to communicate to the other person before they were embraced by them but that they did not try to stop it from happening.

Angela, mentioned in chapter 1, was initially a long-term volunteer, staying on with the Dilley project for weeks or months at a time before becoming staff of the project. She was an undergraduate student and gifted cellist from Juárez, Mexico. She became a favorite among many clients, more than a few of whom treated her like a daughter, some even trying to set her up on dates with their older sons. Her warmth and closeness with clients produced a natural intimacy and, as might be expected, frequently led to moments in which clients attempted to embrace her. Sometimes she let it happen; other times, when in view of guards, she would try to avoid it. She told me,

> There was this one mom I worked with . . . she had been raped when she was little and was bullied and abused by different people throughout her life because of it. . . . So I went with her to her interview, and it was a really hard interview. Afterwards, we walked out together, and she said to me, "Thank you, you've been more to me than my own family; you've done more than my family has ever done for me. You take care of me." Then

> she just fell into my arms. Like, I know they can't give us hugs, but when someone falls into your arms, you can't do shit. They just fall apart in your arms. So I was holding her, and there were so many guards around us. She was just crying on me, and I cried too.

In a way, Angela's story speaks poetically to what advocates did and how they interpreted their practices. This was not an ideal caregiving situation. Advocates and detainees were relative strangers, and advocates both recognized and struggled with this fact. They met briefly before having to manifest some sense of trust and comfort in order to exchange necessary care. Because the trauma experienced by detainees that led them to leave their homes was compounded by the harm created by the carceral environment, caregiving sometimes looked less like an intimate embrace and more like someone keeping someone else's body from falling to the ground.

As seen here, advocates were subjected to their own form of bodily punishment or management. In some cases, their care was constrained by the facility's purported interest in the well-being of detainees. Physical contact was prohibited because it was framed as a threat to the imprisoned body. Although not made explicit by administrative entities or these legal projects, the source of this punitive action likely relates to one of the regulations concerning physical abuse in carceral spaces. In 2014, the Department of Homeland Security released a regulation—known as the Prison Rape Elimination Act (PREA)—that, coupled with ICE's policy known as the Sexual Assault and Abuse Prevention and Intervention, was meant to expand oversight of physical abuse concerns in migrant detention facilities (see ICE n.d.). Although my research did not find clear evidence that this constituted the legal reasoning administrative officials used to not only ban Alejandro but also to then justify new practices denying advocates and detainees the right to hug each other, this possible explanation is based on conversations I had with legal advocates over time.[1] Regardless of official intentions or stated justifications to protect

1. It should also be noted that despite institutional policies and regulations, evidence has shown that claims of sexual assault in carceral spaces are rarely adjudicated in favor of the prisoner. Assault claims are widespread across migrant detention facilities in the United States, including in family detention facilities. This was one of

vulnerable groups like prisoners, a hug, as an expression of intimacy, is important for the caring relationality between advocates and their clients. Denying them this appears part of an extensive punitive strategy aimed, in part, at the advocates themselves, which advocates then interpret as harmful to both. Yet in this instance, administrators' actions are not defined as punishment against advocates but are justified through care for detainees. This showcased how those "visitors" of detainees are, in fact, "not passive witnesses to their friends' or loved ones' suffering, and this is critical to the injuries they incur. Within detention, visitors are made to be instruments of deprivation, as their relational attachments to the people they visit are [weaponized] in the service of deterrence" (Peterie 2024, 96). These supposedly caring actions deprived detainees of the sort of care they themselves sought in their interactions and that advocates desired to provide for them.

Such troubled feelings of care that advocates experienced in response to being denied a small but important element of relationality with their clients illustrates the necessity of recognizing care not just as a feeling but as a practice and mode of thought, acknowledging the ways that we imagine or think through care (Puig de la Bellacasa 2017). Facility administrators' actions align with what Miriam Ticktin (2011, 5) calls the "antipolitics" of care in which "brutal measures may accompany actions in the name of care and rescue . . . [and] ultimately work to reinforce an oppressive order." Other scholars have charted how violence may be evoked by acts intended as care, sometimes through expressions of indifference or uncare (Gupta 2012; Mulla 2014). So, too, is a regulation to police sexual assault that punishes advocates who hug their distressed clients. These incidents demonstrate how, in situations in which multiple actors participate with care, everyday practices contest what counts as care or harm. Care, here, is not a solid object with clearly defined boundaries. It is best understood in this exchange not as a moral good but as something interpreted and entangled within the discourses surrounding its use. The very way in which advocates found themselves in caring exchanges, in this case through physical proximity, became the site on which administrators built a counternarrative, thus denying meaningful

the reasons why the Artesia facility was ultimately shuttered, advocates claim, and it has continued to plague detainees in other family facilities.

contact. The hugging ban thus lent evidence to the frictions between regimes of rights-based processes—determined by administrative officials and carceral regulations—and advocates' caregiving. The arbitrary application of such rules, of course, belied legitimate concerns for the care of detainees and reinforced perceptions of punishments born out of those, and other, frictions between parties serving cross-purposes.

ADJUSTMENTS

Chase's experience at this chapter's beginning offered a glimpse at one of the forms that the "contested terrains" of detention can take; specifically, when an advocate recognizes that a detainee requires attention other than their own, and yet they are in a much less powerful position to manifest it. Yet, participating in caregiving in such spaces doesn't just take shape as competition. In the correctional system, "power is unevenly distributed and some abuse it," though "in the daily life of the facility, compromises constantly occur" (Fassin 2016, xiv). Such "adjustments," as he names them, "contribute to keeping the peace within the prison for the evident benefit of all." Compromises, so-called peacemaking efforts, or "adjustments" were an integral part of the work that advocates did to continue to aid detainees. Migration scholars show that in immigration processes every day, within and beyond detention, state and nonstate actors interact "in collaboration, collusion, conflict, and contradiction" (Mountz 2010, xxiv). In certain ways, then, legal advocates came to "live with the erratic" (Mol, Moser, and Pols 2010a), unpredictable world of the family detention center via such practices, actively recognizing the significance of tending to all sorts of interdependent relationships to afford the continued flow of their caring labor.

In keeping with one of the defining qualities of everyday experience inside, the population of detainees at the Dilley center remained unpredictable. In a month, the facility would shift from being "at capacity" (meaning detaining over two thousand persons) to housing only a few hundred, with virtually no given institutional explanation. During a week at the start of 2016, the population had boomed again. On a Tuesday, the energy in the visitation trailer was buzzing. Not only was it packed to the gills with women and children waiting to be helped, but there was a new illness going around the facility, so many of the kids were sick and staying sick for a few days. Coughing and sneezing added to the regular cacophony of sounds—papers shuffling, printers churning out documents, chairs being slid back and forth across the tile to form *charla* circles, children laughing and crying. As usual, the trailer felt small and frenzied.

When the activity was at a fever pitch, there was a loud and uncharacteristic thump. Many of the women sitting in one of the *charla* circles started to stand up and look toward the front of the room. A client was laid out on the floor. Her body rippled with convulsions. One of her stiff arms kept shooting up and down, flailing; her head rolled back and forth, from side to side; her legs bent, then straightened. The guards got up from their desks a few feet away and walked toward her, yelling at the women nearby watching that they needed to move. They slid the chairs away from her, saying that they needed to make room. Before the guards left their desks, however, Alejandro and Cynthia, who both worked for the legal project, went to her. They appeared angry, and Alejandro said something indiscernible but with a sharp, furious tone to one of the guards. As the guards sputtered and bleeped across their walkie-talkies, the woman's body stopped jerking and someone from the medical staff arrived. They knelt over her, asked if she spoke Spanish in Spanish, and then asked where it hurt. She brushed a weak hand over her forehead, saying simply and repeatedly that her head hurt. They helped to stand her up, then took her to "medical," or the medical care office in the interior buildings. This was just one of the many territories of the facility untraversed by legal advocates, as their movement within was limited to spaces relative to "legal" encounters, like the asylum office or court.

Cynthia and Alejandro quietly began to move the chairs back into the circle. Cynthia looked very angry. Moments later, she would say softly, almost just to herself, "That just happened because of stress, not because of anything else." She then explained to the rest of us watching the scene that the woman had come in exhausted, not feeling well, and not sleeping. She had then been informed that she had received a negative decision by the in-detention judge on the appeal for her case. She became extremely upset and just as she was leaving the trailer, she collapsed. While Cynthia fumed about the turn of events, Alejandro quickly walked over to the guards' desks. He knelt beside one of them as she sat in her chair, facing him with a cold, silent stare as he spoke softly and calmly. His demeanor had changed entirely. He now appeared apologetic, not necessarily remorseful but focused on explaining his reaction to a moment of frustration in a calm, gentle way. His physical position—squatted below her as she sat above in her chair—expressed the work that he was now evidently doing: trying to smooth out the potential effect of what just transpired and how he, and maybe other advocates, had reacted in anger.

On another day, a few of us sat in the project's office room, again in Dilley, talking about cases, snacking, and resting, when Angela stormed into the room, brow furrowed and cheeks flushed, throwing the door closed behind her. "Hey, what's up? Are you OK?" Jaclyn, a volunteer student from Florida, asked. "No, I'm pissed!" Angela spit out. She started to tell us why. One of the clients that week had grown particularly close with Angela, meeting with her often just to talk. As Angela would later describe her work, she felt like she often served the role of "friend" to women she worked with. On that day, her client came back into the trailer that afternoon to let Angela know that she had received a *positivo*, or positive or passing decision, and that she would be leaving the next day. The client was thrilled and wanted to gift something to Angela for her help, so she used what little money she had in her *saldo* account to buy her just a few food gifts, some soda and some cookies.[2] She came in with these things, handed them to Angela as they spoke, and they were both immediately accosted by the guard sitting nearby, watching them. "Did she give you that?" he shouted at Angela. She replied, "Yeah, she wanted to give me those as a gift." "No, no, no. That's a big no-no," he said, adding, "You cannot be given stuff from them. They cannot give you stuff!" The client was confused, then standing meekly and flush against the wall nearby. He said something quickly to her, then continued scolding Angela. The client began to cry, and Angela quietly shot back at him, "It's just cookies and a Coke." She had received other gifts from clients in the past, and never before had she (nor any of us) heard of any such rule against this practice. However, like with the crayon ban, the sudden appearance of these sorts of ill-defined or undocumented rules was quite common in this environment.

2. A "*saldo* account," as it was called at the family detention center, was a kind of bank account used by detainees, where individuals, usually family, outside of detention could send money to a detained person.

Angela was furious, though she tried to disguise it. The guard had made her client cry, thinking that she was the reason that he was now yelling at Angela. Angela took her into a private room and told her that it was OK and that she hadn't done anything wrong. Angela even asked one of the project staff members if this was, in fact, a rule, and they immediately confirmed that there was no known rule against clients sharing snacks with advocates. Nonetheless, the damage had already been done. Walking with her to the exit, saying goodbye, the guard interrupted them again, saying that Angela needed to sign her client out on the sign-in sheet through which all detainees checked in and out while passing through the building. He tossed the pen in her direction, and Angela snapped. "I already signed her out," she quipped at him, angrily. As her client left the building, she walked close to him and shouted, "Don't you ever yell at me again!" She then threw the pen across his desk and strode straight into our office.

How advocates made "adjustments" in light in frictions with facility administrators took different forms, as these incidents show; considered together, we see the complicated ways that people negotiated their caregiving. The significance in the exchange specifically between Alejandro, Cynthia, and the guards, I would argue, is not to be found in Cynthia's angry response or what Alejandro said to the guards after the fact but rather how the different moments of this singular encounter are shot through with manifold articulations of care. The client who had collapsed had what advocates often described as a more "complicated" case than others: her experiences didn't fit neatly within legal asylum categories, and as a result, that client went through more work than most others to move forward, beyond detention, with her case. Undergoing multiple rounds of interviews and courtroom appeals, receiving repeated negative decisions, had understandably caused her a great deal of stress. Volunteers and staff of the project spent tireless hours working on her case, with and without her; in this way, part of the stress of her case was shared with them. The effects of this sense of anxiety and worry over legal outcomes, shared between advocates and clients with different associated stakes, had a significant impact on them, a point to which I will return.

That brief moment when Alejandro shifted his attention from the detained client to the guard represented an act of both necessary emotional labor (Hochschild 1983) and care for another important relationship. One lesson advocates learned immediately in the practice of this work was that maintaining relationships with facility administrators was a part of what they did, an integral aspect of navigating this world. This is why it was rare to see advocates express their frustrations either directly at facility staff or even simply in the open areas of the visitation trailer. Such behaviors could, and had been, used as retaliative fodder in the omnipresent struggles between legal advocates and administrators, who often made their disdain for the legal advocates' existence there clear. The perception of the harm that could be done, because of so-deemed inappropriate behavior, was directly linked through the advocate and the project and onto the detainee. The detainee would be the ultimate recipient of retaliatory efforts, as they could be deprived of legal services. In this way, detainees and advocates were linked, similarly though not equally caught in mechanisms that conscripted behaviors. Thus, while care was extended to the relationship between advocates and administrators, such compromising acts of care were committed with another in mind: the detained client. Yet, as Angela's reaction to such frictions shows, advocates sometimes refused these compromises.

A former staff member of the legal project once noted that so much of their work on the ground was simply "reactionary." By this, they meant that they hadn't the power to control or even predict changes to their working environment, and they did not have the authority to outright reject abusive behaviors or false narratives about rules in the center. This was such a source of frustration for those, like Angela, Alejandro, and Cynthia, who spent extended time in these roles and longed to make significant changes to the harmful practices they witnessed and dealt with every day. For some, there was still the hope of ending this modern practice of family detention altogether. Alejandro himself shared these abolitionist visions when he began working in Dilley after having his first experience with family detention volunteering at the Karnes facility. Not long after working there, he met a woman with a baby who was severely sick and not yet one year old. Aware of a rule that ICE was not to detain children of such a young age, Alejandro thought he would simply need to notify someone on the "outside" that administrators were obviously in violation of this rule. "I thought, wow, I'll just tell everyone about this, that they're doing this, and this place will get shut down immediately," he told me. "Of course, that was the rude awakening. I realized later that it didn't matter and that things like that just happen all the time down there. Nothing changes."

As each of these incidents demonstrate, in responding to practices like this and others, advocates' work was laden with heavy emotion work. Angela was neither reprimanded nor retaliated against in any way for her explosive encounter with the guard, and unlike Alejandro, she never apologized to the guard in question. To be fair, it was exceedingly rare for her to act in the way that she did that day in her interactions with guards. She spent extensive time with the project in Dilley, so she was aware of the interest in maintaining relationships with facility staff. In this moment, though, it appeared as if her interest in both her client's and her own self-care superseded her concern for potential retribution. She had become so enraged by the fact that the guard not only tried to castigate her and the client but also tried to counterpose them against each other. He implied that the client's behavior, in buying a gift for Angela, was the cause of Angela's castigation, eliciting guilt from the client. This unnecessary and abusive reaction pushed Angela to her limits, and she reacted strongly.

Part of the challenge in the work of advocates involved navigating around current issues with an eye to potential future trouble. Donna Haraway (2016, 1) argues that although it is our task to "make trouble, to stir up potent response to devastating events," it's also our responsibility to "to settle troubled waters and rebuild quiet places." The everyday challenges faced by legal advocates correspond with Haraway's dual calls. Angela and Alejandro responded differently to the problems they encountered in those instances, and those responses were, in part, informed by their different roles and experiences in this environment. At the time, Alejandro was a staff member of the project, while Angela was an unpaid volunteer. These different roles affected advocates' relationships to the work and their perceptions of how relationships between the various actors involved in the management of these spaces needed to be negotiated. Particularly for those working as staff for these projects, negotiations around these sorts of everyday frictions also depended on how they managed volunteers' behavior in detention.

FRACTURED ROLES

A month before the crayon ban, I sat with a mother and her young son at Karnes, helping her fill out basic informational intake forms. At the other end of the room, Margaret paced the floor, clicking her pen and looking anxiously toward the separate entrance for clients behind the guard's desk. Margaret was an attorney from Austin and a long-term volunteer with the project. She had been waiting most of the day for a client to be "called up," meaning that the client would be notified by the guards of her appointment with a legal advocate. This was the standard process in both Dilley and Karnes, since we, as advocates, had no way to contact any clients directly. Up until that point in the afternoon, she had been able to work with only one client on her preparation for court, putting off working with any other clients because of how much time she was going to need to dedicate to the one "complicated" case that should arrive at any moment. She was visibly frustrated but without any other option than to wait.

As I sat quietly with the mom and her sweet, curly-headed son, he kept looking at me and smiling. His mom informed me that he wanted to play with the toys from the play area, a corner of the wide, open room that contained a rectangular-shaped green rug with various toys. I walked him over to the spot, where he tentatively picked up a small truck and started to follow me back to where we sat with his mother. He didn't want to play in the play area, it appeared, because it was at the opposite end of the room from where his mother was working, and he was obviously anxious to be away from her. Before he could reach us, however, the guard—an older woman with whom many advocates had negative encounters—left her desk and stood in his path. Speaking in Spanish, she sternly told him that if he wanted to play, he had to play on the carpeted area. As an aside, I heard this same directive shouted at children many times during my time as a volunteer, and on many occasions, children responded with confused or fearful expressions. This young boy also appeared confused and slightly nervous, quietly returning the truck to the carpeted area and sheepishly walking back to his mother and me.

"What is this rule?" Margaret abruptly interjected toward the guard at her desk, after having witnessed the exchange from across the room. "Is there a rule that he can't take his toy over here?" "Yeah, it's a rule," the guard replied defensively. "He can't go over there with it. We all know that. You know that." In fact, none of us in the room knew of such a rule. Again, like with many of the center's administrative "rules," advocates rarely knew which truly existed, in some sort of clear, documented form, adding to the fantastical, dynamic nature of working in these facilities. "This is fucking bullshit," Margaret whispered under her breath, while looking over at me. She turned away from the guard, threw her hands up in the air, and stomped back to her desk. "I'm going to DC on this. This is totally ridiculous," she uttered angrily, to no response from the guard. By "going to DC," she meant that she would notify those advocates who were involved in "off-the-ground" litigation work against the facilities in Washington. The mother continued her paperwork, and her son sat quietly, patiently at her side.

At the time, I viscerally understood Margaret's frustration. Incidents like this happened every day, and being engaged in such an environment long term and thus observing the repeated instantiations of seemingly small slights like this took a special toll on those who felt powerless in bearing witness to them. In the moment, however, I wondered, is something like this incident worth trying to fight against? Will the fight you make do more damage—to the client, the work, or both—than help? The environment engendered this way of thinking, encouraging the measuring of actions of protestation against the potential damaging aftereffects. Carlos, a project staff member in Dilley whose role directly involved the management of volunteer groups, described this conflict in his position:

> I don't know that you get jaded, but your priorities definitely adjust. Volunteers, they will freak out about little things. It's hard, I know, but what the volunteers don't understand is the big picture. The big picture of what we're doing here, or what other things are going on at the time. So they'll say stuff, they'll complain. And even I remember freaking out then when I was a volunteer. Now, on the other end, I feel like some of these things are just not a big deal. They'll just get so upset, and all I can think about is how I don't need this right now.

This is just one way in which managing the friction that resides in this environment especially dominated the work of the project staff and implicated that of volunteers. While maintaining a sort of peace with the facility administrators, staff also must maintain a sense of peace between volunteers and administrators. They worked to direct the shock, anger, and disgust of the temporary volunteers toward efforts that had demonstrable positive effects on the lives of the clients. They managed the behaviors of the volunteers, in what ways they could, so that volunteers did not inadvertently negatively impact their continued efforts. Friction, then, should not be perceived as limited to only interactions between advocates and facility administrators, as it also resided within the advocacy group.

"These people are not reading the emails we send out," Maggie huffed angrily one day in Dilley. Maggie, one of the project attorneys, quickly stood up from her seat on the floor where she was working on her laptop and closed the door to the "PB" (pro bono) room, privately enclosing herself, Allie, another project attorney, and me. "They have way too many questions, and they're not figuring out how to do anything on their own," she said softly, so as not to be overheard by those working outside the office. This was a complaint by staff that came up numerous times regarding many different volunteer groups. Some groups, they would say, were more adept than others at conducting their work independently and figuring out how to locate answers to their questions without the consistent aid of project staff. When individuals or groups of volunteers required more "hand-holding" with their labor, staff were deprived of time devoted to their own efforts. For project attorneys, this frequently involved intimate and time-consuming legal work on various complicated issues with clients or late-stage cases (meaning those who might be closer to the commencement of deportation processes). Those lawyers staffed by the advocacy projects, like Maggie and Allie, were often deeply involved in these complicated issues while also trying to aid volunteers with their individual case questions. The nature of the advocates' working environment—as one in which most of the work was done by a temporary, circulatory workforce—contributed another layer to the perception of this overall environment as erratic. This also led to ongoing frictions between project staff and volunteers.

"You start fresh [with volunteers] every week," Carlos explained, "and it's a gamble. Some weeks it's good, and others, not as good. Every single week you gotta do the same thing and answer the same questions." Carlos's frustration stemmed not only from the exhaustion of having to retrain and repeatedly answer the same questions from weekly volunteers and remain subject to the uncertainties of advocates' varying aptitudes in the work. It also stemmed from the knowledge that more, and likely better, work could be done if the structure of the care work was different. He explained this paradox and his conflicted feelings about it:

> We couldn't function without them, the volunteers. They really *are* the project. But at the same time, the way that it's set up and the way that it has to be holds it back. We could be doing so much more if we could have people volunteering longer term, where we weren't training everybody every single week. So that gets frustrating, but it's an impossible thing to overcome because there's just no way you could get that many people to volunteer like that. But then it's just so frustrating, with the same questions all the time, the data management system being confusing to people, and nobody knows how to do anything out on the floor, and every week we're just starting over from scratch. Some groups will pick up everything right away, like last week, and run it all by themselves. But then like today, we had fifty CFI preps to do, which was very manageable, and we should have been able to do them all, but we didn't. And so now, we [the staff] have to go back in tomorrow, Saturday.

In their reflections, Maggie and Carlos capture both a frustration with the fractures between short-term, temporary volunteers and longer-term volunteers or staff as well as a meaningful critique, which this book deals with more substantively in later chapters. Although it was undeniably crucial that detainees received the kind of care that advocates could and did give, it's also irrefutable that their care was, but should not have been, dependent on voluntary caregivers, often with very minimal training. Even though those associated with the projects broadly supported the work they did, most agreed that better, more standardized care should have been provided by the institutions charged with the care of those held in detention while simultaneously contending that families should never be incarcerated.

With some volunteers, a change in attitude or approach over time was apparent, shaped in part by either longer commitments at the facility or return "visits" after an initial engagement with the work. Sue, an immigration lawyer from Tennessee who had volunteered on multiple occasions, loved to crack jokes to lighten the tension inside, even though she also often found herself infuriated by the behavior of various officials at

Dilley, particularly guards and asylum officers. "Sometimes you're laughing out of rage, just to get that energy out," she explained,

> though my emotions were more managed this time than the last time I was here. You start to see things more in perspective. Even though the guards acted like bigger jerks than when I was here last, I felt more of a responsibility to try to let things roll off my back. If you don't, it can either hurt the project and their access to people, which in turn hurts the [detainees].

Sue's commentary points to the interplay between emotional labor and peacekeeping efforts. A semblance of peace, in her characterization, is maintained through emotional control, through the repression of harmful emotional expressions. "It's all about the women," she went on, "and I would continue to say that to myself. It's all about them. It's not about how I feel or what such-and-such guard said to me. How are you an advocate if you fight them?" This recalled other advocates' comments on the importance of embodying a sort of "selflessness" or avoidance of emotional expression within the bounds of the work. Both value acts of "self-control" with respect to emotions. For some, this mattered most in interactions between advocates and clients, while others, like Sue, emphasized these restrained behaviors in relations with administrative actors. They effectively contended that these emotion "performances" (Goffman 1959) led them to better, more effective care of clients, while others recognized that without restraint, in some situations, their care might not be afforded at all. Still others, like Angela, refused to effectively ignore abusive or obstructive behavior. Here, small-scale, mundane expressions of care—including the minutiae of everyday frictions and emotional reactions—are directly linked with the macroscale of their efforts—securing and maintaining the provision, or flow, of critical care through the management of working relationships among interdependent actors. The question Sue poses, concerning how a person is an advocate if they "fight" administrators, seems to capture the way that they perceive this conflict in simple terms. Such comments and claims about interdependency that have been raised here naturally evoke important questions that have yet to be addressed. Later chapters will take up this work, unpacking the various meanings of "good" versus "bad" care, as understood by these legal advocates, and explore how facility administrators might be seen as dependent on the labor of legal caregivers.

INTERDISCIPLINARY MECHANISMS

On a bright morning in May 2017, a collected crowd of advocates in Dilley were pissed. It was yet another week where facility administrators changed the rules around where they could physically be within the visitation space throughout the day. The new rule deemed that volunteers could not be in the open space, as opposed to the private meeting rooms, unless they were meeting with clients, but there was also a new limitation to the number of people allowed to wait in the PB room for client meetings to occur. That week, it so happened that there were many volunteers. This practically meant that advocates, if they wanted to remain in the building, had to meet with clients continuously, without break, until they left for the day. One of the staff, Cynthia, knew the disruption that would result from having to wait while advocates moved in and out through security all day and thus complained about these changes to administrators. "You can't tell us how many people are allowed in here," she said curtly to the two guards standing in the doorway of the front entrance. "They've all been cleared to be here, and they can't be doing something every single minute." The guards temporarily relented, allowing those advocates waiting to pass into the building, but one returned later to speak with Maggie. Late in the afternoon, he softly yet sternly told her that he was sorry but that "what happened today couldn't happen again," that they were breaking the (new) rules by keeping so many advocates inside. Maggie, sitting as usual on the floor of the PB room with her computer on her lap, to my surprise, apologized and consented. "I get it . . . they're under pressure too," she exhaled exhaustedly after he walked away. "There are cameras all over, and they're being watched all the time." Alejandro had once shared that they had been told that the guards' supervisors could pull up any video feed from those cameras, even remotely, at any point during the day and watch them (though it was unclear if this was true). If guards were caught allowing something to take place that shouldn't, according to whatever new or old rules, they could be reprimanded, and this did appear to happen on occasion. "I can't imagine how edgy that would make a person feel," Maggie said. This was the same for administrative staff at Karnes where, as a project staff member once cautioned, "Somebody's always watching."

This exchange speaks to something that both impacts frictions between advocates and others in these facilities and is, again, unfortunately not explored in this book. This is partly due to the fact that other administrative actors were not included as official participants in this study, and so their perspective on these environments and resultant conflicts is inherently absent. Yet, it's important to note that in considering frictions among advocates and administrators, specifically guards, such encounters should not be misconstrued as simple indictments of individual administrators or administrative groups. Carceral regimes and the concomitant forms of suffering they cause are not simple or singular; many migration scholars have demonstrated how the "project of immigrant detention dehumanizes not only immigrants but workers in the system as well" (Furman, Epps, and Lamphear 2016, 9, referencing Bosworth and Fili 2016).

Advocates, when going through their orientation before entering the facility, were informed of the fact that there were cameras placed throughout and that administrators observed these recordings daily. While project staff emphasized the existence of these cameras in order to prepare advocates for an environment in which they, and their work, was under constant surveillance, the simultaneous surveillance of administrators themselves was recognized less frequently as potentially playing a role in conflicts between the two groups, as implied in Maggie's comment. Constant and omnipresent surveillance of guards, advocates, and detainees alike, like Bentham's panopticon, are part of the all-encompassing "disciplinary mechanism" of the facilities. The effect is to induce in those being observed "a state of conscious and permanent visibility that assures the automatic functioning of power" (Foucault 1977, 201). Together, these groups share, albeit at different scales, in the position of the "inmate," and through this observation (and awareness of observation), the watched individual inevitably "becomes the principle of [their] own subjection" (203). Yet, surveillance is only one of the ways in which administrators experience friction while also bringing it into being. Tensions and anxieties resound in such "unstable places" (Greenhouse, Mertz, and Warren 2002), affecting all in distinct ways.

Ultimately, many elements affected the relationships between facility administrators and advocates, and there was much information, particularly around the experiences of those administrators, that was inaccessible to me, primarily because of research constraints. It was also true, however, that this was simply an integral part of the environment itself: knowledge about inner workings, rules, and the distributions of power was similarly partial. These gaps in understanding led to unquelled anxieties that affected all relationships. At a particularly stressful time at the Dilley facility in which multiple advocates were being banned and changes in rules were occurring at a rapid pace, a new group of student volunteers arrived for work, as usual, on a Monday morning. Once in the visitation trailer, a high-level administrative official walked in and informed both project staff and volunteers that they were to line up with their backs along the wall. Confused, they did so, and he proceeded to inform them of "new rules." He stood close to their faces, walked along the line of their bodies, and shouted at them about how he was "in charge" and that if they wanted to work in the facility, they had to abide by "his rules." Some found this extreme aggression almost comical, particularly because they had never met or been in the space at all, as they were new volunteers. Others were disturbed by the ways that they felt as if they were being treated as prisoners, or "quasi inmates" (Comfort 2008). It was a bizarre experience for many and, oddly, did not recur. In considering this, some interpreted it to be more of a sort of theatrical expression of disciplinary power, an aggressive yet awkward attempt to display authority over the legal advocates.

Thinking about negotiations in the provision of "good care" in inherently fraught environments, like these, inevitably leads to larger concerns about the unavoidable paradoxes of humanitarian labor and the role of care as an organizing force for resistance. Considering the critiques of humanitarians for expressing "functional solidarity" (Agier and Fernbach 2011) with punitive state actors, a discerning observer might ask, what is the relationship between peacekeeping or compromising "adjustments" and actions that contribute to the "management" of detainees? In other words, do peacekeeping efforts reflect a more deeply ingrained relationship between legal advocates and facility administrators in ways that do harm to their own efforts of resistance? This research shows that care is, in each of these relationships, a central organizing force. If not for an interest in the continued provision of care for detainees, advocates would likely not concern themselves with caring for administrative relationships, sometimes even empathizing with constraints under which they labor. Interest in providing care for detainees also shaped how advocates individually conceived of care and how they responded to other advocates' comportment. Even though this discussion of the relationship between care, conflict, and resistance has only begun here, my research does demonstrate some of the frictions between the practical constitutions of this relationship and how it was negotiated by advocates.

CONCLUSION

Like many other institutional spaces, carceral spaces abound with frictions, taking formal and informal shape (Ibsen 2013). The frictions leading to the incidences documented here illustrate how figurations of power can be understood more intimately through, or alongside, care. The right to give care and the ability to receive it involve expressions of power. Here, both the provision and reception of care were controlled by administrative figures, deployed as means to control and punish legal advocates and detainees. Friction itself resulted from the existence of advocates, as caregivers, in these spaces. It was precisely both their active contestation of what administrators implicitly or explicitly defined as care and their attention to the diverse needs of their clients that caused frictions. While administrators repeatedly deployed putative care in ways that reinforced oppressive orders, legal advocates redrew the borders of care through practice to resist. Power was effectively asserted and contested through care.

Legal advocates recognized the inherent conflict in their existence within these centers, one that hinged on some cooperation with the figures they resisted. This situated them, confusingly, in a role shaped by contradictions; for advocates in detention, "their own in/action—their very presence or absence—is not entirely within their control. Despite a desire to not abandon the people they visit, institutional processes often render [such] visits unpredictable, capricious and difficult to sustain [and] visitors not only witness others' wrongdoings but are also made to feel morally complicit in them" (Peterie 2024, 96). While advocates possessed a legal right to meet with potential clients—though ambiguously defined—administrators wielded significant power in allowing their continued presence beyond the front doors. Thus, one can see how advocates' responses to the conflicts they experienced in detention simultaneously created both traction for their work to continue and barriers for its continuation. "You know, our project struggles, at times, because it has these two kinds of contradictory functions," Carlos said as he sat exhausted on the floor of the PB room. His stickered laptop and a messy stack of client paperwork rested on his legs. He continued, explaining to a new volunteer,

> These functions conflict in that one, we have established this working relationship with ICE and CoreCivic, so that we can get the women the help they need so they don't get steamrolled, forgotten, deported, whatever. But then we have this other work that is all about ending family detention. It seems paradoxical to me because the one sort of hurts the ends of the other.

While trying to effect the collapse of the facility's operation, drawing attention to how these forms of incarceration should not exist, advocates' everyday work involved managing operative mechanisms. This created a form of friction, as one goal, ending family detention, grated against another, providing daily legal care to as many detainees as possible.

CHAPTER 4

ACCOMPANIMENT

On a Wednesday, I went with Elena, a middle-aged Guatemalan mother, to her interview, which was conducted by a new asylum officer (AO), AO Moreau. Jillian, one of the project staff, asked me to accompany her, to help her feel more comfortable but also to make sure that the interviewer didn't misunderstand her when she shared her story. Elena had but a few years of formal education and seemed to struggle with communicating her experiences in a clear way. I was nervous for her but also because the advocacy team had already lodged complaints about this new AO, having observed her being rude with clients and improperly conducting the interview. As we walked into the office, AO Moreau instructed her in simple Spanish to sit in the seat directly across from her own, closing the door behind us. The AO quickly informed me that I was to sit in the corner of the room near the door, several feet away from them both. This was curious to me, as there was an empty chair right next to Elena. I stepped out for a moment to use the bathroom, and when I returned, AO Moreau had already begun her questioning with the usual phone interpreter service.

AO Moreau asked her questions quickly, aggressively, and seemingly counterintuitively. She moved erratically through different topics, asking one question about the rape Elena had experienced by a gang member, then jumping immediately to an unrelated question about family members. She would ask Elena where her other children were living currently, then ask about her own childhood experiences of abuse, then immediately to questions about what kind of work she did. I felt the whiplash from the way she flitted through lines of questioning. Her questioning appeared to have no natural trajectory, and it felt as if the swift shifts between topics made it more challenging for Elena to respond. I watched silently from the corner taking notes, recording questions and answers, tones and behaviors, and listening intently for errors I might pick up in the phone interpreter's translations. Elena sat far back in her plastic seat, her small feet dangling above the linoleum. She held the manila packet that contained important documents about her case in her lap, nervously tugging at its corners. She expressed confusion several times with questions AO Moreau asked, looking over to me, seemingly for clarity. The interpreter had to repeat many of these questions, and the AO was visibly frustrated, huffing and sighing.

At a certain point, AO Moreau decided that she wanted to speak with just Elena's son, Marcos, who had his own asylum claims apart from his mother's. Marcos was outside the office, in the waiting room full of toys for much younger children. As Elena quietly left the room, Marcos walked in. He was only twelve years old, but he was much taller than his mom. He was quite shy, but when he walked in, he held a sweet smile on his face. "Wow, you're really big!" AO Moreau exclaimed, grinning. "How old are you?" He responded softly, shyly, taking his mother's seat. She spoke in a notably friendlier manner with him, leaned back in her chair and staring at him with her bright blue eyes. "Do you know where you are?" she asked. He smiled widely but was silent, staring headlong at her with a squint, like he was trying to think. She continued to smile and asked the same question again, this time more forcefully. "Do you know where you are?" He remained silent, smiling, searching for the answer, when he looked over at me in the corner. "Que es . . ." he said softly to me, but before he could finish his thought, AO Moreau interrupted. "No, no, no, don't look over there," she said sternly. The comment certainly caught me off-guard, and it appeared to rattle him as well. The impersonal language was odd, as if I was some sort of threatening apparition that only he could see but that she knew was "over there." He looked back at her, not smiling. He seemed embarrassed now, like a child being scolded, and still didn't know how to answer her. "OK," the AO said with a sigh, "do you know what country you're in?" He burst out enthusiastically, "Oh, Texas, Texas!" AO Moreau laughed. "OK, Texas is the state, but you are in the United. States. Of. America," slowly exaggerating the last few words, which the phone interpreter repeated in the same way. He nodded gently.

Marcos told his own story in small pieces for the AO, and like Elena, he struggled to offer the sort of details AOs were usually looking for. He talked about how local gangs at his school had been trying to recruit him; he, of course, was now of the right age to be recruited and his stature lent additional desirability to the gangs. His classmates constantly told him they were coming for him. His answers to her questions were short and he looked down at his feet, one foot folded on top of the other. His hands fidgeted in his lap, and he started sniffling. His brief answers frustrated the AO, who spoke to him in an impatient way. She started to end the interview, asking him if he had anything else he'd like to say. "I don't want to end up dead from these gangs," Marcos said softly with tears rolling down his face. "Just like, buried in the ground . . . where no one will ever find me." My heart broke, and although I was just a few feet away from him, it felt like a hundred. He started to silently cry, and AO Moreau stopped typing, crossed her arms, and looked at him. "You don't need to cry," she told him flatly. Yet Marcos did have reason to cry, reason to be afraid. As he explained, his older brother had to leave the town in which they lived previously because of gang recruitment efforts, and another brother had been killed by the gangs. His body was found buried in a shallow grave, covered by loose dirt. Marcos had good reason to believe these weren't empty threats.

When the AO had finished with her questions, Elena was brought back in and the interview abruptly ended. Officers typically offered a "summary" of each client's case to them at the end, noting the main elements of their claim. Some allowed the accompanying advocate the opportunity to offer a brief, prepared "final statement" of sorts, drawing the officer's attention to the claim through the language of the law and thus, effectively, helping the officer make sense of that claim. Sometimes, as with this occasion, neither of those happened. This time, after she finished her questioning, AO Moreau smiled again and dismissed us all, never looking at me. I walked out of the building with Elena and Marcos and told them that they did a wonderful job before my facility escort walked me back to the visitation trailer.

Kristin Yarris's (2024, 105) claim that "engaging with the immigration detention system means contending with its illogics and cruelty at every turn" was frequently and diversely illustrated in family detention. The interview was just one moment within that proved this to be especially true, as another expression of the entanglement of violence and care taking place in a carceral environment (Sufrin 2017). This interview centers on an applicant's fear of harm or persecution in their home country, thus justifying asylum protection. Although its purpose is to define a specific narrative around this fear, the interview itself was often a fearful experience. This chapter looks at how, as for detainees, feelings of fear and impotence played roles in the experiences of legal advocates in these critical yet differently configured spaces of the facility: the asylum office and the courtroom. Whereas previously I focused on caregiving tensions with facility administrators, here I explore such caring frictions in encounters with both asylum officers and judges who presided over the less common courtroom proceedings. The most significant struggle advocates faced in their "accompaniments" and in courtroom proceedings concerned how to give care in settings where their actions and participation were severely limited. As this opening anecdote shows, the functional role of advocates in these contexts differed greatly.

Many advocates found these to be particularly frustrating spaces, primarily because they were often forced to remain nearly silent observers. In courtroom proceedings, their role was defined by the concept of amici curiae, or "friends of the court." In each setting, they were not meant to speak on the client's behalf, to direct the officer's or judge's questioning, or to instruct the clients' answers. They were officially confined to mostly nonparticipatory roles. In such constrained environments, I felt compelled to ask, what can care look like when, either by official rule or ruling custom, an advocate is essentially muted? When they are relegated to "mere" observation, is caregiving even possible? If so, how is it reconfigured, and how would that shift our understanding of how care is practiced by legal actors? Paul Farmer (2005, 26–28) recognized the significant critiques of "bearing witness" in ethnographic works discussing the observation of atrocities, and yet, in appropriating the concept for his own work, he also called for its rehabilitation, primarily because of its undeniable usefulness in encompassing different "ways of knowing" people and contexts. I identify this concept as similarly useful in making sense of certain aspects of advocacy labor in family detention, while addressing another set of questions: In what ways does the practice of bearing witness contribute to our understanding of "ways of caring"? More to the point, is witnessing caring, and if so, how does this take shape in these environments?

In both material and symbolic ways, we can think of spaces like those of the interview or the court as kinds of borders that inflict various forms of "legal violence" on applicants (Menjívar and Abrego 2012). Asylum officers and immigration judges are distinct decision-makers that make determinations for detainees in relation to many boundaries: membership in legal categories, so-called credibility, and legal status, among others. Officers and judges effectively determine where a detainee will be released, either into the country to continue their case, transferred to another facility to continue while detained, or deported elsewhere. In this way, they serve alongside other federal and local officials as additional border gatekeepers, and the spaces over which they preside are "border zones." Cheryl Mattingly (2010) refers us to another, different sort of border zone—the clinic—that I often found relevant to what occurred in family detention. She notes that in such spaces, "actors find themselves uncertain about what others are up to and struggle to be understood by their interlocutors. While much of life may be fraught with ongoing misunderstandings, interpretive trouble is particularly pernicious in clinical spaces where a great deal is at stake" (11). In the clinic, she illustrates, misunderstandings occur as different languages or ways of communicating—from doctors to patients to their caregivers—come into contact.

Such "interpretive trouble" was a notable characteristic of these spaces. A great deal, sometimes life or death, was also at stake in asylum interviews and courtroom proceedings, as legal advocates were uniquely positioned as deeply constrained participants. Furthermore, while the performances of advocates were marked primarily by nonverbal formulations of care (Mol, Moser, and Pols 2010a), and as they were often subject to disruptions in their work, interruptive behaviors on their part in these spaces also served as vehicles for care. Even under constraints, they participated in these encounters, troubling the often-dehumanizing, sometimes violent processes of asylum adjudication through the limited mechanisms available to them. While their care was transfigured in these high-stakes spaces, typically taking subtler or quieter forms, it was nonetheless present via other “tactics” (De Certeau 1984).

Advocates’ care here can be understood as falling within a few practical, tactical configurations: presence, witnessing, and documenting. In addition to presence, or accompaniment as a form of being-with (Horton 2024; Yarris and Duncan 2024b), the acts of witnessing and documenting are also kinds of care strategies, ones that might be understood, particularly in these sorts of spaces, as forms of “countersurveillance” (Walsh 2013). James Walsh (2013, 286) notes the ways that im/migrant rights activists and advocates engage in different forms of countersurveillance in order to “promote transparency and democratic accountability by ‘watching the watchers’ and turning the gaze of authority against itself” (Walsh also cites Huey, Walby, and Doyle 2006). Looking at how such care practices unfolded there provides important insight into how advocates navigated shifting roles and resisted constraints along new borders. The work they did in these heightened moments—in accompaniment, bearing witness, and documenting observations—was different but no less significant than what they did elsewhere in these facilities. Rather than as official representatives, their roles in these spaces, as more akin to friends or allies, extended the possibilities of how we might draw the boundaries around legal care in more muted but no less fractured encounters.

EL ASILO

Beyond the security and visitation areas, the asylum office, or *el asilo*, and courtroom were virtually the only other spaces in which advocates were allowed, though their movement within was even more strictly monitored. In the Dilley asylum office, advocates would wait with clients to be retrieved by the assigned AO, who would then escort them to a private room. The waiting room also doubled as the space in which newly arrived families would watch their orientation video. Each room was slightly different, though most were quite cramped. They were sparsely furnished with a large office desk on which sat the AO’s largest desktop computer, two or three chairs for clients and advocates, an outdated landline phone for interpreter services, and an almost always empty bookshelf in one corner. Some rooms had high windows looking out on the inner landscape of the facility, while others did not, feeling more like large closets. The offices, like much of the facility, were kept at a low temperature, and a box of tissues was positioned, expectantly, near the clients' seats. Familiar sounds resonated throughout each interview: harsh fluorescent lights buzzed along with feedback from interpreters on the line. The walls of each office were especially thin, allowing various sounds to permeate. On more than one occasion, I sat next to a client as they cried, recounting their experiences to an officer amid the raucous sounds of laughter from guards on the other side of the wall. Such sonic incongruity was unsettling, so much so that on occasion, the officer conducting an interview would pause to angrily tell the guards they needed quieting.

Throughout my fieldwork, advocates' abilities to accompany clients varied widely. This was a source of frustration for them, as it was difficult for both advocates and clients to cope with the fact that only some clients could have an advocate accompany them. The informal rule was that advocates would attend interviews for which there was special concern for a particular client, determined by several factors. If a client appeared to be especially emotionally fragile in their interactions with advocates, suggesting that they were in particular distress in recounting experiences, or if they struggled to recall or articulate details or events in what they determined to be a significant way, the advocacy team would send someone to accompany them. At times, when the volunteer pool was large, advocates accompanied many. Alternatively, when the team was stretched particularly thin, they would reserve accompaniments for the direst situations, as an interview could take an advocate away from the intake and prep work for anywhere from one to a few hours. A loss of even a single advocate when the facility population was high had a noticeable impact.

To be sure, accompaniments were not only meant as support for those clients who needed another supportive presence in the room, which was important; they were also meant to observe how asylum officers conducted interviews. Specifically, advocates documented the sorts of questions that were asked, the ways they were asked, and clients' responses. Families often reported to advocates that they experienced issues. Asylum officers sometimes misinformed them—telling them that they could only respond to questions with a "yes" or "no" response—which severely hindered applicants' abilities to communicate their cases. There would be interpretation issues, wherein, for instance, the phone interpreter was speaking an indiscernible dialect of a client's language, or the interpreter would speak in a confusing way, cutting them off before they could respond appropriately. Advocates would thus take extensive notes as they silently observed and, if given the opportunity by the officer, advocates would offer a final statement about the client's case at the interview's end. In this moment, they might also comment on the officer's missed conversational opportunities to draw out important case details or misinterpretations before it concluded.

Chapter 2 discussed what work advocates did to prepare clients for the complexities of the interview, mainly learning how to articulate their experiences in terms of a story—which, for many people, isn't necessarily a "natural" skill (Fobear 2015)—and drawing connections to legally relevant details of their cases, among other things. Many advocates I spoke with who had attended interviews remarked on how they wished they had been able to know more about how it practically functioned, and how it felt, before they had met with clients to prepare them. Karla, a graduate student originally from Honduras, was fortunate to accompany a mother early in the week she volunteered in Dilley. "I really think volunteers should go with a client to the interview so they can see how intimidating it is and see how the process functions," she told me. "That helped me in prepping women for their interview. It helped me to know that they weren't going to get someone in their interview who was friendly. Someone who may not be expressive with their body. They may seem cold. If I hadn't seen that, my approach to the prep might have been different, possibly not as effective." Although advocates were provided with a view of the broad outlines of the interview by project staff, as Karla notes, it felt important to also prepare clients for the feelings experienced in it, which were difficult to understand fully without having witnessed it. Delving into the discursive microdetails of such encounters helps to illustrate why applicants were prepared by advocates in the way that they were, while also demonstrating how the environment, like so much else there, could be unpredictable, both for detainees and their advocates.

Despite the continued legal and conceptual obscurity of the central subject of the asylum interview, "credible fear" (Augustine-Adams and Núñez 2021), it is certainly an unambiguous claim that fear was embed-

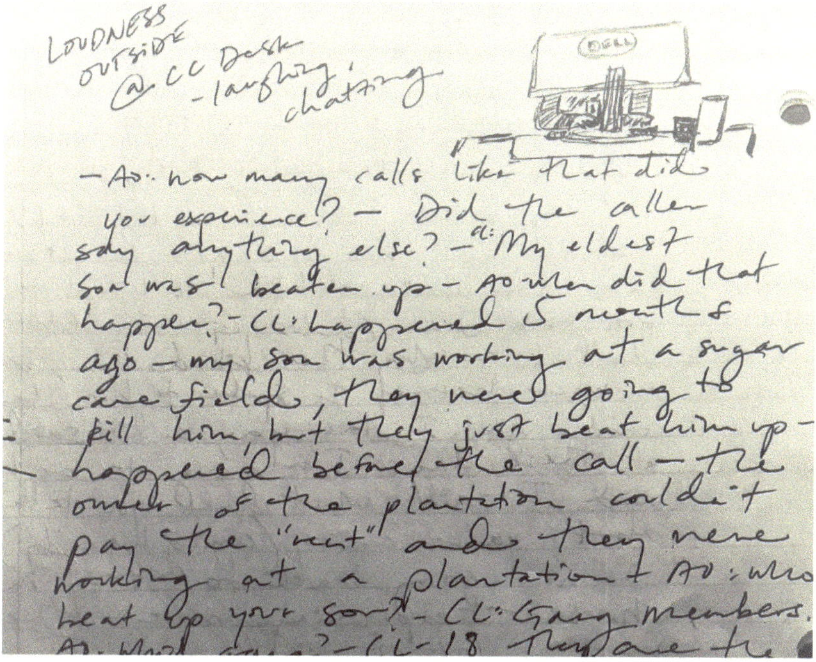

FIGURE 14 Excerpt of notes taken during interview accompaniment, with rendering of asylum officer from advocate/client perspective. Credit Erin Routon.

ded within and around this space. While generally we speak about this in terms of the fear instilled in asylum applicants, primarily about the possibility of a negative decision, I would also argue that fear is relevant to a discussion of legal advocates' experiences and feelings concerning this encounter. As it functions to determine the existence of a potential asylum claim and the credibility of the applicant, explaining fear in relation to experiences, and thus a claim, is critical. In the moment, fear becomes expressed through language, narrative of experiences, and the body. Like applicants, fear was also expressed by advocates in relation to the interview, even though its stakes affected each in different ways.

Advocates were understandably anxious around the "performance" of clients, rather how well someone they prepped would be able to communicate their narrative and respond to questions in ways helpful to their case. They also worried over how they would be treated by their asylum officer, and how the asylum officer would translate that interaction into a decision about their case. Advocates feared that they had "failed" the clients with whom they worked, by, for instance, underpreparing them or giving them incorrect or improper information, unintentionally. Their fear was based on the idea that despite their interest in helping, they either had not sufficiently helped clients or harmed their chances of receiving a positive decision.

Daphne was an undergraduate student from Maryland who happened to be volunteering at a time when her skills were especially needed. She came with her friend Raquel at one of the times in which Dilley received a large and unexpected influx of Haitian asylum seekers. She was Haitian American and was the first volunteer I met who spoke Haitian Creole. Over time, a substantial reserve of voluntary remote interpreters for the language was established, but none had visited the facility in-person yet. Her presence there, if only brief, was incredibly meaningful in establishing trusting relationships with this already isolated community at the facility, where most services and documentation were in Spanish or English.

While most advocates expressed some form of performance pressure, Daphne felt a special responsibility to connect with Haitian clients and prepare them for their interview. "Personally, I was very nervous imagining a woman that I had prepped going in and sitting in front of an asylum officer," she explained.

> It felt like a responsibility that was resting on my shoulders. Knowing that even though I believe she has "credible fear" and that that may not come across to an officer, it feels like it falls back on me. It took a bit of communication with the CARA [DPBP] staff to understand that a *negativo* is not the end of the world.

Raquel herself echoed this anxiety, saying that she was constantly worried on that first trip about whether she was doing a good enough job preparing clients:

> One of my friends who was volunteering and I were checking the online database what felt like every five minutes to see if any negatives had come in. All of the women that you work with come in saying can you help me,

> can you help me. You try so hard to help, but in the end, it's not my decision to make.

Many expressed similar thoughts about the online database that was used to store client information, including case decisions. For Raquel, as for others, their continued connection to their clients through this database created a kind of virtual tie, allowing them, even if only temporarily after they left, a way to do something with their worries for clients. Even if this meant learning that a client had received a negative decision or, in the worst case, had been deported, the database served as an outlet to assuage the anxieties of the unknown.

There was also, however, the fear associated with a clear awareness of what could occur. "I felt like I was in a circus," Chase told me, on the edge of laughter. "I thought to myself, this is crazy, this is absolutely crazy." Chase was the volunteer in Dilley who spent much of his time entertaining the children during preps, including that time that a child collapsed in the middle of the visitation trailer. On one repeat trip, he was able to accompany many clients to their interviews. In the one he referred to as being like a circus, the officer was talking to the client about the client's own kidnapping, which had been perpetrated by a gang. She explained that her brother had started seeing this married woman, and that woman was affiliated with the gang. "The AO, though, kept misunderstanding what she was saying," Chase explained. "It wasn't a misinterpretation, just a misunderstanding. The client and the interpreter didn't notice the mistake. The AO kept repeating that it was her brother that was a gang member, and that it was him that kidnapped her." In that moment, he leaned forward from his seat in the room and tried to interrupt, interjecting that the AO was misunderstanding this. Her brother didn't kidnap her, he told the officer, but

> this AO would just scoff at me, saying, "Whatever. It doesn't matter; he kidnapped someone." So I kept having to jump into the interview to try and correct this. I told her that I wanted to put it in the record that neither she nor her family was involved in her own kidnapping. [The AO] kept telling me that it's fine, that she didn't need to change it, and I kept telling her no, it's not fine, you need to correct that. I told her that while I understood that

> it might not be relevant to her interview at the moment, it should be on the record for, like, credibility purposes and possibly establishing a humanitarian case. Her family wasn't a family of kidnappers; they didn't do this.

Chase was understandably incredulous at the fact that the AO neither understood nor respected the need to maintain accuracy for this client's record. In their preps, advocates often reminded clients of the importance of remembering that what was said in the interview could "follow them" throughout the length of their asylum case, were they to continue it outside of detention. Accidental or unintended discrepancies like this could have substantial impacts in later, more nuanced stages of their legal case. "It was at that moment," Chase continued,

> that I thought about saying to the AO, "You really do see these details as irrelevant. You just see these people as numbers, and you're just trying to get this over with." At that point, I put myself in our client's position, and I thought, this is scary as fuck. . . . I literally looked around the room and thought, "Is this all that this boils down to? Literally, one extra human on the other side of the desk trying to convince this person of her story?"

Chase was clearly unsettled, both by the lack of concern or accountability in the asylum officer as well as by the fact that he, a volunteer who simply happened to be there that day with that client, happened to catch this error. The phone interpreter, asylum officer, and client had not noticed this. What was even more concerning for Chase was that when he tried to course-correct, the asylum officer exhibited resistance to spending further time trying to make sense of the apparent disconnect. It was alarming for many, myself included, to be made aware of the major implications of these seemingly small details. A client's case, her future success in establishing an asylum claim, could depend on these little moments of misunderstanding, and an advocate's presence to recognize these issues was critical and, for many, unnerving. Laurie, a business immigration lawyer, was similarly disturbed by the precariousness of the client's situation in this space: "I just realized how quickly it all could blow up for them. It seems like if things don't go well or if the officer doesn't understand the client in the interview, they're subject to this uphill battle from then on."

Chase's experience also demonstrates how advocates' position was configured in sometimes contradictory ways. From his perspective, he was simultaneously figured as an irritant or interruption to the quick completion of an interview as well as an individual knowledgeable enough about the asylum process to know that such errors could make a critical difference in a case. Advocates were variously treated and interpreted by officers as knowledgeable, sometimes as aids, other times as silent observers offered the privilege of presence, and in still other encounters, as intrusive or adversarial forces.

INTERPRETING ROLES

"I see you as my helper," AO Hart said with a smile to me as I walked into his office with Saidy, a Cuban mother who, before having to flee her home, had worked as an economist. This was my first time meeting this officer, a young man with wrinkled clothes and a booming voice. In this interview with Saidy, who was calm and well spoken, AO Hart was the one who struggled, which consequently clarified the surprising comment about me being his helper. I felt that Saidy's claim was quite clear, and she rarely misunderstood any of his questions. Nonetheless, he frequently looked to me when asking his questions and after receiving answers. "Am I doing this right? Should I ask more questions on this?" he would ask me. He would also ask me questions as if he was required to defer to me. As someone simply accompanying an applicant, of course, this was not the case. "Is it all right if I ask this? I don't want to get in trouble," he said, again to me. In these moments, Saidy would turn to me, confused, then look back at him, as he did not deploy the interpreter for translation. Somewhat bewildered, I helped in leading him through his questioning, confused by the sort of highly participatory role I was being afforded, which up to that point, I had yet to experience anything even remotely of the sort.

On another occasion with the same officer, Esmy, an Indigenous mother from Guatemala, began talking about how her father was recently murdered by one of her cousins, a gang member, when AO Hart suddenly leaned back into his office chair, yawning loudly. Esmy seemed confused but kept trying to speak over the sound. She had only a year of formal schooling and seemed to struggle to understand many of his questions. It was possible that there were language barriers, as while she identified as being part of an Indigenous community, she didn't want to proceed in the interview with an Indigenous language interpreter. Navigating conversations with clients about which language they should choose for their interview could be challenging; some clients believed, or were told by officials, that if they were to ask for an interpreter in their native language—especially if that language was considered "rare," meaning rarely spoken, like many Indigenous languages—they would likely have to wait days or even weeks to reschedule. It was true that some Indigenous languages had so few professional interpreters that scheduling their services sometimes required significant lead time; it was also true, however, that some advocates believed this to be a tactic by officials to convince detained clients to go forward with an interview in order to "process" them more quickly. This happened an unfortunate number of times with ethnically Roma clients who passed through Dilley or Karnes, sometimes with disastrous interpretation issues.

There were multiple issues with interpretation in Esmy's interview, including loud feedback sounds that delayed conversation. Several times I intervened, trying to clarify the errors of misinterpretation. Esmy continued to be confused by the phrasing of questions, and AO Hart visibly appeared to swing between frustration and boredom. "I'll ask this question one more time," he said looking at me, in reference to a line of questioning about her father's death, which she was quite confused about. "And then I'm done. They said all I had to ask was three times, that's it," he said shortly. I understood what sort of answer he was looking for, but he was failing to get there through his phrasing of the questions. I was worried that he would abandon this important part of the discussion simply because of this, so I suggested an alternative approach for his inquiry. This did, in fact, end up helping to break through the impasse. Advocates, even when they weren't welcomed to speak or were explicitly told not to, often found themselves interjecting at moments where they observed sometimes critical errors being made. Like with AO Hart, the burden to obtain pertinent information for a client's case, beyond what they themselves could provide, was more heavily placed on the accompanying advocate.

From my own and others' experiences, advocates' positions in the interviews conducted by this officer were interpreted as a sort of dependency or assistantship. At times, officers like him openly recognized this type of relationality—in this case, by referring to legal advocates as helpers—and others when their apparent ineptitude in the role seemed to call out, itself, for assistance. This highlighted both the potential incongruences of encounters within this part of the process as well as the ways that administrators came to rely on the voluntary labor of these advocates, to aid them in work that they were neither meant to do nor direct others in doing. Although this could be seen as a more productive form of relationship between advocate and adjudicator, to the potential benefit of the applicant, this was neither the desire nor intention of advocates. As was made repeatedly clear in trainings for advocates, their work aimed to help applicants communicate their own case, not to speak on their behalf. While Officer Hart was not explicitly asking advocates to do this, he was encouraging a kind of discourse that effectively left applicants out. Another implication in this officer's comments that challenges a positive evaluation of the exchange regarded his reference to "getting in trouble," which speaks to a perception of advocates as powerful and threatening. This perception—of advocates as adversaries or subversives to the work of adjudicators—was familiar, and it would be made more explicit in other encounters.

Raquel rushed up to me, placing her hand on my forearm. "Can you go to my client's interview, Erin?" she whispered to me. The woman, Bessy, was sitting at the front of the visitation trailer, waiting to walk over to the asylum office. Raquel, who had prepped her, had promised her that she would go with her to the interview, as Bessy was very anxious. Raquel, unfortunately, was in the middle of prepping another woman and couldn't leave at the moment. I told her I would go, and we spoke briefly about Bessy's claim, in preparation. This awareness on the part of the accompanying advocate was important, especially in the rare but possible case that the interview completely derailed or the client froze, unable to talk about their experiences without specific direction. Raquel then quickly introduced me to Bessy, and we walked over to the asylum office together with our guard escort and sat for a few minutes waiting for her officer to retrieve us.

When I saw the familiar officer walking up to us, I felt my body tense. AO Jones was a short woman who had an intimidating presence. I had accompanied someone to an interview with her the week before, and it did not go well. In that accompaniment, she barely acknowledged my existence apart from, strangely, mocking my poor handwriting after she asked me to write down my last name for her records. She also repeatedly cut the client off when she responded to answers. She, like many other AOs, wasn't particularly friendly with advocates and often expressed coldness and impatience with applicants. Other advocates in then-recent weeks had upsetting run-ins with her, including one in which she told an advocate that they weren't allowed to take notes—which, in fact, wasn't true, but because temporary volunteers weren't necessarily aware of their own rights in this space, they didn't protest—and another in which she instructed an advocate of how they needed to act within and beyond the interview in order to be a "good advocate." Her attitude toward applicants, however, was unpredictable; sometimes she was in a good mood, playfully joking with them or attempting to build rapport. Sometimes these "jokes" veered sharply into uncomfortable terrain, like when she told a young child, in apparent jest, that they should behave or she would "have to call the police" (in this case, meaning the guards standing outside the room) to take the child away. The advocate who observed this exchange came back to the visitation trailer furious, complaining about her astounding obtuseness. "How could she think that would be funny?" he said incredulously. "To a little girl who only knows the police to be bad people?" Patiently enduring what many felt were detestable or uncomfortable jokes made by officials at the facility—either adjudicators or guards—wasn't an uncommon experience for advocates. At the end of another client's interview, an officer even joked to a mother that maybe she'd rather leave her child behind at the detention center. He laughed, saying that some parents "would rather ditch their kids." I stared at him in shock, appalled at his insensitivity and failed awareness of the qualities of the context in which he suggested an asylum seeker would leave her child incarcerated. The client awkwardly smiled, shaking her head and responding simply, "No, my son is my life."

The interview that day with AO Jones was particularly difficult, primarily in that Bessy's experiences were quite traumatic, and she was in an emotional state. Her boyfriend had been murdered, after which she had been pursued relentlessly by a man who then assaulted her. After one incident, she had tried to file a report with a police officer, who then assaulted her as well as a kind of "payment" for filing the report. Fortunately, AO Jones appeared sympathetic to Bessy's story, making eye contact with her and refraining from using harsh language, and the interview didn't last longer than an hour. As Bessy and I stood up to leave the room, AO Jones stopped me. "Ms. Routon, can you hang back for a minute?" she asked. I was confused and nervous, but I said goodbye to Bessy and sat back in my chair.

I had an idea of what she might want to speak about. Earlier, Bessy had used a legal phrase to discuss a part of the framework of her case. Legal advocates, in preparing clients, presented them with legal categories for asylum. Individually, advocates discussed with them the relevant categories for their cases. For Bessy's case, Raquel discussed the concept of an "anti-gang political opinion," as it functioned in asylum law. She explained to Bessy the meaning of this concept and how she believed it related to Bessy's case, and Bessy chose to use the phrase when discussing her case in her interview. When she used this, AO Jones appeared surprised, looking over from her computer screen with raised eyebrows. I thought that this might be what AO Jones had intended to discuss with me, as previous advocates who encountered her expressed that she had accused the advocacy team of "coaching" clients on what to say in their interviews.

As it turned out, I was right. "This isn't official or anything," she said with a slight smile, leaning forward from her side of the desk, "but I just wanted to give you some advice. I can see that this 'anti-gang political opinion' thing has come up a few times in different interviews. This is what I call 'CARA [DPBP] coaching.' I just wanted to say that I don't think this 'anti-gang political opinion' thing is going to work later down the line [with applicants' cases]. I don't even think there's any case law out there for that sort of thing." I nodded and thanked her for her advice before returning to the visitation trailer.

It is important to question not only the validity of this officer's critique but also what this critique had to say about officers' considerations of asylum seekers. The implication of a "coaching" claim was that the applicant being questioned had been instructed on what to say and precisely how to say it in their interview. This would lead the officer to question both the credibility of the detainee and the ethics of the legal advocacy team (and thus, in turn, their continued interaction with detainees). This begs further questions: Why was an applicant's use of legal language suspect? What did that communicate about how officers thought about asylum seekers, and what did it say about how officers thought about legal advocates? One of the obvious implications of this accusation was that the officer questioned the capacity of an applicant to deploy complex legal constructs for their own ends, using specific institutional language. Another problematic assumption was that advocates were simply telling clients what to say rather than allowing them to communicate their experiences in their own words, which, as noted earlier, ran counter to the training and orientation of advocates in their roles. In this critique, applicants' use of legal language and advocates' involvement in the knowledge-sharing of these terms challenged the interpretive authority of the officer. From the perspective of the officer, this interfered with her work, creating friction between the three actors participating in the encounter. In this case, AO Jones responded to this friction by leveling unfounded accusations that implied subversive behavior on the part of advocates.

In spaces like these, where advocates were restricted in their caring roles, they recorded and observed what occurred between the interviewee and interviewer. They noted failures to pursue relevant lines of questioning, a client's disregarded discomfort, and mistakes or misinterpretations made. Such ethnographic-like attention to detail in this encounter is another articulation of care. These details could be used to contest negative decisions potentially made later by the officer, but they also could be deployed, in more serious cases of client mistreatment, as fodder for lodging complaints about AOs and their behavior toward clients. In instances where advocates were given some participatory leeway, they could make more critical interventions. As Chase's story showed, advocates could intervene in moments that were indeed important for a client's future case, even when disregarded by the officer. Advocates' care was displayed through their attentiveness and observation but also their presence. Clients asked advocates in their preps if they could accompany them, even being aware that they could not speak on their behalf. Ari, an undergraduate student who was studying abroad in Florence when they learned about Dilley and signed up to volunteer, described how they felt they could sense the impact their presence had on clients.

> I felt their energy in that way that like, if I'm there, they're more confident. The way that they talked to me, their body language . . . it was less tense

> than I think it would be if I wasn't there. I think they were also a little more relaxed that a native Spanish speaker was there with them, to make sure everything was going smoothly.

Although it was effectively impossible to know whether a client would truly be more confident or relaxed if an advocate accompanied or hadn't done so, without grounded data to support such a claim, it was apparent, from many clients' expressions and advocates' own "sense" or reflections on the context, that their presence served a positive function.

Other asylum officers, it should be noted, exhibited much greater care in their conduct in the interviews than others, sometimes through small gestures, like making eye contact with an applicant while she told her story, rather than looking away at their computer screen. Other times, their caring moves were more substantial, like when they patiently worked with applicants to help them make sense of their legal claim. These stories were not meant to negate the real existence of officers who expressed care in their work; rather, they were meant to show what legal advocates often observed, reflecting the unpredictable ways that applicants and advocates were treated. This unpredictability was itself harmful, requiring advocates to sometimes improvise care, remaining adaptable to the particularities of individual encounters.

Advocates' experiences in this moment illustrates how "care work requires recognition," and even more specifically, how it requires "fluctuating kinds of recognition, in which different aspects of the person and context need attention at various moments" (Coe 2019, 11). Recognition, attention, and at times, boundary-crossing interventions are all reconfigured care tactics in spaces like these. In a way, this follows the everyday tactical subversions of state power and various forms of boundary maintenance realized by migrants who, as Reece Jones (2017) reminds us, engage in a political act of refusal simply through movement, crossing sovereign borders. Even accompaniment, without explicit interventions, served to offer "an alternate vision as a form of praxis rooted in a feminist ethics of care, one grounded in universal humanity and explicit acknowledgments of power, privilege, and the responsibilities of our subject positions" (Yarris and Duncan 2024a, 14). In other words, accompaniment itself is an act of refusal as well, one that draws additional attention to how asylum seekers are made vulnerable by the state and by everyday legal processes (Speed 2019).

EL CORTE

Although most detained families who received preparation for their interviews received positive decisions, a *positivo,* allowing them to continue their cases beyond detention, some inevitably received negative decisions, or a *negativo.* This meant they would need to appeal the decision within the facility's court, determined by an immigration judge, to avoid deportation. To begin this part of the discussion, however, exploring advocates' unique care in this moment, I will recount an encounter between a judge and a volunteer lawyer that occurred at the Artesia detention center mentioned in the introduction to this book. As a reminder, the Artesia facility was the first center to usher in the new era of family detention in the United States. Even though the facility existed for only a short period, it was also the site of what would become the legal advocacy projects at Dilley and Karnes. The story below depicts an exchange involving lawyer Stephen Manning, who, as previously noted, both founded Innovation Law Lab, the Oregon-based organization that created and managed the digital client database, and was part of the initial group of volunteer lawyers in Artesia. This story appeared at the opening of a report that documented the inner workings of that center, including the mistreatments of detainees and misapplications of the law, as well as the work of legal volunteers.

> "You are a mute observer. You may not speak on the record," the Immigration Judge says. "I know you attorneys think you have a role here. But you do not." The attorney tilts his head and begins, "Your honor—." "No" [replied the judge.] The judge's image flickers; his voice sounds distant. "If you begin to speak, I will stop the recording. You may watch. I will not hear argument from you." The judge is a floating image, 8 inches diagonal, on a computer screen. In the courtroom, the guard glances at the lawyer. The lawyer turns to M-, his client, and starts to whisper in her ear. The lawyer means to explain what has just happened. "Stop that counsel. You may not speak to her," the image says. "But she is my client, Your Honor." On the

computer screen, the image shakes its head. It simply scolds, "No." ("The Artesia Report" 2024)

Although this tense exchange occurred beyond the scope of my own field research, it reflects a deeply familiar experience for those legal advocates who attended court hearings at Dilley or Karnes. It also makes plain one of the characteristic threads between the roles for advocates in these spaces: silence. In the courtroom, legal advocates were considered "friends of the court" rather than official legal counsel. Their ability to participate in this space was deeply limited and yet, also unpredictable. This section speaks to the environment and unique experiences of advocates in the in-detention courtroom, as often "mute observers," including how they managed support for their clients around such forceful constraints.

The court, like the asylum office, was situated in a separate space within the facility, and the judges that presided over cases appeared remotely on a screen, as in Artesia. Such physical absences contributed to feelings that advocates often expressed regarding both asylum officers and judges: that they were not attentive to the person whose fate they were deciding. Many detainees never needed to attend this court, as they received positive decisions on their cases. Nonetheless, most weeks saw at least a couple of negative decisions, which meant that those clients were able to appeal those decisions and go to court to continue with their case, rather than face deportation immediately. Judges, in responding to clients' appeals, would elect to either uphold or reject them, or "affirming" or "vacating" the officer's decisions. They were meant to base this decision on their consideration of an appeal document or series of supportive documentation and questions posed to clients directly in court concerning why they had received a negative decision from the officer and why they deserved to have that decision overturned. There were typically specific days reserved for court cases, and each judge's "docket" or schedule for that day would be shared with the advocacy team. Typically, those volunteers or project staff who accompanied clients to court were professional lawyers. Volunteers would sometimes spend the greater part of their day sitting through the processing of different client cases in court, returning to the visitation area later to share what had occurred in court with each case. Sometimes, those who had worked with clients to prepare their appeal documentation or even those who had worked with clients prior to their interviews weren't those that attended court with them; they, especially, anxiously awaited news on how judges had treated and responded to specific clients' appeals.

A form of documentation, known as a "declaration," for court was an opportunity for advocates to go into greater depth on a client's case, to express nuance or additional experiences that might never have come out in an interview, to explain issues with asylum officers, or to clarify misunderstandings, among other things. In prepping the declaration, advocates would pore over the transcript of the interview of their denied client, searching for misunderstandings or missed opportunities by the officer to get into relevant details of a claim. As already illustrated, the interview was, truly, a fleeting moment in which much could be misinterpreted or even go unsaid. Other things, like asylum officers' language or behavior, could disturb the conversation or elicit inhibitive reactions. Many things affected why a client would have received a negative decision from the officer, and advocates needed to work with the client to create strong explanations and support for overturning this decision. The stakes naturally increased in the courtroom. As a result, the characteristic instability and arbitrariness that permeated much of the inner workings of the facility at-large effected a new level of anxiety in those who participated in courtroom defenses.

"I love it, I love it, I love it," Charlotte said to me enthusiastically. Charlotte, an immigration lawyer from Kansas City, was not talking about her experience with Dilley's court, but about how happy she was in her new role. As a freshly minted lawyer, she still had a background image on her laptop of Sylvester the cat sitting at a desk with bloodshot eyes, drinking coffee and smoking a cigarette. She told me that was what it felt like when she was studying for the LSAT, the Law School Admission Test she had recently passed. Her work in Kansas involved family-based and humanitarian petitions primarily, and she had a diverse caseload of asylum clients. Prior to this, she had worked in both English as a Second Language (ESL) education and policy with the Department of Education. She characterized her work now as more of a calling than that previous work, especially policy, which felt "too far removed from people." She, like many other volunteer immigration lawyers, spoke of her interest in the complexity of immigration law. For them, the complexity was a pull; the dynamism of the field was, in a way, exciting and deeply engaging.

Charlotte went with clients to court on two of the five days that she was volunteering with the project. "It was kind of like a boot camp for me," she explained. "The first day, all of the women I went with got their decisions vacated, but it seemed like it was completely just luck of the draw." Before she went to court, she was extremely nervous. She was expected to attend the court of a judge who had a particularly harsh and unkind reputation with project staff. The day before she first went to court, she explained,

> Another volunteer went to his court and he affirmed every single case. But when I went just the next day, the same judge told one of the women that he vacated her decision because it happened to be her birthday. That one I was excited about, but I was also quietly very angry about. When I went back to the visitation trailer and told the project staff about it, they were astounded. It's ridiculous, and so arbitrary.

In this case, as Charlotte rightfully pointed out, even positive feelings for the outcome of a case could be tempered by the fact that decisions like this were not made even remotely fairly, a point that disturbed many lawyer advocates.

Others' experiences drew attention to the upsetting ways that not only the law was applied but also how clients were treated in courtroom encounters. Most of my conversations with Max were about his feelings about court. He was an immigration lawyer with a degree in international human rights, having written his thesis on Central American gangs. Max was exceedingly familiar not only with legal categories for asylum and asylum seekers' rights but also with the contexts through which these cases were formed. Thus, he thought he knew what to expect coming to Dilley; unfortunately, he was wrong. "I didn't get sad as much as angry," Max said plainly, continuing,

> What was most surprising to me was the misapplication of the law. In one day, I watched a judge deny four cases without merit to do so, one which I thought would've won all the way through, would've gotten asylum. That day, that judge was just awful, and I told the project staff about how he was incredibly condescending to clients. It was so frustrating to have to not interrupt or say anything back to him. The legal standard is just so low, so

> I couldn't even fathom all of those women's appeals being denied. I mean it was sickening. I know the law is discretionary, but that was just beyond what I had braced myself for.

Max opined that the arbitrariness of judge's denials was most clearly evidenced by the obvious variations between the different judges. On a day when he was in court, he observed that

> all the women across the hall with the other judge had their decision vacated.... They got to go back to their rooms and rest. And their cases were so similar to the others. But [his] judge said that what these clients' cases were about were just "generalized violence." He said that over and over. There was this one mother who told her story *perfectly*, explained herself *perfectly*, she said everything that she needed to say. Another woman had a strange case where her guardian was seriously physically and mentally abusive to her, and the judge just wasn't having any of it. He didn't believe her or believe that the way her guardian had treated her was unreasonable. His first question for her was, "Do you think it's abuse to expect you to do chores when you're living somewhere for free?" She looked over at me, confused, and said, "Yes?" and he just moved on. For another woman, he simply dismissed her case, telling her that what happened to her family wasn't worthy of asylum, that it was just "undesirable to live in her country" and that he "wished her well." That was it. To be fair, there was one mother who just couldn't articulate her claim clearly. He could've worked around that, however, but it was obvious that he chose not to. He never even interviewed any of the children despite the fact that at least a few of the mothers' claims were based entirely on their daughters' persecution.

In his view, it wasn't simply that claims were denied—though that was surprising, considering that these cases had reasonable merits—but the qualities of the encounter that were upsetting. "It was horrible," Max said. "The whole concept of having to tell some white man all the abuse you've suffered, that's bad enough. But his tone was so incredibly condescending. I've never heard someone be that disrespectful to people that have gone through that much trauma."

For lawyers like Max, the practical applications of the law in this unique court were often bewildering, even destabilizing. Yet, at the same time, many were also acutely aware of how they needed to deftly manage their position in those spaces, as it could impact decision-making. Anita, a volunteer attorney who worked for the NGO Human Rights Watch, reflected on the special delicacy with which she approached her interactions with judges. "It's about learning where the boundaries are," she said.

> Then you want to behave in a way that shows them that you respect them and those boundaries. If I were to go to the court and tried to defend the client or offer feedback to the judge, he or she would just tell me that I couldn't talk at all. You don't have the luxury of arguing for the client because, in this scenario, they're not really your client. The point is that you want to appease them and placate them, the judges, because you want to keep the conversation going.

Efforts aimed at "keeping the conversation going" seemed to be another articulation of what advocates did with guards, officers, and other administrators in their management of relationships. Management of those relationships, which was dependent on many factors, supported the continued flow of legal care. In this setting, as with the interview, advocates attended more as supportive observers. Similarly, they could potentially clarify questions the judge might have, catch interpretation mistakes, and serve as a supportive presence for clients. In their training, volunteers were reminded that they were indeed only attending as a friend of the court rather than as a representative. This was an important clarification, especially for those attorneys who attended court but weren't used to this legal position. The advocate sat in a sort of uniquely vulnerable position in which achieving their aim—to, as Anita phrased, *keep the conversation going*—depended on their ability to express awareness of and adherence to expectations around positional boundaries, even when this meant they were often muted. Their relational status—as a friend—defined the challenge.

Generally, advocates believed that judges either misunderstood or intentionally misinterpreted asylum law. However, when they spoke negatively of their encounters with judges, it wasn't simply about their knowledge or interpretation of the law but also their behavior toward clients and themselves. Advocates' precarious positions in court shaped these uneven and uncomfortable encounters. "I believe he was misapplying the law," Lillian, a volunteer attorney, said of one of the judges, "but I was also just frustrated with him. One day in court, I tried to ask him a question about the case I was there working on, and I waited until we were 'off the record' to ask it, just to be safe. I didn't want to insult him or hurt the outcome of the case in any way," she said. Advocates spoke about the ways that they tried to cautiously move through their interactions with judges, to avoid potentially negatively influencing their decisions on cases. Yet, despite their best efforts to manage those relationships, responses remained steadfastly unpredictable. "So I was talking to him, and all of the sudden, he just snapped at me," Lillian continued,

> saying that he wasn't going to answer my question, and that it was a privilege that he even let me in his courtroom. So, of course, I immediately apologized and thanked him for that privilege. It was nothing like the interactions I had with the other judge. She'd allow me to help answer questions, we'd have conversations about case law. She was a really interesting person. And she was really fair in her decisions.

The unpredictability of "fair" adjudication, as Lillian described it, was hard for advocates to accept, but bearing witness to the kind of disregard practiced by those decision-makers, in their constrained role, was also deeply challenging. "Maybe it was naive of me to expect otherwise, but just to see what little time the judge spent deciding on someone's case and possibly their life, was gross and sincerely wasteful," Max said with frustration, continuing,

> There was this case I was working on where the judge only spent ten minutes making a decision. The [declaration] that we put together was thirty pages long, and he even commented on the length of it. But still, he only picked out certain bullet points that he wanted to talk about. And his tone, that was the other thing. So the facts of her case were that her partner had been targeted by gangs, they tried to kill him, and he left in order to protect her and the kids. It was kind of unclear whether or not her partner actually left to protect the family or if he just left. To her, it was about protection. The judge's tone, however, and the way that he spoke to her about what happened was "Well, when he left you, blah blah blah." As soon as he said that the first time, I could just tell, she froze up. Already before that, she

> wasn't able to talk about a lot of what happened, but when he made that comment, she looked at me like, *That's it. I can't do this anymore.* By the end of it, I was shaking with anger. And you know, if this were to take place in a real trial setting, I could have redirected the judge's comments, asked questions. All I could do here was just take notes, writing down every bad thing he said.

Expressing care in apparently careless exchanges like this, especially when boundaries are sharply drawn between those who are allowed to participate and those who aren't, is difficult, to say the least. In the space of the prep, advocates frequently went to great lengths to establish comfort and trust ahead of clients' interviews. They expressly assigned value to clients' experiences and choices and took seriously the need for care in bringing out discussions of trauma. This was also true in prepping clients for court. In engaging with specific instances in interviews and courtroom encounters, my work illustrates the contrast in the approaches of asylum officers, judges, and advocates in obtaining information with which to build or envision an asylum narrative. Advocates' care practices are made clearer through the ways that positional boundaries are drawn in these encounters, distinguishing friends from gatekeepers.

MUTATIONS

Legal care in these spaces did not disappear because of these apparent and often substantive limitations on their participation, but it was transfigured. Advocates were effectively muted unless afforded the rare opportunity to comment on their client's behalf or to fulfill other helpful roles. In trying to resist this constraint, they sometimes risked upsetting tenuous relationships with adjudicators, the outcomes of which had the potential to harm either the continuation of legal assistance or decisions on their clients' cases. Advocates, individually, were forced to weigh those risks against others, sometimes with just a split second to decide on what to do. Familiar experiences can be seen running across different fields of care work, especially those that depend on voluntary labor. In the context of volunteers working at a rape crisis center, Leslie Thornton and David Novak (2010) demonstrate how such participants are forced to engage in emotion work, managing both their own and those of others, in unexpected ways. Their interlocutors had to navigate

> the delicate balance of displaying one emotion . . . to influence a service provider (and, in doing so, showing support to the client), while tempering one's affect with another, more favorable emotion . . . directed to the client. Interestingly, advocates often found themselves performing the role of shock absorber when paid service providers failed to engage in emotion work. Volunteers absorbed the shock of inappropriate comments made by nurses and law enforcement officers, apologized to survivors on behalf of paid providers, and tried to protect survivors from harmful effects that emerged from the actions (or lack thereof) of paid providers. (443)

Emotion work was a key part of what legal advocates did in various aspects of their labor, and their own articulations of how they navigated these spaces demonstrate its continued centrality. Indeed, the stakes for managing one's own and others' emotions were notably higher, putting the pressure to remain attentive and flexible on the shoulders of advocates.

In making sense of what unfolded in these spaces—again, as kinds of metaphorical border zones—it's important to recall that "while borders provide order, they also are structures of, and environments for, disorder" (Wilson 2024, 8). This was first touched on in chapter 1, when I discussed some of the "disorienting" practices and processes of the facility at large. The disorder here, the unpredictability of the interview and court experiences, shouldn't be understood as accidental but rather by design, not unlike that of ongoing "crises" at the southern border. What consistently occurred was a reflection of that design; they were varied expressions of authoritative control and power, rather the kind of "power to make oneself unpredictable and deny other people any reasonable anticipation, to place them in total uncertainty," which defined applicants' very "detainability" to begin with (DeGenova 2016, 7).

While legal advocates may have been muted or deeply inhibited in their caring roles, their "mere" existence within them informed the encounters. In such spaces, "accompaniment conditions the pathway through which our bodies enter the room, the amount of time we spend there, and the commitment we feel. Accompaniment amplifies the stakes and thickens the air [and] can heighten awareness of mise-en-scène at the same time that it meaningfully transforms the room" (Castañeda and Crabapple 2023, 20). Yet again, this effect left advocates at a kind of crossroads: their presence had the potential to heighten the tension—particularly in cases where they were perceived by adjudicators as a kind of threat to their authority—but as so many anecdotes illustrate, their presence was predicated primarily on either the desire of applicants for being-with or a notable concern for accompaniment, as determined by advocates working in preps with clients. And because of the unpredictable nature in which advocates were perceived by a given adjudicator, it was often impossible to include this as part of the calculus for accompaniment.

Part of the perception of threat presumably derived from this awareness on the part of adjudicators of advocates as "watchers," and potential complainants, either officially or unofficially, of their work. Surveillance, importantly, should be understood as "a dynamic and interactive process in which the boundaries between watcher and watched are often indeterminate and where, despite inequalities of power, subordinates are able to contest and challenge gatekeepers, order enforcers, and other formal authorities" (Walsh 2013, 299). This challenging threat was at times realized by advocates, while other times it might have been perceived to be just resting under the surface. Although adjudicators were not themselves the direct subjects of my research, and as such I hesitate to assign such interpretations to them, based on my own and others' interactions, I believe it makes sense that advocates could have been perceived in such a way in those encounters. Unknowingly or unintentionally, then, what I would characterize as forms of advocates' care labor—observing and documenting these encounters—had the potential to build tension while also offering a necessary form of aid. This complicates our understanding of how what might be deemed spaces of "uncare" (Gupta 2012), those quintessential places in which legal violence is enacted, are transfigured into spaces of care, even if that just means having another person present, watching and scribbling notes on a legal pad. In such spaces, the "audacity of accompaniment" (Kleinman 2024)—meaning that in which a caregiver is meant to "step inside" the experiences of those most in need of help—can seemingly function at counterpurposes, and advocates are left trying to pick a path: not one, necessarily, of least resistance but one that leads toward better care.

CONCLUSION

"Accompaniment," Josiah Heyman (2024, 174) reminds us, "is particularly drawn toward these sorts of present but potentially disappeared circumstances, because it is a method of knowing, connecting, and morally and politically affirming humanity and mutuality in contexts where such connections fully exist but may be suddenly destroyed." Whereas previously I showed how advocates' work was constrained by the constant frictions that often permeated everyday encounters with facility administration, this chapter showed how their care and influence was particularly inhibited during the interview and court. Although advocates attempted to prepare clients for what would likely come, this was primarily focused on the sorts of questions they would receive and how they might be expected to narrate personal experiences. The work thus involved building a narrative that fit with legal allowances for asylum. However, it was impossible for advocates to predict exactly how a client would be treated by an officer, or how an officer would approach conducting their interview. As affirmed in scholarship on this subject (e.g., Millbank 2009; Schoenholtz, Schrag, and Ramji-Nogales 2014), the adjudication that takes place in the interview is unpredictable, inconsistent, and marked by sometimes widely varying degrees of expertise, professionalism, and subjectivity. The sort of relational environment established by an officer was unpredictable as well and thus made it quite difficult for advocates to prepare clients for what they might experience in that space. Having advocates accompany clients, when possible, was one way to respond to that uncertainty.

With this chapter, I again recognize one of the shortcomings of this study: that asylum officers and immigration judges, like facility staff, are presented in a limited and partial manner. My research does not explore their backgrounds or positionalities, nor does it attempt to speak to the actual intentions of officers or judges in their comments or decisions. It further does not offer the final word on how their actions should be construed, as interpretations are admittedly variable. I offer here only interpretations of those encounters from the perspective of advocates who often struggled to support clients because of administrators' behaviors. To be sure, there were officers and judges with whom I and other advocates had positive experiences, some of whom expressed a high degree of professionalism and empathy in their work. Advocates and clients alike expressed gratitude for these caring and careful individuals. The deeply complex nature of the work of officers, judges, and even guards, I argue, deserves greater attention than I am able to offer here. Nonetheless, the perspective of advocates on these many encounters is also valid, even if it misses a part of the story.

"I *loved* going to the interviews," Chase told me. He was one of only a few advocates I knew who used such effusive language to talk about accompanying clients, though his reasoning matched others' perspectives. He admitted that he was aware that most advocates didn't exactly enjoy this part of the work and that some saw their impact in this space as minimal, and yet, he said,

> I really feel like there's nothing more "advocacy" than to literally sit on the same side as your client. You sit on that side of the table and outnumber the [other side], so at least it's two against one. It feels like real advocacy when you're sitting right next to them, and they look at you, and you're able to help them with that a little bit. . . . Selfishly, it just felt good to have the client working right next to me, you know? It feels like I'm saying, "I'm here for you."

In giving care, advocates were entangled in the narratives and everyday experiences of their detained clients. In addition to feeling fear for the things that might happen to them, especially those that appeared just beyond their influence, and frustration with those often unreasonable limitations, they also wrestled with conflicted feelings concerning exactly how they should practice accompaniment (Castañeda and Crabapple 2023). This had the effect of making advocates, at times, question the true impact of their work, including how they might be causing more harm than good.

Nonetheless, even under remarkable constraints, an advocate's presence alongside their client was meaningful. This wasn't just evident in the reflections of advocates but also in the various forms of deep appreciation frequently expressed by clients to those advocates, for agreeing to accompany them, to be there in those spaces by their side. Their presence also potentially entailed correcting critical errors made by decision-makers or interpreters that might have gone unnoticed or at least unchallenged. Thus, their material and attentive presence were each impactful in different ways. Furthermore, in those spaces they were able to both bear witness to material injustices and document them. Unlike with those encounters recounted by applicants that occurred upon crossing the southern border or in other spaces of the facility, in the interview and court, advocates were able to witness the mistreatments and abuses they experienced.

Advocates' presence alongside their clients, sometimes on the literal "same side," and their ability to observe, to bear witness, and to record were all clear markers of their care. Their witnessing and documentary efforts—effectively, efforts to countersurveil—demonstrate this point most obviously, but I also argue that their even relatively minor expressions of sensitivity, attention, and closeness were also forms of resistance in that they challenged operative norms that commonly treated applicants with both disregard and suspicion. As illustrated, indeed these forms of treatment were extended to advocates themselves, albeit in different articulations. The interpretation by these decision-makers of advocates as potential impediments or even adversaries in those spaces further highlights both the impact of their presence as well as the perceived threat of their care work; it is only in part this repeated tension or friction that articulates their care, in these spaces and others, as resistance.

CHAPTER 5

THRESHOLD

On a hot August evening in 2015, I walked out of the facility in Dilley and waited, leaning against the side of my dusty rental sedan. It was the end of the first week I volunteered in the detention center, and it had simultaneously felt like one of the longest and shortest periods of my life. My body was weary and drained, but it was also still buzzing with energy, like some long-distance runner mid-marathon. Earlier that day, as I sat uploading client documents, Matt, a project staff member, rushed in. "Can anyone take a family to San Antonio tonight?" he asked loudly, with a wide grin. A client family—mother and daughter—had received their release (NTA) paperwork, and while they were able to acquire bus tickets to take them to their new home city, they didn't have the means to get from Dilley to the bus station in San Antonio. Legal advocates frequently helped arrange travel for families who needed additional support as they left the remote center, sometimes driving them to the airport or bus station, and sometimes offering to board them temporarily. As I was leaving town that night and had already offered a ride to San Antonio to Maddie, another volunteer, I offered to take them to the shelter in the city where released families in transit stayed and were cared for.

Maddie was the first advocate I met when I started my research in Dilley in 2015. Even though she was only in her mid-twenties at the time,

FIGURE 15 The end of author's first week volunteering in 2015, in front of the Dilley facility. Credit Erin Routon.

Maddie was an intimidatingly impressive person. She was working in a legal fellowship after having finished her undergraduate studies at a prestigious university, had interned at the United Nations, and was fluent in multiple languages. While I initially struggled to find my way around the role, Maddie seemed to glide through different aspects of the work as if she had been doing it for weeks, speaking to clients one minute about their cases and seamlessly navigating the online database the next.

Facing the metal door of the security trailer, I saw them exit: Maddie, and a mother, Esther, and her seven-year-old daughter, Tatiana, carrying large plastic bags full of their belongings that had been confiscated upon entering this facility. On the way out of town, I stopped to gas up and buy snacks for Esther and Tatiana, as they were only given a few bottles of water upon leaving. I quickly grabbed a few fried pies and icy jelly pastries made by a local bakery. On the drive, Tatiana snacked on the pastries while Esther, Maddie, and I chatted about Esther's hometown in Guatemala. Tatiana was quiet but smiled through her snacking.

Esther and Tatiana planned to leave for North Carolina the following morning, and so we were to drop them at the shelter. Called the "Mennonite House"—for its relation to a local Mennonite Church—it was a large, older house located in the artistic King William district of the city. As we drove up, we could see kids and adults playing basketball and a woman walked out of the back door to greet us. The four of us followed her in through the back to the kitchen. The house was full of people, sitting and talking in different rooms, laughing and eating, kids running all around. There were big pots cooking on the broad stove, and the comforting, earthy smell of rice and beans filled the room. After ensuring they were well situated, Maddie and I began our bittersweet goodbyes to Esther and Tatiana. Esther embraced Maddie, and I knelt to tell Tatiana goodbye. She swiftly wrapped her small arm around my neck and squeezed me close, holding on to me more tightly and for longer than I would have ever expected. I was taken aback. She had barely said a word before this, and even in that moment, she didn't speak and neither did I. Tears welled in my eyes as if the strength of her embrace had squeezed them out, and I felt the lump in my throat that would come to be a constant companion throughout fieldwork. She eventually let go, we left, and I made my way to my sister's home in Austin late into the evening. Sailing through the small towns and farmland that connect the two cities, awash in the glow of twenty-four-hour gas stations and lustrous starlight, I realized I could not let go of that hug. In some ways, I still haven't.

Nearly two years later, I found myself leaving again, though this time, it was at the end of a long, challenging year of fieldwork. As I left, I had conflicted feelings: excitement about the future, as I was soon to get married, but also an overwhelming sense of grief at the thought of leaving. I was distraught at the thought of leaving these projects, my friends and colleagues, and importantly, all the women and children who were still detained and those who were still to come that I would never meet. The loss felt great, and the full effects of secondary or vicarious trauma I had experienced in the field were yet to be understood. At the time, all I knew was it felt like my heart was breaking; I couldn't understand just why it hurt so much.

Although this chapter doesn't offer a definitive answer for why I and many other advocates felt this way upon leaving the work, it does take the experience of "crossing over," including those concomitant, often conflicted feelings associated with leaving, seriously as an integral part of this story of legal care. Here, I consider the threshold, or a point of crossing that is both symbolic and material, as it relates to the work and experiences of these advocates in different ways. Whereas previous chapters focused only on their labor with and for detainees, here I consider the ways that advocates themselves were, in a different manner, accompanied by disturbing or unsettling experiences inherent to this work. I describe this as a kind of "haunting," in part demonstrating how "emotion[s] temporally [extend] beyond the immediacy of the scene, [revealing] a post hoc element to the emotional landscape of volunteer advocacy" (Thornton and Novak 2010, 444). Thinking with and through haunting also allows us to consider the variety of post hoc, lingering expressions of power, so characteristic of carceral spaces, as haunting itself "is one of the most important places where meaning—comprehension—and force intersect" (Gordon 2008, 194).

Inevitably, this is a chapter partially about trauma: how this work engendered a traumatic response and the different shapes that trauma took for advocates specifically. What the book has presented thus far is not just how advocates worked to mitigate the harms that asylum seekers experienced as a result of the environment and legal procedures but also how they were subjected to their own forms of harm in the process, impacted by various frictions built into the environment and everyday encounters. In this way, I've argued, we must consider how legal caregivers themselves are similarly and uniquely impacted by the "continuum of violence" (Scheper-Hughes and Bourgois 2004, 1) that informs asylum and carceral norms, and how they are exposed to consequences of the "structural shrapnel" of destructive immigration processes (Caswell and Ruehs-Navarro 2023). I consider here the impacts of leaving this work in these facilities. Rather than making a sort of "clean break" with that violent continuum, advocates' experiences around crossing this threshold make further evident the wide variety of ways that the "collateral consequences" or "spillover effects" of migrant incarceration and related punitive immigration processes, like deportation, inflict harm on communities that surround those most directly impacted (Golash-Boza 2019; Martinez-Aranda 2020; Patler and Golash-Boza 2017; Peterie 2024). As I came to believe, the story of legal care here is not only defined by the being-with as well as the being-there, but it's also about the going, the moving on, the aftermath of care.

RELEASE

La salida, or exit, was the term used in discussions, particularly in the "release *charla*" presentations, to refer to detained families' exit from the detention center. In this interactive presentation, advocates would address clients' questions about how they would be able to leave after receiving their positive interview decisions, explaining the differences between leaving via parole (*por palabra*), bond (*la fianza*), or with an ankle monitoring device (*la grillete*). In the release *charla*, advocates would explain much of what would come next in the progression of their legal case, what was expected of them, and their rights as asylum seekers. Unsurprisingly, this was often a joyous, even humorous moment in the centers. Both women and children expressed relief and excitement that they were soon to leave the center, most to move on to greater comfort and security with family and friends. Although not all families were given this opportunity, because of the efforts of the legal advocacy teams most families were released to continue their cases; thus, *la salida* generally carried it with more positive connotations.

At one point in Dilley, the release *charlas* were held in a separate building, near the back entrance of the legal visitation trailer. The space was a large rectangular room with a couple of desks situated at the back and a miniature plastic playset with a slide and stairs set up across from the entrance door. Most of the space was taken up by old church pews, three rows of them, in which the women sat as they listened to the advocates give their presentation. The presenter would discuss how families needed to prepare as they left the facility and where they could potentially get help when they finally arrived at their new home destination. After typically one to three hours, mothers would leave the trailer with stacks of papers in their arms, documents that explained which legal services provided pro or low bono support for families in Virginia, New York, Utah, and so forth. They would have sample copies of important legal files they needed to submit upon leaving. At Karnes, women were given a booklet that outlined the most important aspects of this information, and usually one advocate would sit with one small group at a time discussing each of these in detail.

Because these *charlas* were not quiet moments of seriousness but, in fact, were often some of the most joyous moments in the entire ordeal of family detention, some advocates described doing them as their favorite task. During her time in Dilley, Betty, the long-term, undergraduate volunteer from California, conducted many of these *charlas*. She spoke about how often she found herself laughing with the women, sometimes making jokes. "There were so many hilarious women," she said. "For instance, when I would show them pictures of the ankle monitor, just so they knew what it looked like, some of them would laugh and throw their hands up, pretend like they were walking out of the room, being really dramatic." Women would joke about how they had to charge the monitor, plugging themselves into the wall, and laughed at the idea of how they would bathe if they could not get it wet. Once, when Betty described the necessity of filing paperwork if they were to ever change home addresses so that the government would know where to send legal materials, a mother surprised her and the group by jokingly musing on whether that was necessary for one-night stands. "There were so many funny things that happened in the *charlas*, and because I was doing it for so long, I got to see a lot of that."

Most advocates with whom I spoke held few illusions about the serious legal challenges that faced asylum-seeking families after their release. During the release *charla* and in the actual moment of exiting, though, a sense of lightness, a glimmer of hope punctuated interactions, as it did when I drove away from Dilley with Esther and Tatiana. While advocates shared joyfully in this moment of "release" with clients, their experiences of leaving were conflicted and often reflected a measure of pain. Back at her home, Carolyn, an immigration attorney who had volunteered in Dilley the week of the 2016 presidential election, explained how this played out for her:

> I didn't even necessarily realize what I was going to be feeling, you know. . . . I got to the airport on Friday night and just started sobbing. I think it was a combination of everything I saw all week and just working these long hours and seeing what these women had to go through. But it was also

> about, of course, the election and what that meant and whether or not we could continue to offer asylum to people coming to the border.

Tara, the volunteer attorney from Colorado introduced in a previous chapter, interpreted her unexpected response upon leaving as the result of a kind of "stockpiling" (Thornton and Novak 2010) of emotions during the work:

> I think that taking in all that trauma so quickly and not having any time to process it, all I can figure out is that as soon as I got out of there, it all came pouring out of me. . . . I cried for days. I couldn't even talk about it. I just . . . was a mess. And I feel like, it's the only way that I can make sense of why I was so emotional when I came back. It's just taking it in, taking it in, taking it in, don't cry, don't process it, just move on to the next one, keep going, keep going, hear another traumatic story and then crash out at night, then wake up, do it again, and then finally just. . . . Whoa. As soon as I was driving away, just tears, you know? It all came out after.

Paula, the paralegal originally from El Salvador, also found herself in similar circumstances. She explained,

> It hit me sooner than I thought, when I was at the airport. I felt kind of weird, like I was really disconnected from everything and everyone, being at the airport. . . . I wanted to cry so bad because I felt like I needed to go back to Dilley. I was thinking, "I can't leave, there's so much more stuff to do," and it was really hard for me to kind of let go a little bit. I felt like I had been in a place where nobody would really understand what I'd been through.

For Paula, Tara, and Carolyn, feelings of discomfort and sadness manifested immediately. For them, crying or the desire to cry arose suddenly, without a clear connection to the exact impetus, though they all pointed to different reasons. A common refrain in my interviews was that volunteers often tried to stifle emotional reactions, such as crying, in their work with the families. Many considered this to be either an act of self-preservation or, more commonly, an act in support of their client. They saw themselves as doing a "disservice" to those who needed both their emotional and professional support—something they considered less possible were they to allow themselves to cry alongside their clients. Much of this speaks to how volunteer advocates experienced post hoc emotions as they left the role, having previously denied themselves the opportunity to express their own emotions within the sorts of heightened exchanges common in the work. And yet, because of the unexpected nature of these reactions, when they found themselves unexpectedly upset, it could be interpreted as a kind of estrangement from themselves. This was particularly pronounced for Paula, as she described feeling "disconnected" and that others wouldn't understand "what she had been through," which would be a common comment. Each of these effects, differently articulated but existing along the same continuum, were prompted by the act of leaving: leaving those for whom they still wished to provide care and abandoning a self-invoked practice of emotional restraint. It was upon crossing the threshold that the repercussions of the work began to take new forms.

For some, a strong emotional reaction coming out of this experience made sense, in a way, because of the particularly jarring effects of the environment. June was a weekly volunteer and came to Dilley, along with her partner Francisco, a policy specialist in Mexico, with a wealth of international refugee work experience. She had worked with survivors and refugees in Uganda and Guatemala, among other places, and made a comment one day that, considering her experience, surprised me. "This feels like frontline work in war," she said.

> Working with refugees, you hear some really bad stories and then some that aren't so bad, kind of similar to the different types of stories you encounter in Dilley. In that way, it's similar. It's also similar in that this is more like humanitarian work, because of the sense of emergency. When I was working in Jordan, at the Syrian border, other aid workers would talk about how they had people coming through in like hordes like this, but in the past. People doing that kind of work would burn out after three months, just because it was so exhausting and intense.

For June, though, it was the differences between her prior work with refugees and her experience of Dilley that disturbed her.

> This feels different, though, because everything's different when it's happening because of war. When there's a war, eventually the rebels will leave, and those who have fled can go back to some kind of normal life, like the families I worked with in Uganda. War is meant to end, and when it's over, there can be peace, even if it's not until the next generation. But this, what we see in Dilley, isn't the result of war. It's harder to cope with the problems we see in the women's stories from Guatemala and El Salvador, because most of these problems are the result of just how their societies are now. This isn't an event with a beginning and an end. I've worked with women in Latin America but in the context of war, and I'm telling you, these [domestic violence] cases were harder than anything I've ever had to work on. War, and what happens to people in the context of war . . . it fits an already existing narrative that we have. But with this kind of violence in Central America, there isn't a narrative like this. It feels like there's no hope, no end. It feels very bleak.

June's reflections on the hopelessness of the situation extend well beyond the context of family detention and asylum in the United States, though they echo the kinds of "legal cynicism" engendered within and through migrant detention spaces (Ryo 2017). They also offer an important window into the ways that even those with significant prior work in refugee or asylum law found themselves unsettled by what they experienced in these centers. Ultimately, the experience for June and Francisco in Dilley led to an early departure from their volunteer roles, after working on an especially traumatic case that involved the kidnapping of a child of a detained parent, in real time during their detention, an incident she described as something she "just wanted to forget." While some advocates described this desire to forget particularly painful encounters or observations in detention, at least for some there appeared to be a kind of psychic tether that complicated fully leaving the work behind.

HAUNTED

In *Sanctuary and Asylum: A Social and Political History* by Linda Rabben (2016, 14), a refugee formerly detained in Yarl's Wood Immigration

Removal Centre, England, recalls their experience of leaving: "'When I left detention, Yarl's Wood followed me to Manchester. Sometimes I feel like I'm in a trance, I feel I hear the footsteps of the officers, I hear the banging of the doors and the sound of their keys. Even though I'm out of detention, I'm not really out—I still have those dreams. I wish the politicians could understand what they are doing to women by detaining us like this when we have already been through so much.'" Advocates, both legal and medical professionals, have repeatedly and in various forums made the case that incarceration is invariably harmful, and refugees are particularly vulnerable to traumatization in detention (AILA 2014; von Werthern et al. 2018). They argue that by the nature of their arrival in the receiving country, they have already experienced trauma, some greatly so, and detention compounds this in significant ways (Mares 2020). By locking them away, keeping them from critical mental and physical health services, from family and friends, and, for those in family detention, causing them to parent while incarcerated inflicts unnecessary and utterly avoidable trauma. It is thus unsurprising that refugees are, in a sense, haunted by their time in detention.

This demonstrates that this experience of haunting was not just isolated to the direct recipients of the harm reproduced in and by detention. Volunteers and staff of these legal projects, as their reflections show here, were themselves haunted, sometimes by the upsetting stories or cases encountered—experiences not uncommon for aid workers (Malkki 2015)—sometimes by the pressures or immediacies of the work, and sometimes by the simple fact of having left the work and the people, both detainees and other advocates. In this way, then, it was not just the detainees that are haunted by detention but their advocates as well.

Avery Gordon (2011, xvii; also citing Gordon 2008), in her vital exploration of the subject, helps us to understand the complicated relationship between haunting, which itself is not equal but rather "kin" to trauma, and violence:

> What's distinctive about haunting is that it is an animated state in which a repressed or unresolved social violence is making itself known, sometimes very directly, sometimes more obliquely. . . . Haunting raises specters, and it alters the experience of being in time, the way we separate the past, the present, and the future. These specters or ghosts appear when the trouble

> they represent and symptomize is no longer being contained or repressed or blocked from view. The ghost, as I understand it, is not the invisible or some ineffable excess. The whole essence, if you can use that word, of a ghost is that it has a real presence and demands its due, your attention. Haunting and the appearance of specters or ghosts is one way [that] we are notified that what's been concealed is very much alive and present, interfering precisely with those always incomplete forms of containment and repression ceaselessly directed toward us.

Many advocates interpreted what they experienced in the work through language that pointed toward, or explicitly denoted, a sense of haunting. In articulating how encounters or stories followed them beyond detention, advocates would speak of effects like nightmares, flashbacks, and sudden feelings associated with memories. Often, these hauntings would be connected with recent experiences in these facilities, while others involved concerns for the future, of what may come for their clients, or what Derrida (1994) conceptualized as the "arrivant" (also discussed in Chiovenda and Chiovenda 2018; Blanco and Pereen 2013).

Betty and I spoke again after we had each left Dilley, having returned to our other lives. I was back in New York, and she had returned to her home in California. "I've had a lot of trouble lately feeling safe in new environments," she said. Immediately after she left Dilley, she went on a brief vacation with her family to Hawai'i. "Even at the hotel, or walking alone on a street, I didn't feel safe. Now that I'm home, though, I'm OK." She talked about how this feeling of a lack of safety was also something that she struggled with while she lived and worked for those couple of months in Dilley. "I had a lot of sleepless nights," she explained. "I would think that MS-13 was out to get me in Dilley, Texas," she said with a sheepish laugh. "I have no idea why. I think the work can just become pretty haunting." Betty also described other ways that Dilley haunted her. "It has been hard to sleep at night, though, here at home, knowing that I'm not there anymore. There are so many women that need help, and with some of the stories I heard there, it's been hard to come back here and live a normal nineteen-year-old life." Like others describing their sudden emotional reactions upon leaving Dilley, Betty noted how her experience of haunting involved a fear of what harm might come for those detained clients she'd "left behind."

Some advocates found these hauntings in less predictable, more immaterial realms of existence: in particular, within their dreams. Jaclyn, the undergraduate volunteer from Florida, had previous refugee aid project experience and was hoping to go to law school after her summer volunteership in Dilley, during which she and a few other undergraduate students had ended up sharing a small rental apartment in town. After that first week of work, leaving the facility at the end of each day came to feel less like relief and more of a different form of stress. "There were always moments where I felt like I just couldn't do it anymore," she explained.

> But at one point, it felt like the weight of everything started to be too heavy. The things [the clients] were talking about every day were things that I had never experienced in my life, and I wasn't used to hearing about. I would get back to the place we were staying, and I would hear the stories replaying over and over again. I would have nightmares about them. I felt like I was experiencing what they were experiencing because I was trying to empathize with them. When you empathize with someone, you put yourself in their situation, you know? You think, "How would I react in their situation?" Then you picture those things happening to your own friends and your own family, and that is what kind of messes with your mind. It made me break down and cry sometimes. I just kept picturing what I would do in their situation. It was really emotionally draining.

Without explicitly identifying it as such, Jaclyn related her experience of haunting through nightmares in which she envisioned living through the traumatic stories of others in the center. For her, this resulted from relating empathetically to her clients, imagining herself in their positions, which she expressed feeling a compelling desire to do. This led to nightmares in which she no longer determined the boundaries of this sort of imaginative work.

Jaclyn certainly was not the only advocate afflicted with nightmares about the work, as others expressed similar dreams, some in which they imagined living through clients' experiences. Evan, a volunteer attorney who came to Dilley with a group of thirteen from his law firm, was not unfamiliar with trauma-centered work. When he was an undergraduate psychology student, he worked for a crisis hotline. "When I did that job," he explained, "I learned that you have to be dispassionate in order to really help them. You can't be overly emotional, and it's really hard to be empathetic, but you can show them that you care." Although Evan was also familiar with family detention, as he had worked on building bond requests for detainees in Artesia, Dilley, he noted, was different. Dilley was the first time he had worked directly with detained mothers and children on their asylum claims. "Their stories . . . they were very upsetting. Some women would talk about being raped while [their] children were sitting in the same room. One woman I spoke with had to prostitute herself just to have food for her children. It was just impossible to be dispassionate there." Despite Evan's previous work experience, the unexpected impact of these conversations followed him, like Jaclyn, to unexpected places. "After I would leave, at the end of the day, I would have these dreams about the women. That continued even after I left Dilley and went home. I would re-create these scenarios from their stories in my dreams, horrible things we had talked about during the day. I was really surprised at how that persisted for so long afterwards."

Hilary, a first-year undergraduate student at Florida State University, had similar experiences as Jaclyn and Evan. Her two-week stint in Dilley led to varying experiences:

> That second week, the team was delegating more to me, so I talked to a lot more people. Everything from that week was more memorable, even though the first week was more emotional. In the second, when I felt emotional, I tried to lock myself in one of the offices to do data entry, to get away from it, but they were just too busy. I knew I had to figure out some way to deal with the feelings; they were really getting to me. Once, I was helping another volunteer, this attorney Jim, do this prep, and while he was talking to the mom, I was playing with her four-year-old son in the corner, to distract him. I asked him to draw me something, and he drew a bunch of these little circles, and then more and more circles. I thought they were stars, so I asked him about them. He told me they were bullets. That was upsetting.

Eventually, as Hilary left, the stories and related feelings that she had suppressed to continue her work manifested as they did for others.

> At the end of the trip, I started to have these nightmares about the stories. I had them for a while. I don't have them anymore now, but it was difficult to have them so often. I really don't think there's a way around having these feelings or these nightmares or whatever. You have to find a way to use what you've got to try to fix this problem, to help these women. So, in my opinion, you have to find a way to bury these things.

As with Hilary and Evan, many other advocates either explicitly stated or implied a perceived necessity in "burying" these sorts of experiences and feelings, to continue the work. In attempting to deny those experiences, even temporarily, some advocates found them returning in spaces, like dreams, where they lacked a kind of narrative control.

With this haunting form, advocates experienced one way in which they could encounter harm related to but beyond the walls of the facility. This was due, in part, to the kinds of "vicarious witnessing" (Keats 2005) of the past traumas of others that they regularly performed in their roles, clearly demonstrating how "trauma . . . accrues over time and spreads through social networks of care and empathy" (Beckett 2019). In relational contexts like these, it is instructive to examine the relationship between dreams that might be deemed "nightmares" due to their disturbing nature and experiences of trauma (Barrett 1996; Kirmayer 2009): "Whether or not disturbing dreams or nightmares reported in the aftermath of traumatic events give us an undistorted re-presentation of those events, they tell us something very important about the dreamer's state of self, perhaps at the moment the trauma occurred, but certainly in the present, as the person copes with memories or reminders of past experiences" (Hollan 2009, 319). While such experiences are not uncommon for other caring professions (McNeillie and Rose 2021), it is uncommon to consider how this unfolds in primarily legal encounters as well. Looking at these kinds of experiences as they occur through these different sorts of encounters, then, adds to our understanding of both legal work as care and the "variable nature of trauma-related nightmares" (Hinton 2009, 217).

Speaking to the blurred boundaries explored in the new "hauntological" literature, including between metaphorical and nonmetaphorical ghosts, Hollan (2019, 452) suggests an attention to the significance of emotion, and specifically the emotions of those who experience hauntings: "The relational and interpersonal aspects of haunting . . . suggest that our analyses of the dynamic forces contributing to the emergence and disappearance of ghosts must always include a concern with the complex emotional lives of the haunted." Not all advocates were haunted in the ways that I've presented here, though I would argue that the fact that many were deeply disturbed by what they experienced suggests a few important points in relation to their specific care. It shows the degree to which such legal encounters were intimately bound with deep and complex emotions, often effectively requiring meaningful expressions of empathy or emotional intelligence to properly care in this environment. It demonstrates how, because so few were prepared for what they would experience in this work, again as effectively unrecognized caregivers, as well as the fact that there were so few resources to handle their immense responsibilities, advocates remained somewhat vulnerable to traumatic repercussions. The specters produced through these experiences followed advocates as they left, building a kind of immaterial connective tissue. Advocates described how the experience of this work, which led to unsettling, sometimes confusing hauntings, was itself exceedingly difficult to express in adequate terms to others. This apparent ineffability was another form of haunting, one that could feel incredibly isolating.

LOST IN TRANSLATION

Chapter 2 discussed the everyday forms of translation with which advocates were tasked in their role. Beyond interpreting from one spoken language to another, they importantly served as "legal brokers," operating in a "legal translational role" that helped their clients understand and respond to the institutional processes they had entered (Coutin 2000; Galli 2023; Lakhani 2014). When advocates left, they returned to their preexisting lives at home or, for some, began to forge new paths, changing careers or, especially for outgoing project staff, taking breaks to rest and reflect on an arduous experience. In moving beyond these spaces, advocates reencountered their communities: friends, family, acquaintances, and colleagues. To those unfamiliar with this experience, this might not seem to result in any effect worth noting, but it was precisely that unfamiliarity with family detention that inspired a repeated type of frustrated refrain among my interlocutors. "Everyone who wasn't there doesn't get it," Hilary said to me, with a slight irritation in her voice. "I've told my parents and other people all about it, and they just don't understand. You try talking to people about the terrible things you hear and see there, and all you get is, 'The world is a sucky place.' I don't know what I was expecting. I didn't really want any empathy for me, though. It's not my trauma; it's theirs, the women. I don't know . . . I just can't brush over the experience."

Advocates seemed to be of different minds when it came to talking about the experience with others who had not done this type of work. Some characterized it as a "responsibility," an obligation to talk about what occurred in these places as much as possible: the legal work itself, the contexts of the asylum seekers' situations—meaning what they had fled and what they went through in order to get there—and the qualities of their detention. Those advocates believed that this responsibility was tied to their commitment to change conditions for the detained, believing that if broader publics were made more aware of what these detainees experienced, they would be more inclined to do something to effect changes. The common assumption in their comments was that to care—meaning, for them, to be invested in another's well-being—translated to some sort of practical action for change. Some, like Hilary, noted a desire to talk about these things with others they were close to, though with unclear motivations. Others would share that while they wished to talk about it, they were more selective with whom. Even though some expressed feeling quite uncomfortable with talking about the experience, especially with the idea of sharing details of clients' experiences, many attempted to have such conversations with others once they left, frequently leading to disappointing kinds of responses.

Jody was an attorney and was involved in these projects from the beginning of the expansion, in Artesia. Although she had not worked as a project staff member, she had served in a leading role with one of the projects' funding organizations, and as a result, she frequently took trips to Dilley to check on how conditions changed over time and how the on-the-ground staff were dealing. Jody had a wry sense of humor and spoke directly. She explained to me how, after all this time having been associated with this work and having witnessed so much, she had come to carefully approach talking about these places with "outsiders." "I'm always very cautious about talking about the experience to others, just because I'm concerned about 'cheapening' the women's stories," she said. "It's not cocktail party conversation for me. It's too painful, and it really feels like a violation to recount the details of individual stories. I mean, I shared some of my experience on [a radio] show once, and I've presented about the work to an undergrad class before. I do want others to know that these women have viable claims." Jody's articulation of why she shared at all, and why she felt uncomfortable to share certain details, speaks to the struggle in sharing that many felt. Talking about the experience was not seen as something that should be self-serving in any way but should point to a broader, more substantial purpose. In other words, sharing was meant to do something. Otherwise, as Jody opined, it cheapened both her experience, as someone who also felt pain or trauma in this work, as well as that of the women and children who had entrusted her with those deeply personal narratives.

Sue, the repeat volunteer attorney from Tennessee, also felt conflicted about sharing the experience with others, especially her more conservative relatives, but certainly also believed doing so was an obligation she needed to fulfill:

> I talked about it with a couple of really close friends. . . . You know, with people who are only tangentially interested in this, it feels like whenever I try to bring it up around them, it's like I'm dwelling on a funeral or something. My family is just like, "Can't you just let this go already?" The experience, for me, becomes so precious that I don't want to share it with you if you can't value it. But then, part of the bargain in going there is that you have to talk about it when you come back home.

Sue's attitude toward sharing the experience and what she witnessed as a part of the "bargain" of being involved in these projects was, in a way, constituted by the projects themselves. One aspect of the work that staff did was to encourage advocates to share their experiences, following the same assumption that if "outsiders," people who hadn't encountered these spaces, were only to know of its injustices, they would be more likely to support campaigns that aimed to effect things like the cessation of family detention. Throughout my fieldwork, this would be articulated in different ways, from asking volunteers to write blogs or op eds to engaging in fundraising or presenting their experiences to other communities, from university students to law firms or religious groups. These were encouraged alongside the many awareness-raising anti–family detention campaigns devised by these projects' organizations, including actions like holding mock "baby showers" outside of ICE offices and sending postcards to then–DHS director Jeh Johnson (CLINIC 2019).

Sue's comments about discussing these places with her loved ones demonstrate not only that this personal and sensitive experience for advocates was quite difficult to communicate to others but also that they could receive kinds of feedback that would exacerbate the pain they felt. Rebecca, an immigration lawyer in Texas, echoed these frustrations with the kinds of opinions she would hear from those unfamiliar with these spaces and their inhabitants: "It's really hard to bite my tongue," she said, "when I heard the sort of rhetoric out there, on the 'outside,' from people who don't know anything about these detainees or what they're going through." Carlos, the project staff member in Dilley, shared a similar sentiment after having taken a brief trip back home to Kansas City to attend a friend's wedding, during which he described feeling "blank," as if he was unable to enjoy the event. Speaking about people there wanting to talk to him about his work in Dilley, Carlos expressed frustration. He, like other staff, expressed how others, those that hadn't experienced being in these places, could not understand what they or detainees had been through and that, as advocates, they did not desire to spend their time trying to explain it to them. "If people who I know are conservative or whatever, I don't want to have to listen to their bullshit opinions or noncare for these people," Carlos argued. Staff member Norah agreed: "I don't want to listen to why some people don't care about these women or have to explain why I care so much."

All advocates, as they discussed their struggles and conflicted feelings about talking about the experience of these places with others, seemed to face what was a central dilemma in this pursuit: How *should* one talk about this experience? The question seemed to flow from the problem of bridging the gap between two simultaneous, yet sometimes counterintuitive, concerns after leaving: one, a need to share stories of the realities facing asylum seekers, including the unnecessary and cruel legal experiences they faced here, and two, a desire to properly respect painful and private stories by not sharing those details with others. Speaking implicitly to this last concern, one of my interlocutors opined that it simply "wasn't her story to tell." This evoked a point made earlier by Hilary, that it was not "her trauma" to talk about. Yet, what I and others have attempted to show in contrast is that advocates' trauma is an integral part of the story of these places. Recognizing how other communities of nondetained caregivers or loved ones share in the material and emotional collateral consequences of detention (Martinez-Aranda 2020) is a contribution that this book has tried to offer in its portrayal of legal advocates in detention.

Yet still, their quandaries in speaking to others about their experiences raises some necessary questions: How do we, as advocates and caregivers, inspire the feelings and actions of "outsider" others with the sort of details of encounters that moved us, in having these experiences firsthand, while also not exploiting those deeply personal, sometimes intimate encounters? After crossing, what responsibilities do we have to those left behind, both other advocates struggling through constrained care work and detainees quietly being harmed through legal and other institutional means? What kinds of stories should we tell if our goal is to get others, who can presumably impact the lives that reside within these spaces, to care? As I've shown, these questions were answered, in practice, differently by different advocates, though there were a rare few I met that seemed unburdened by such concerns. For many, it seemed that even if it took some time to cope with the experience, there was a desire to dwell among these memories in renarrations. Their desires expressed a kind of paradox, just one of many that characterized legal advocacy in family detention: to be rid of painful memories but also to have a continuous connection with the work that was so affecting and thus, ultimately, haunting.

One constant among many of my conversations with advocates was an ongoing desire to explore the experience with those who, like myself, had a substantive understanding of the context, recalling Liisa Malkki's (2015, 6) fieldwork with aid workers: "They needed to talk just as the genocide survivors in Tanzania had needed to talk. Many aid workers said it was worth talking with someone who had lived and worked in the general region, and with genocide survivors specifically. There was some shared understanding." Legal advocates struggled to find that sense of shared understanding after having left the work. The experience was truly meaningful, even transformative for some, and unsettling for most. They expressed this desire, sometimes a need, to talk about all of this, and struggled to find the right opportunity to do so. Part of this translational struggle has to do with the lack of recognition of legal work as care. If framed through care, advocates' efforts in these environments would not only be given a more adequate language—thus making the details of their experiences more translatable to outsider audiences—but it would also help to create an assumption concerning the need for legal care of incarcerated individuals. In these contexts, the inadequacies of asylum law and constraints inherent to incarceration, without guarantee of legal representation, effect serious consequences, and yet because of the normalization of these sorts of "crimmigration" (Stumpf 2006) practices and obscurity in asylum law, it could be difficult for others outside of these "worlds" to imagine the complex harm they inflict.

SPECTERS

On a busy spring afternoon in Dilley, a grieving mother handed me photos of her dead child. I had been asked by another advocate to make copies of the documents this mother had brought with her on her journey to support her case. Usually, in the rare, best-case scenarios, these were police reports, death certificates, medical records, news stories: these things that were "attesting to" their claims. For obvious reasons, we immediately helped clients make copies of these crucial documents. The mother pulled out a big stack of papers from a manila folder, which were curled up in a way that I could not see their contents. Before handing them to me, she tried to communicate what these contained, quietly and somberly, pressing the pages against her chest. She was struggling to find the words, turning her tearful eyes down from me, but it was clear she was trying to prepare me for the graphic nature of the images. I unfurled the stack and saw him immediately.

Her son was a teenager when he was shot only weeks prior by gang members on a street in Honduras, which was why she and her other young son—the second "target" who was at the time incarcerated separately in the nearby adult detention facility in Pearsall—had left home. The first photo, taken by police or the coroner at night, was of his naked and bloody body sprawled on the gravelly ground, face down, covered partially by a sheet. The second photo was a close-up image of his hands, also spattered with what appeared to be blood. The third was of his young face, eyes closed, his bruised skin a bluish-gray. I held the photos flat in my hands, temporarily frozen, forgetting what I was supposed to do with them. As I walked into our office room to make copies but also to hide my shock, I considered the fact that she had warned *me* before showing them. This mother, someone who had traveled for weeks from Honduras with the images of her child's violent murder in her pocket, in part because she knew that this served as evidence for her legal case, concerned herself with preparing me for seeing them as well. Truly, I don't know what I could have done to prepare to see such images up close, but then being unprepared for the kinds of traumas that circulated throughout these facilities was one of the few certainties of our daily experience.

In a sense, asylum seekers are forced to repeatedly reside with various specters from their lives prior to leaving: the moments—with their sights and sounds, smells and feelings—and the people, both loved ones and those others whom they did not love, those that hurt them. In recounting the different configurations of trauma, discomfort, or pain that led them to resort to this convoluted and suspicious legal process, far from their homes or what is left of them, such things are given the opportunity to live on with them, showcasing in an albeit more figurative way how "specters are very much part of the legal domain" (Dayan 2011, 12). Recalling and repeatedly having to defend such experiences, attesting to the credibility or legitimacy of their fears, certainly isn't therapeutic; it can and has caused what advocates and mental health professionals would refer to as retraumatization (Ryan, Kelly, and Kelly 2009). A mother having to carry the visual evidence of her child's death certainly has the potential to cause this alone. These processes themselves helped reinforce traumatic attachments that clung to them far beyond these spaces, picking at their wounds, as one advocate described it, and repeatedly demanding recognition of their existence.

Here, I consider other haunting specters that were raised for legal advocates because of their time in or proximity to these spaces. I have previously associated their work with the physical space, or spaces, of family detention. The work itself was deeply entwined with the particularities of the space, and the space could not be fully understood without accounting for this legal work that shaped how daily processes were managed *and* contested. In these ways, work and space overlapped, and one could not be understood completely without the other. This also played an important role in the haunting effects experienced by advocates. Again, June's experience working with similarly affected communities pointed to this relationship, though through contrast. "Working with those people, like in Uganda for example," she explained,

> there were stories I heard that were worse, stuff that people were made to do in those situations. But this here is a different environment. It's harder. In Uganda, when we'd have these similar types of conversations with people, talking about the violence they experienced, it would be in someone's home, or sitting under a tree. That's, of course, not what's happening here. The environment in which you're meeting someone and talking about this kind of stuff, it matters.

Most advocates would agree with this sentiment, as this aligned with one of the central contentions of these projects: that proper care, whether it be health or legal assistance, could not be adequately offered to asylum seekers while incarcerated. The space mattered, and this was evident not only in how it impacted detainees' abilities to defend their cases but also in how it impacted the work of advocates and the subsequent traumas they experienced while laboring under such conditions.

One obvious illustration of how this affected advocates comes from chapter 3's discussion of a staff member's "banning" from reentering the facility, a permanent form of spatial refusal that, for Alejandro, was deeply hurtful. Months before this occurred, when those working for the Dilley project offered Alejandro the job, he found himself considering the reality of living in the rural town of Dilley. He had previously volunteered at Karnes, where we first met, but with that project, staff advocates did not live near the detention center. The offer in Dilley, at the time, was for him to live in the communal staff house—the ranch—near the facility. For him, neither Dilley nor the ranch were particularly enticing; both were extremely isolated, with few options for activities beyond the work. There were wild things like scorpions and snakes both in and around the house, and because it was a communal space, privacy was in short supply. It was also the space where trainings and meetings with volunteers would take place, which made it even less private. But for him, one of the benefits of being in such a place was having access to the sort of breathtakingly dark night sky a small Texas town affords. "I told myself," he said to me, "I could live out there, at the ranch, if I could just get to see all of those stars at night."

After taking the job, however, he quickly learned that this was just one of many refusals. At the end of their long workdays, he and other staff would drive back to the ranch, begin their "second shifts," sitting at a long dining table while they individually faced the glowing blue light of their laptops, continuing to work on clients' cases and other project processes long into the night. When the sun had set on the day and that big sky had lost its bright hues, staff might finally sit outside or on the roof of the house, accessed by a ladder propped against the overhang covering the entryway. Instead of the glow from millions of stars, they saw half the sky awash in the light of the detention facility's floodlights, which remained lit until morning. "It really bothered me, seeing those every night," Alejandro explained. "I hated thinking that the kids there never got to see the stars." The effects of these lights were striking. Excessively tall and bright, the posts that held multiple lights cast an overwhelming glow, which extended far beyond the facility, beaming across acres of farmland that surrounded.

Most advocates, like Alejandro, expressed their frustration with the lights through the experience that was denied to the families detained under the glow, especially the children. His initial comment, which was the first of its kind I heard from staff, drew out another effect of this continuous illumination. While Alejandro was frustrated by the fact that this refused children the opportunity to observe that beautiful night sky, he was similarly denied this opportunity. Staff like him struggled with not only the final *salida*, the day when they would leave this work and move on to something else; there was also the daily *salida*, the weekly *salida*. For staff of these projects, especially, there truly was no end to the work: no end to the cases that hung by a thread or to the clients who needed more attention and more defenses against authorities who were denying them proper care. There was no end to the amount of client data that needed entering into their virtual case tracking system or to the email communications they needed to send or follow up on, with volunteers,

FIGURE 16 A constant glow emanates from the floodlights of the Dilley facility. Credit Erin Routon.

one another, or various administrative officers. More than that, though, they struggled to let go of occurrences with clients inside, awful things that were effectively beyond their control and yet they were forced to witness, like deportation proceedings. As noted previously, the work of such advocates was wounding, and their "emotional wounds [were] not incidental but [arose] from the very logic of deterrence-based detention policies" (Peterie 2024, 87, also citing Martin 2012). In this way, as I saw it, the lights took on another meaning. Their ghostly glow was less a figurative haunting and more a material reminder of both their work and the pain it inflicted on detainees and those who tried to help them. This spectral presence reached across the sky, linking the detention center, and all the thoughts and worries that it conjured, with a temporary "home," unsettling spaces intended for rest and relief.

In other ways, however, these specters of detention took much different shape and had quite the opposite effect. Staff of the project rarely took time off, and even when they did, it was difficult to escape the mental burdens of leaving, knowing what even a brief absence would mean for those left to carry the immense workload. Nonetheless, they all found some time to get away. One weekend, Alejandro decided to take a quick trip home to visit friends and family. "I took just thirty-six hours to go to Boston and then come back to Dilley," he said, laughing.

> And in the airport, on the way out, I ran into three families [from Dilley] who all recognized me and were like, "Oh, *muchacho*!" We all had connecting flights through Charlotte. So I went up, talked to them for a bit, but then I thought that maybe they wanted some space from me. I wondered if right after leaving Dilley, they maybe wouldn't want to immediately have someone from there talking a lot to them, you know, someone who reminded them of detention, so I backed away pretty quickly.

After that immediate encounter, they all got on the plane and sat in different areas, with the women occasionally waving to Alejandro throughout the flight. They arrived in Charlotte, and he gathered his things, preparing to go on his way. "Then as I was getting off the plane, I walk into the terminal and all three of the families are standing there waiting for me." He laughed again loudly, with an incredulous smile.

> I was like, "Hey, guys, what's going on?" And they were like, "What do we do next?" So I said, "Well, where are you going?" And they told me about their connecting flights. So I brought them over to the big board, trying to figure out where their flights were. It just turned out that their gates were right next to mine, and they only had fifteen minutes to make their connecting flights, so we had to run across the whole airport together.

One of the important elements of this encounter involved the relationship he had already developed with those detained families who recognized him in the airport. While my field research initially focused on just those relations of care in the detention center, care, as evidenced in that instance, was truly best understood as existing along a continuum. Alejandro's concern, that he would be interpreted primarily as someone associated with the families' misfortunate experiences as detainees, was upended by their continued expression of trust. In this exchange, he experienced even clearer recognition as a caregiver, demonstrating how the advocate-client relationship was intimately marked by a kind of care not limited by the boundaries of detention.

Jaclyn considered herself fortunate in that she was also able to see her relationship with some families continue beyond the threshold of the facility. "There were certain women that I ended up getting really close to," she told me.

> Like I worked with them for hours and hours, prepping them like three or four times. Sometimes we would have to delay their interviews because they needed more prep, sometimes I'd have to bring in other staff members to help, and there were some that we'd just work with continuously for days. So I was leaving Dilley finally, going to Phoenix to visit my boyfriend before going back to Florida, and one of those women that I got really close to happened to be seated right next to me on my flight. It was amazing. I had worked with her on a Saturday, and I hadn't heard back on how her interview went because I had to leave for my flight. When I saw her, I realized that she had gotten her positive [decision] and was released, and I just started crying. We worked together for so, so long, me and her and her daughter. I got to know them so well. I was so emotional. After we arrived in Phoenix, I got to walk them through the airport and *actually* welcome them.

Jaclyn appreciated not only the fact that she was able to see the positive results of their hard work together, the shift in spatial context also meant something important for her, as it did for Alejandro. "Leaving Dilley and then seeing her again in a setting that wasn't a detention center was so great," she explained, "because I felt like we were actually able to interact just like normal humans, like friends." Being together beyond the space of the facility afforded a kind of reconfigured relationship that Jaclyn and so many other advocates expressed a desire for in this work. The environment of the center, which in part informed the inherent, deep disparities between advocates and clients, limited the development of what felt for some like more authentic caring relationships between the two. I have already identified how this was both built into the structure of these spaces as well as shaped by administrators' actions. These sorts of encounters beyond the facilities, instead, represented moments of continuity in care, and although sometimes continuities in caregiving practice serve to reconstitute harmful forms of relationality (Kehr 2018), advocates articulated moments like these as an important shift in relationality.

For them, seeing clients on the "other side" afforded a reconfigured and much desired spectral relationship of care.

CONCLUSION

"The anthropologist working in prisons," Fassin (2016, 300) reminds us, "is affected by what he sees and what he hears, by the suffering and the violence he witnesses, by the individuals who confide in him and the fragments of life they offer him. To take up the neologism proposed by Jacques Derrida [1994], we could say that all ethnography of the carceral world is a hauntology." Advocates in contexts such as these are engaged in similar forms of work as an anthropologist: listening attentively to others, learning to pose generative questions, observing and taking notes on not only detainees' responses in their intimate conversations but also on the qualities of the interactions and spaces. They conducted kinds of interviews, in their preps, observed the environment around them, sometimes for critical care-related ends, and while neither they nor I could truly participate in the experience of detainees, they typically conducted their work with great empathy. Thus, I would argue, Fassin's contention about the hauntological, repercussive aspects of ethnographic research in carceral spaces extends to these communities of advocates as well.

"I hope I never see you again," Matt said to me, followed by a slight laugh. I was initially taken aback by his comment, but he quickly explained further. "That's something I would say to my clients at the end of their cases, and that's kind of how I think about Dilley." Matt had been a public defender for twenty-five years and was now retired, exploring his newfound extra time. He had come to volunteer with his wife, Billie, and a friend of theirs, Tina. As a volunteer in Dilley, Matt drew many parallels with his previous work. "It's like what I used to do every day, just on steroids," he said.

> The thinking on your feet, the nonstop action. Talking to people about their situations and stories and trying to shape those things, with integrity, to meet certain legal standards or requirements. It was like when I would prep people for court. I would go to the jail with twenty folders of different cases and would have to prep all those people for court. But it's also very

> much a short game; we're just trying to get people through the first step of the process.

Matt also believed, as with his previous job, that moving on or letting go was an important part of work like this. "As a public defender," he offered, "you need to develop a very short-term memory because someone else needs your help. That mode of thought really stays with you. You have to let go of the stories. And if you experience a big defeat, you can't dwell on it. This is the public defender mentality." Some advocates expressed similar ways of thinking about their roles, particularly those who had closely related jobs, like Matt. Experienced immigration lawyers, especially, seemed accustomed to this operative mode.

Most others, though, struggled with this idea of letting go for a number of different reasons, which calls us to question, how *do* you cross that experiential threshold? What does it mean that some want to hold on to those feelings or memories while others desperately want to let go? What does that tell us about the reverberations of trauma, the shrapnel caused by these institutions and processes? It's undeniable that in making sense of the sort of traumatic effects my interlocutors described, such things cannot be understood outside of the context of confinement and institutional violence caused by exclusionary legal mechanisms. The production of trauma in migrant detention, both direct and indirect, is not incidental. As this work and so much other scholarship have demonstrated, "harm is not a failure of [the] system, but one of its core functions" (Peterie 2024, 97). This book also further justifies the claim that "when workers stand so close to the unfolding of violence, they themselves find that the violence becomes embedded in them" (Caswell and Ruehs-Navarro 2023, 191).

Post hoc "ghostly" experiences and feelings are inextricably linked with these violences, proving that "haunting is one way in which abusive systems of power make themselves known and their impacts felt in everyday life, especially when they are supposedly over and done with" (Gordon 2011, 2). The fact that many advocates in this work struggled to let go, in different ways, to communicate the experiences they had to others or make sense of those themselves, or to "just get over" what they witnessed and heard points to something more substantial than individual reactions to harmful encounters. What legal advocates experienced in their roles as caregivers was deeply informed by the ways that they were interpreted and treated by administrative actors as potential threats, challenging exclusionary processes and narratives alike. Their very presence created a kind of friction, and this carried over even as their work ended. I would argue that we might better understand those unexpected, often uncomfortable experiences advocates expressed after leaving, then, if we were to think through those as forms of haunting or spectral encounters, rather of a type not coincidental but closely connected to the ways in which abusive institutions exert their power, sometimes from afar.

CHAPTER 6

NOMADIC HOPE

In 2017, a former U.S. immigration attorney, Jawziya Zaman, published an article online titled, "Why I Left Immigration Law." In it, she explains how after four years of practicing as an immigration lawyer in San Francisco, she no longer felt as if she was serving the sort of justice she had desired as an attorney. She was deeply uncomfortable with how the U.S. immigration system, as she put it, "demands penance" from immigrants who hope to remain in the country (Zaman 2017). She argued that it was challenging for her to continue to participate in such a repugnant system that, through its many arbiters, often blames and performatively shames immigrants for their status, reifying positions of vulnerability and abjectivity, and expecting inordinate professions of fealty to their new home country, not only from immigrants themselves but their families, friends, and community sponsors as well. Playing a role within this system was something that made her "feel sick" as she, for instance, trained clients on how to perform a kind of victimhood for those making legal determinations. She argued that "as lawyers, we are often locked in a fast-paced process whose daily urgency inhibits our thinking critically about the complexity of lived realities, the global structures that lead so many people to come to this country in the first place, and the insidiousness of a legal system that looks upon immigrants with suspicion or pity."

In truth, Zaman's concerns are reflected throughout the previous chapters, as advocates witnessed the ways that detainees were forced into positions of abjection while detained and throughout the early processing of their cases. Zaman quite fairly critiques the urgency produced by a deeply flawed, chaotic, and clearly punitive legal system that, as further confirmed by other immigration scholars (e.g., Hiemstra 2019; Golash-Boza 2010), functions with far too few resources and shockingly little oversight, and it is entirely understandable how this inhibits legal actors' freedom, in a sense, to think more critically about their participation in such systems. Yet despite this, legal actors who participate in these processes *are* engaged in thoughtful reflection on both the complex conditions that have led to their clients' circumstances and, as I observed, their roles in admittedly unjust legal structures. While this wasn't the case for all I encountered in my research, advocates in family detention earnestly discussed this dilemma and frequently reflected on their own role in these processes and how to respond to systemic injustices most effectively, either through direct legal service work or through other modes, like protests, public campaigns, or litigation as well. Being critical of and participating within these legal structures are not mutually exclusive modes of engagement (Galli 2023), and looking at and through care helps us understand their sometimes uncomfortable, other times fractious coexistence.

What we can observe in this context challenges some of the ideas intimated in Zaman's article, though it is also true that legal advocates vocalized their struggles with their place in this work, including their involvement in oppressive processes, which often led to conflicted feelings. Recognizing their lack of expertise in the everyday matters they encountered, legal or otherwise, was a commonly expressed form of discomfort. Many volunteer advocates, as noted, were not immigration lawyers; even with those who were, many were not deeply experienced with asylum law. Most were not trained in trauma response, therapeutic methods of speaking, or working with often recently traumatized individuals. *Who am I*, some advocates would ask, *to be giving advice to these women and kids?* They would also articulate their discomfort in reflection on the privileges they possessed in the face of their clients' vulnerabilities; this was true even of advocates who shared much, personally, with detained clients. "Like anthropologists," Malkki (2015, 53) reminds us, "aid workers are sometimes left feeling ambivalent, inadequate, and even impure about the work that they have done, despite their best efforts to fulfill the standards of their profession and their personal ethical commitments." Such conflicted feelings, of course, are not uncommon for especially frontline caregivers (Luz Ibarra 2013), though this also attests to the overall ambiguity in care practices (Sufrin 2017).

And yet, what I have also attempted to show is the exceptionality of these spaces and the kinds of work that engaged legal advocates. The practice of offering universal legal assistance to clients, regardless of the merits of their claims, was one such marker. I encountered many advocates who worked specifically in immigration law that noted the disparity of care from Dilley and Karnes to the legal world beyond their walls, including other detention centers. Many would note that if certain clients they met in Dilley or Karnes had come to their office or firm with their cases, asking for assistance, they would likely have to turn them away. In some situations, this would be a result of the weakness of the "merits" of an individual's claim. Many would lament that limited pro bono resources needed to be reserved for cases that had stronger merits. Additionally, as many who worked in immigration law would tell me, depending on where a client was headed after detention—meaning, essentially, to which court they would be pursuing the rest of their case—many would not have a strong chance of actually winning their cases.

All of this pointed to their explicit recognition of a system built on the differentiation of applicants through widely varying, subjective determinations of things like personal "credibility" and case merits as well as the well-documented fact that where and by whom an asylum case was tried mattered substantially (Sanchez 2021). A report by the Transactional Records Access Clearinghouse (TRAC), covering the period 2016–21, documented these diverse outcomes in decisions, based on the location of the court (TRAC 2021), with cities in the South/Southwest having especially low rates of success. This, unsurprisingly, has remained true over the past several years. According to a 2024 study by TRAC, the overall denial rate of asylum applications across the United States was at 57 percent, with rates continuing to vary extremely widely across different locations and courts, with some judges' denials at 100 percent while others were at 1 percent (Sanchez 2024c; TRAC 2024). Although multiple factors influence rates of denials among judges or within particular courts, this has led lawyers and advocates to characterize certain immigration jurisdictions as effective "asylum-free zones" (Washington 2017).

Although we rarely had extensive conversations about their feelings or perceptions of their role in such exclusionary norms, a reference to these things helped to clarify part of both the pain and pleasure that advocates expressed in doing this sort of work in this environment. In this exceptional space, they themselves were afforded the opportunity to experience a moment in which success was the norm and where no clients were denied legal care because of arbitrary merits or financial constraints. Legal advocacy in family detention, in a way, offered a moment that breathed life into long-sought hope.

The work there was also exceptional in the landscape of typical legal practice because many of the people engaged in it were not experts in asylum law or even legal professionals. Though a serious critique arises from this fact, there was also a kind of unique benefit in that a variety of different skills and personal and professional perspectives were brought to bear on the work. The collaborations between different knowledges, experiences, and sensitivities helped lead to what I interpret as caring exchanges as a result of legal needs. Although not impossible within other legal contexts, the unpredictability, and importantly urgency, of expanded family detention and the resultant organizational responses came together to form a uniquely collaborative environment in which the problems of caring for incarcerated asylum seekers were approached and contested from a variety of activist and advocacy-oriented angles. I suggest here that, while unintentional, this may in fact have contributed to a unique care response.

I have already explored various mutations in care in this space, as well as how advocates themselves were entwined within and subject to both punitive action and trauma. I examined the unexpected and unpredictable intimacies that marked advocates' experiences, challenging the solidity of experiential and sentimental boundaries. This chapter speaks to how those ambiguities, inadequacies, and even impurities in legal advocates' care were informed by the broader implications of their presence in detention. I also engage more directly with the question of how "care proceeds amid uncertainty in contexts of relative scarcity" (Livingston 2012, 6). This was shaped by the ways that their labor was at times co-opted for aims that ran counter to their own, leading potentially to a kind of "erosion" of care on their own terms.

At the same time, I look at how hope played an important, often implicit, yet also paradoxical role among advocates, particularly those familiar with the challenges that lay ahead for applicants. Additionally and in response, I consider the presence of a different kind of hope, one not fixed on a specific goal, like ending the practice of family detention. In doing this, I return to Reece Jones's (2017) claims about movement as a political act; thinking about this may be a useful conceptual way to imagine hope as mobile, or "nomadic." I consider what their years-long, continuous presence in these spaces means for how we think about their care in relation to their goals, and how the commitment to care without the promise of ending family detention left them, for good or bad, caught in a kind of trap with no exit.

TO MAKE NICE

"I love what the Dilley project is doing down there, don't get me wrong," Patricia, the retired lawyer from Illinois, said to me, continuing,

> I'm glad that they're there. I'm also annoyed that they're there. They're doing too damn good of a job, and you know, these prison companies have these long contracts now to keep these places open. Maybe if things there were worse, things didn't look so great, these companies wouldn't have been able to get these contracts extended, because people wouldn't have seen them as being successful, like many do now.

When Patricia said this, I didn't know if the "they" to which she referred doing "too good of a job" referred to the organizations behind these legal projects or the on-the-ground aid workers, like herself and project staff, doing the daily labor of direct client services in the centers. As a reminder, I have intentionally not used this book to assess or critique the functionality of the organizations involved in this work. Even though this would be an incredibly valuable study, I wanted my research here to focus on the everyday, grounded experiences of those who came to do the work organized by these groups. To be sure, the echo of depersonalized, careful, nonprofit messaging reverberated throughout trainings, Big Table meetings, and emails as a kind of constant reminder of the additional constraints under which we all labored.

To consider the potential entrenchments of this form of care work in these environments requires, in at least some small way, broadening the scope. It requires some form of examining these caregivers and the work they do as representative of larger issues related to the increasing institutionalization of what might be deemed unpaid legal care work. The situations presented thus far illustrate more than an example of the growing overreliance on the volunteer sector, or "shadow state" (Wolch 1990) in the United States, operating to fulfill what have historically been state or federal responsibilities relative to the care of their citizens and noncitizens (Wacquant 2009). Nor are they simple illustrations of collaborations between the "velvet glove" of nonprofits and the "iron fist" of punitive entities but rather the problematic associations between the carceral sector and the "nonprofit industrial complex" (INCITE! 2007). Although these critiques are certainly relevant for this context, I focus on how this is also a reflection of the underrepresentation of caring labors. Scholars of care, particularly feminist researchers, have long supported the idea that care work, especially that done by marginalized or migrant women, is undervalued and often unrecognized as work, as effectively invisible labor (Kaplan 2022). This is true even in cases in which communities of migrants themselves are the receivers of care (Hannaford 2023). What I've argued here is not only that legal advocates were caregivers and deserve recognition as such, but that this present lack of recognition helps explain why their work became both co-opted by facility administrators as well as increasingly entrenched within the constitution of facility processes.

When Patricia commented on the worry she had for the "good job" at work, she expressed a concern for this relationship between caregivers and facility administrators. While the question of how advocates' work benefited detainees has already been illustrated, it's also important to consider how administrators—facility employees, asylum officers, ICE officials, and others—benefited from the work of legal advocates. Much of my own and others' observations in fieldwork emphasize the antagonistic treatment, even punitive measures that characterized how administrators often interacted with advocates. But were there benefits that administrators reaped from their work, and if so, how does that complicate this story of care? Did the work of advocates contribute to something that would run counter to their goals? Or is this another manifestation, directed at advocates rather than detainees, of institutionalized abuse? Although I intend to make a case for the latter, it is true that advocates aimed to improve temporary conditions for their clients while detained; as a result, their work led to a kind of improvement of these facilities.

"Gracias a Dios, por este lugar, por ustedes," a mother said to us one day; I couldn't stop thinking about it. On an afternoon in Dilley, Angela and I spoke with a mother, Adriana, and teenage daughter, Carolina, from Cuba. Carolina had met Angela days before to prep, and she had told her that she wanted to become an immigration lawyer when she got out. She showed up to the visitation trailer and asked us if there was anything she could do to help us. This wasn't uncommon: many detained mothers and their older children, especially, offered their services to the group, from helping other families fill out their intake forms to translating for those who didn't speak Spanish or English to helping clean up the desks that were constantly a mess of scattered papers and pens. When the daughter asked if she could help us, I asked project staff member Cynthia if we might want to ask her to draw us a map, of sorts, of the rest of the facility. Our team was always interested to know the layout of the rest of the facility—what their rooms and other spaces looked like—to better understand how they were being treated. It was rare for advocates to be allowed to enter spaces in either facility beyond the three legal-specific buildings—visitation, asylum office, and court—so we thought this might be a good opportunity, especially as Carolina was eager to help us.

Carolina returned to the trailer in the early evening with Adriana. As Angela and I sat with them, Carolina started to sketch out a layout of the rest of the facility, showing us the size of their rooms, how they were separated from others, and other spaces. We asked them questions, and they both spoke about how "nice" the place was, comparing their experiences in Dilley with other facilities in which they had been held previously. Those were much worse, they explained. They had spent some time in a detention facility in Tapachula, Mexico, and spoke of the horrible conditions there, explaining how the only thing that was better there was that there were family visits available at any time, for however long, with people on the outside. Beyond that, though, everything there was worse. They described how the only seating they had was made of concrete, how there was a pregnant woman held there with them and that they had to use toilets with no privacy. In contrast, in Dilley, they had much more privacy and comfort. They both gushed enthusiastically about how they loved sharing a room with people from other places around the world, appreciating the sort of conversations they would have with one another, that they were able to have, even, because of the circumstances. Carolina talked about having a conversation with a young Brazilian girl they shared the space with, how she was learning Portuguese from her, and how they loved to dance and sing together. They were happy here, they told us, and they were grateful. They thanked God for this place, and they were thankful for us.

After talking for a while, they got up to leave for the facility's dinner service. Angela and I walked over to Cynthia, explaining to her what Adriana and Carolina had told us, including that they were sharing a room with three other families. Cynthia expressed anger at the fact that multiple families were being crammed together in small places with little personal privacy. I tried to explain that while they said they shared a space, each sleeping quarter was separated with a kind of accordion-like barrier. Cynthia had asked that we speak to them about whether they had experienced guards coming into their rooms in the middle of the night to perform unexpected "night checks," wherein staff would turn on lights and wake them up, to ensure all members were accounted for. This was something we had previously heard about happening from other families. We explained to Cynthia that Adriana and Carolina dismissed this fairly quickly, though, saying that no guard had ever entered their room while they were in there without knocking.

Rather than relieved by this information, Cynthia seemed frustrated. I understood that Cynthia was not disappointed that these things had not happened to Adriana and Carolina, but there was also a kind of reticence in her expression, a frustrated reluctance to fully accept the reality that they were describing. Cynthia was a deeply devoted migrant rights advocate, both throughout this project and long before. Many times I observed as she argued with guards about detainees' mistreatments or seemingly meaningless bureaucratic processes that slowed or stunted our work, like when packs of legal documents would be sent back to us to be stapled and then the following week they'd return, with a rule change, requiring that all staples be removed. She would sit on the phone for hours repeatedly explaining to journalists why these women and children should not be detained. She laughed and cried often, and I wondered how someone who cared so deeply could stand to do such exhausting, heartbreaking work for many years.

As a volunteer, I heard of and witnessed many mistreatments of those detained, some of which have been explored already. I also encountered, like other advocates, many detainees who would say that they were treated well in these centers. Like Adriana and Carolina, they would state that they were grateful and that they felt safe there. However, as with Adriana and Carolina, the conversations in which these comments were made often involved a comparison. Many detainees viewed their time spent at Dilley or Karnes with fresh memories of the places they were prior to family detention: *las hieleras* and *perreras*, again, the short-term ICE detention facilities at the border that received widespread media attention detailing their abuses (Burnett 2014). Conversations about those experiences, noted already, often involved much crying as women and children reflected on great and unexpected trauma. When they described feeling safe in the family facility, it would also frequently accompany a discussion of the lack of safety they were experiencing in their lives prior to coming to the United States or during their dangerous cross-country journeys. In detention, they were safe from being killed or kidnapped, safe from starvation or dehydration. To this end, scholars of migrant detention have drawn attention to how "viewing detention of any sort in a favorable light is perhaps more suggestive of oppressive and depriving environments outside of the walls of detention centers than a glowing endorsement of said centers" (Furman, Epps, and Lamphear 2016, 9). In drawing immediate comparisons with previous experiences of detention, Adriana and Carolina may illustrate this point.

Although this was not the case for the many other detainees that did not feel safe or secure, this kind of reflection depicted a valid reality for some, and it was not the place of legal advocates to reject their clients' interpretations or sentiments around their incarceration. This also speaks to a sentiment that was expressed by advocates themselves: that they expected the facility to be worse than it appeared. In both centers, women and children were not kept in the same kinds of "cages" as they were elsewhere (most comparing this, visually, with *las hieleras/perreras*). They were relatively free to move about the facility throughout the day, and even with the barriers discussed in chapter 1, there was nonetheless a school and daycare center. These spatial qualities had an impact even on the perceptions of legal advocates who were opposed to family detention.

What, then, are we to make of a place that not only was created and maintained as a response to a manufactured problem but also is one that at least some of those trapped variously within its grasp characterize in good terms? This, I believed, was the root of Cynthia's frustration. It was not that she wanted Adriana and Carolina to have had worse experiences; she was frustrated by the fact that their comments, which did not reflect the horrific experiences of many other detainees, aligned with how facility administrators portrayed their centers. A significant part of the battle that advocates fought to shutter these facilities involved contesting the legitimacy of their existence. Jude McCulloch and Sharon Pickering (2009, 236) note that when the state perpetrates violence on particular groups, that violence also "amounts to an attack on the body politic which turns away or even embraces as necessary and normal the harm committed. The violence of incarceration depends substantially on discourses that mitigate its practice in the public imagination." While advocates and detainees certainly did not embrace detention as necessary or normal, certain comments, by implication, leaned toward normalcy, even decency. It seemed that some of those who, perhaps unwittingly, undermined the struggle against legitimizing these manufactured places were the detainees and advocates themselves. This complicated efforts to end the practice of family detention.

It is important for the purposes of this book to draw attention to the fact that both of these undermining arguments hinge on care. It was the perception of good or decent care that framed these detainees' positive comments, and it was the lack of obviously deplorable care—particularly through material or visual invocations—that framed those of some advocates. This unfortunately supported the detrimental fallacy that material harm is the only, or perhaps the most, significant register for rejecting unjust incarceration. The assumed goodness of care, in other words, whatever that might mean for different parties, superseded justice.

CO-OPTED CARE

Adriana's expression of gratitude for us and for the place where we met was indeed a common refrain. When detained clients commented on this gratitude they felt for advocates, they sometimes used language that overlapped the place *with* advocates. In these and other ways, advocates' work became somewhat synonymous with the facility, which not only inaccurately represented advocates' relationships with administrators and their roles as volunteers but also functionally impeded their ability to support a stronger case for closing those centers, meeting their ultimate goal. The work that advocates did was not just recognized by detainees and others as being a part of what made the centers livable for many, but it was also actively co-opted by administrative officials. In this co-optation, their legal care work came to help produce the kinds of conditions that supported administrative aims to keep those facilities continuously functioning while also being perceived by others as something different from what they objectively were; they became something normal, even caring for some.

This active blurring of boundaries between the work of legal advocates and that of facility administrators, on the part of those administrators, expressed itself in overt and covert ways. In the asylum office in Dilley one afternoon, I walked up to the desk where detainees and accompanying advocates were required to check in ahead of their interview. As I stood next to the mother whom I was accompanying while she leaned down to sign in, I glanced past to the wall behind the desk, my eye catching a familiar acronym: CARA, the name for the legal project at the time. It was in a greeting card, splayed open and stapled to the wall's panel, signed and written by a group of asylum officers that had once rotated through the facility. It thanked CoreCivic staff for "all their help" to them and to the women, meaning the detainees. Last but certainly not least in my mind, it thanked them for the advocacy team, for CARA. As my client finished signing in and we were swiftly and impatiently ushered by the desk guard to the waiting room, I sat down, stunned, trying to reset my attention to the nervous mother I was accompanying. How was it possible, I thought, that asylum officers were thanking CoreCivic staff for us? Facility staff deserved not only no credit for legal advocates having been there to help detained families, but to the contrary, they were often the first barrier to providing legal services to detainees, both logistically long term and at the microlevel daily. In that moment, I felt a surge of anger that not only had the asylum officers misunderstood the fractious nature of the relationship between legal advocates and facility staff but also that those staff had felt emboldened to post this tribute to them in clear view of advocates as they passed through the space. Ultimately, this was a minor, though not insignificant, material expression of how the boundaries between legal advocates and administrators became blurred. There were many other instances in which facility administrators more actively tried to co-opt the efforts of the legal advocacy teams, to either claim credit for the work of advocates as their own or to deploy language in such a way that intentionally misrepresented the roles of advocates.

Many "tour groups," of sorts, made their way through these facilities, from politicians to United Nations representatives to Latin American emissaries or ambassadors. Some of those groups passed through the visitation area, though not all, and for various reasons, these appeared to be rigidly orchestrated events. On one occasion in late 2016, one such group passed through the Dilley facility, led by a CoreCivic staff member. After having toured the interior of the center, passing necessarily back through our trailer, Jason and Amelia, both staff attorneys, gave a brief presentation to them, trying to present the kinds of aid that our group offered. As they finished and the staff officer led the group toward the exit, a few of us stood in the doorway of our small office, listening as the officer continued to explain the nature of our work to them. The officer, surprising to many of us, spoke positively of our group, stating that the legal services we provided were just "one of the services their facility offered to detainees." This was one of the first times I had heard a facility staff member frame our relationship in such a truly misleading way, as something provided by the facility itself, but it certainly was not the last. I later asked Jason about this, recounting what I had heard the staff officer say to this group. "Here, they always try to use us," he said flatly, as he continued to type on his laptop. "They try to take credit for our work all the time. It makes them look better or that they are somehow involved in our presence here in a positive way."

Advocates aimed to shape public perceptions of the facilities in ways that reflected the realities they observed within. Many elements impeded this effort, from the physically obscured existence of these centers and their daily goings-on to the carefully constructed language deployed by administrators in describing these centers while denying more critical interpretations. One of the barriers advocates faced in trying to shift perception, I would argue, involved their very role. One reason that administrators were at times able to lay claim to the efforts of advocates had to do with advocates' liminal position. As clarified already, the individuals who came to work as representatives of these projects were not official legal representatives of any individual client within. Detainees were given legal assistance on their budding cases through the pro bono project itself.[1] As was illustrated briefly during an encounter in chapter 4, many advocates struggled to communicate this somewhat confusing role to their clients, which was understandable. Volunteers who were not legal professionals were frequently referred to as "*abogada*," or lawyer, by clients with whom we worked. Advocates, in their *charlas*, would explain that we were not all lawyers, and yet it was difficult to find another appropriate word to describe our role to the families, so the identifier often stuck despite clarifications.

For a period in the facilities, we experienced a significant influx of ethnic Roma/Romani clients, and I frequently worked with them. Working with these clients required a different approach than working with clients, for instance, from Central America or Mexico, not least because of the substantial difficulties in finding an appropriate interpreter. When I met my first Roma client in Dilley, Dora, she mentioned to me that she had been told by an officer at the facility that she was going to have a lawyer that would help her with her case, a "public defender," she was told. Dora and I subsequently had a long, winding, and confusing conversation in which I tried to explain that she was, in fact, not afforded a public defender. I muddled my way through communicating that while the "lawyers" to which that staff member referred were us, the legal advocates, we were not public defenders but rather volunteers who provided free legal services. Later that same day, I found myself musing on this supposed difference. Were we, effectively, public defenders? Could

1. This was why, on the exceedingly rare occasion that a client had obtained legal representation prior to meeting with either the Dilley or Karnes teams, that person's legal case could not be assisted by them.

CoreCivic, ICE, GEO, or asylum officers not guarantee to detainees that legal advocates and their services would be available to them in a similar way that the government does with public defenders for others incarcerated? We were voluntary aid workers, providing free, nondiscriminatory services through these organizations for years. What might it mean that our labor was considered so integral to the functioning of the facilities' claim "processing" for the care of detainees?

The blurring of boundaries between advocate and administrator naturally leads to a deeper consideration of this conflicted relationship. In many other scenarios, this relationship has been described by some as one of "functional solidarity" between the "hand that cares," meaning humanitarian aid work, and the "hand that strikes," which includes controlling or punitive organizations, like the military and police, as was discussed in chapter 3. We can best think of this functional solidarity through Michel Agier and David Fernbach's (2011) discussion of humanitarian government, where NGOs come to manage the groups confined within various forms of encampments or enclosed spaces. NGOs, then, develop a sort of solidaristic relationship with the state in that their work becomes the localized form of governance, reproducing some of the state's functional roles—care, management, and control—on behalf of the state. Since in many instances, governments retreat from some of the more intimate forms of care and management of these depoliticized subjects, like refugees, humanitarian aid work comes to fill that gap but often in either terms explicitly provided by the state or in some form of alignment with the state's interests.

In the case of family detention, these chapters have attempted to make clear how legal advocates and governmental/private entities were often directly at odds with one another, as administrators challenged the care work of advocates at both micro- and macroscales. While one could rightly argue that legal advocates established a relationship of functionality with facility administrators, it is necessary to recognize their differences in aims and perceptions of care as well as how administrators used their ultimate authority and advocates' precarious positions to co-opt their labor. This was a relationship not of solidarity but one of mostly functional yet competitive and uneven coexistence. The boundaries that divided them could be made unclear as a result of this complicated, ever-shifting relationship. The co-optation of their efforts inflicted a kind of wound, inhibiting their abilities to achieve their ultimate goals while also serving as a reminder of the diverse ways that detainees and their caregivers could be harmed, even when they were being "treated well." Still, despite the wounds the work in this environment inflicted on most, a strange kind of hope was ever present as well.

FRONTIERS OF HOPE

In many ways, family detention felt as if it existed along a frontier, a "contact zone" (Clifford 1997a) bringing together disparate peoples, needs, and interests. "A frontier is an edge of space and time," Tsing (2005, 28) reminds us, "a zone of not yet—not yet mapped and not yet regulated." This characterization might seem contradictory to what much of my research has presented to this point. As spaces of incarceration, family detention spaces were rigidly regulated and controlled, the contours of which were informed by multiple, sometimes competing forces. Legal advocates themselves played a role in that, both in contesting that control and, at times, affirming it. In another sense, though, what unfolded inside these spaces made it feel as if it was always in a state of becoming, unmapped and unpredictable. Mechanisms, rules, and practices changed rapidly, and advocates often discussed how it routinely felt as if the environment was on the cusp of something new. *Were these facilities the first of many like them to come, or would they all be closing within a week?* Such questions circulated throughout the advocacy community, sometimes encouraged by the *chismes* traveling between detainees and facility staff. Whereas facility employees would sometimes express anxieties about a sudden loss of their job, advocates would worry that these centers were just the beginning, that we were on the precipice of a new world in which imprisoning asylum-seeking families was the norm rather than an exception. This fear of an unmapped future echoed throughout advocates' comments, and this only increased as the then-incoming Trump administration took charge of immigration processes. But among that fear and uncertainty, a unique kind of hope also resonated.

"Hope has never trickled down," oral historian Studs Terkel (2003, xi) once noted; "it has always sprung up." For some legal advocates, their experiences with these projects served as an unexpected and strange

FIGURE 17 Note adorning the refrigerator at the ranch. Credit Erin Routon.

wellspring of hope. Amal, an attorney who regularly did pro bono work with refugees in Atlanta, was one of the first of my interlocutors to offer an alternative sort of perspective of Dilley, one that focused on the preservation of the memory. Like others, there were some experiences she had helping refugees, in her nonvolunteer work, that she preferred to try to forget, cases she had worked on that were "horrifying." She had cases with judges that, in her estimation, were so indiscriminately unfair that she would rather not recall them. In her everyday work, she explained, it had become normal to forget. "I've been doing asylum law for four years," she said.

> In Georgia, we're completely jaded.[2] Women will pass their CFIs, get out of detention, and then will get deported within two months. Judges won't even let them present their claims. They need immediate help when they get out of detention, but they don't have any money. Don't even have access to transportation to get to court.

2. Georgia was and is notorious among legal advocates for its extremely high rates of asylum denials (see https://trac.syr.edu/immigration/reports/judge2018/denialrates.html).

In recent years, Amal and her colleagues have experienced bouts of extreme stress with their case denials, and she had learned to "compartmentalize" the emotions she experienced with her cases. "I will be in an interview or a meeting with a client, and I will have tears in my eyes listening to their stories. Then I'll leave, and it's like I'll completely forget. I'll forget the details of their stories, what just happened in front of me. It's like it's gone." This echoed the previous comments made by Matt, the long-serving public defender, on the necessity of forgetting in similar lines of work. Other immigration lawyers shared Amal's opinion. "As an immigration lawyer, I usually give more bad news than good news," Rebecca, the Texas lawyer, explained. "And it's tough. So, in a personal way, going to Dilley is a more uplifting experience. But it's draining in another way in that you have to listen to these really horrific stories all at once. That's really hard to do." For nonlawyer advocates, the liminal qualities of family detention rarely conjured a sense of hopefulness. For those advocates, hope was found in release from detention, the achievement of that first aim of the projects, as, for them, it symbolized progressive movement toward justice, toward reunification with families and loved ones. Advocates in legal professions, however, typically expressed difficulties in sharing this view.

Louis was still a law student when he went to Dilley, though he had already had much experience working with different organizations in the United States that served the legal needs of detained refugees. In contrast with those previous experiences, Louis recognized a strong sense of hope in Dilley's detained families.

> At the stage of detention I was working at with detainees before, they know what their chances of actually winning asylum are. They're more hardened, more realistic even. But in Dilley, they are still really hopeful. And I think that was hard for me, in a way. I know their chances. I know that there's not really any way out. The government doesn't care about them, and there's so little that we can do to change that.

Few advocates expressed this same sort of explicit pessimism. His perspective, at times, led him to speak more frankly with clients about the chances of their case's success, both within the space of the interview and beyond detention. It was rare that advocates spoke in such a way with detainees, even when they questioned the success of a client's case, and Louis's actions were challenged by other advocates and ultimately discouraged by project staff. Some staff would argue, with volunteers in agreement, that it simply was not productive or helpful to share doubts about the future success of a client's case with them at this stage. Liv, an undergraduate student from New York who had volunteered with legal organizations serving detained youth, openly expressed her frustrations with attitudes and behaviors like Louis's. "I feel like it's our job to give them hope for the future," she argued. "They don't need our pity or for someone to tell them that they've got no hope with their cases. They just need someone to respect them."

For Noelle, also an immigration lawyer, it was all about taking "one step at a time." "Being in a detention center is not tenable," she said.

> It's not a solution to anything. Nobody can withstand that for long, so getting past this issue [of being detained] is how you get to whatever the next possible steps are. If it means that they do find the right advocate on the outside who can't win an asylum claim but can reunite them with their families and can keep them in the U.S. on a work authorization for two or three years, I think that's a great solution. And then maybe something changes with their case or their circumstances in the meantime.

While Noelle uses the language of "solutions" in her remarks, the temporary nature of her proposition seems incongruous with how one typically thinks or talks about solutions, as more like resolutions, especially when speaking about immigration processes. Mary, the immigration lawyer who was volunteering the same week, shared a similar sentiment: "If all this work does is only to give these women a few years of security and opportunity, it's worth it. The majority may not win their asylum cases, but they may have other opportunities that could really make a difference."

Already, many immigration lawyers knew the slim chances of families actually winning their cases, being afforded a form of legal status to remain in the United States. Depending on the courts in which a claim was pursued, especially those that constituted the so-called asylum-free zones, like Amal's court in Atlanta, this could be functionally impossible to achieve.[3] The vision, then, as these advocates demonstrated, is rearticulated, shifted from a future sustained by the concrete legal status that asylum or citizenship could provide to an unknown future. Maybe the asylum seeker remained in the United States for only a few years, and maybe those few years of working and earning money while remaining relatively safe, as their case progressed, afforded a different sort of future, even if they were ultimately expelled. Maybe, as other immigration lawyers pointed out, different legal pathways from asylum might be pursued. Perhaps they could get out of detention and just live without legal status, which might be better than having to return to their home. There were many possible futures that entered into this kind of estimation. Hope resided in this unknown space because the known—here meaning the narrow likelihood of winning asylum—failed to provide a path to sustained security.

In *Life in Crisis: The Ethical Journey of Doctors Without Borders*, Peter Redfield (2013) challenges the argument that humanitarian action must involve a sense of optimism about future end goals. Using the example of Doctors Without Borders, Redfield demonstrates how the nomadic organization's nature—of attending primarily to the immediate needs of survival—emphasizes the importance of engagement, of a "presence in the field," and importantly, mobility. As a result of unpredictable outcomes, something like hope, Redfield argues, "becomes embodied and realized in specific individuals and actual lives" (240). I suggest that a mobile or nomadic approach to humanitarian engagement also helps us to imagine a formulation of hope that is not predicated on problem-ending solutions. What I am calling a "nomadic hope" does not require a firm emplacement in time, space, and for the purposes here, legal statuses. While it is "embodied in individual lives," it also resides within and moves throughout indeterminate space and unforeseeable futures because it is in exactly the indeterminate and unforeseeable that hope can thrive. The figure of the "nomad," as several scholars have recently pointed out, is a particularly relevant symbol of our times today, with some, like archaeologist Yannis Hamilakis (2018), claiming that we have

3. "Impact-2018.Pdf," accessed April 21, 2020, https://innovationlawlab.org/reports/Impact-2018.pdf.

entered a "new nomadic age." While we think about this figure as embodied in those fleeing the violence, wars, and climate change affecting their home countries or states, we should also consider those that move throughout space in order to provide aid to those displaced or detained, like the legal advocates at the center of this story, as part of this nomadic group. And although the literal nomad seems a figure emblematic of our present moment in many ways, I think the conceptual nomadic can be deployed generatively as well for the ways that we think about the imaginative engineering work of hope. Hope, for legal advocates and especially for those working in immigration law in these tumultuous eras, appeared not merely a sentiment but more a method (Miyazaki 2004) in their continuous work with those, like asylum seekers, who existed within multiple spheres of precarity.

"In a way, Dilley itself is the middle of nowhere," Cora said to me. Although she was not a lawyer, Cora was used to working with those living in vulnerable conditions in her role supporting victims of human trafficking in the D.C. area, and she repeatedly compared her experience in Dilley with that work. One of those ways involved the stark contrast between the two locations, with the implication that the town of Dilley was "nowhere" while a place like Washington, D.C. was most definitely "somewhere." This, noted in the introduction, was a commonly expressed sentiment, which resonated awkwardly for me as someone who grew up in a place much like Dilley. For Cora, though, the place itself almost evoked a sense of hope precisely because of its liminality, its nowhereness. "Dilley," she explained,

> is also nowhere, to me, in the sense that it sort of sits between the violence and trauma of these women's pasts and their hope for the future. It's like, they are all on the cusp of something better. It's very different in that way than, for instance, the issue of human trafficking in D.C. When I started working with the organization that helps these victims, I didn't know that this happened all around me. I learned that the neighborhoods that I live in, that I spend a lot of time in are these same places of fear and harm for these other people. For them, they are living in their trauma, in those areas, trying to escape it while still being there. In Dilley, though, the women have, for the most part, left the scary things behind. They're safe for the time being, and so you feel this hope that there's something better on the horizon.

For many, that horizon was moving further and further away, testing the hopeful limits of both asylum seekers and their advocates. I would suggest that this calls for a mobile or nomadic formulation of hope, one that moves with the horizon, rather than remaining fixed on a particular end or achievement. To an extent, this is in keeping with both advocates' reflections and current conceptualizations of care, as best understood without a kind of fixed boundary. Indeed, Mattingly (2010, 6) contends that hope, in fact, "most centrally involves the practice of creating, or trying to create, lives worth living even in the midst of suffering, even with no happy ending in sight. It also involves the struggle to forge new communities of care." Hope does not just come into existence, then, but rather involves an active creation, rather practices of and around care even amid suffering. Hope in such environments, indeed, is a kind of refusal of the violence of the "global border regime" (Jones 2017). Advocates, especially those that possessed a keen awareness of the potentially brutal legal outcomes that faced asylum-seeking families once released, reflected on their work and the uniqueness of these spaces through a kind of mobile hope, one that didn't rely on the cessation of suffering. In that way, they denied the rigid conditions under which hope could exist. This was a hopeful politics, and it proved to be an important way of responding to the indeterminate future landscape of family detention.

SIN FRONTERAS

In this final section, I discuss how advocates during this period reflected on the potential future of family detention. Whereas all previous chapters of this book have discussed events of the past, I find it important to note here why I include a discussion of advocates' sentiments about this future. It remains important to reflect on these past perceptions because it offers an understanding of how individuals and groups engaged in such work feel amid ongoing uncertainties. When I began preliminary fieldwork in 2015, the fervor among advocates to end the practice of family detention was high, as was the optimism to accomplish this goal. Even when I returned to begin a continuous year of fieldwork in 2016, that energy was only slightly dampened. Many still expressed the belief that with the right mix of successful litigation and increasing oversight of the

FIGURE 18 A weathered "End Family Detention" sign hung on the fence at the ranch. Credit Erin Routon.

practices that went on inside these centers, particularly being exposed to public attention, the facilities would close.

At a town hall–style interview hosted by MSNBC in April 2016, then-presidential candidate Hillary Clinton sat on a stage, speaking with host Rachel Maddow about her goals postelection. In between questions, an audience member shouted toward the stage, asking what Clinton planned to do about family detention, if she was going to stop the practice. They specifically referred to the Berks facility, which was the only family detention center beyond Dilley and Karnes. Clinton responded quickly, looking directly out into the audience: "Yes, I'm against that," she said firmly, continuing, "Absolutely. I'm against it. I've been against it for a long time. I've said we should end family detention, we should end private prisons, and private detention centers. They are wrong" ("MSNBC Town Hall" 2016). This and other related comments from candidate Clinton helped fuel a sense of hopeful excitement and relief many seemed to express, at the time, about the future of family detention.

In my time working with these projects, advocates articulated different imagined endings. Particularly in the lead-up to the 2016 election, when sudden changes would occur to the environment or legal teams would experience success with broader litigation efforts, advocates on the ground expressed beliefs that the end was potentially near. The end of family detention, as an idea, had a constant presence, especially in the early years; as time passed, however, I witnessed a shift. This didn't occur immediately after Clinton lost, but that was certainly a catalyzing moment. In later discussions with advocates, it became clear that the end was seen as less likely to become a reality. "I don't think anyone is even working on that anymore," Meg said with a slight laugh, as we sat on the floor of her apartment in San Antonio eating takeout and drinking beer during the summer of 2019. Meg was a staff member of the Dilley project and had been with it for just over two years at that point. I had asked her what people on the team were thinking then about the prospect of ending family detention, through the litigation efforts that played a major role in their early efforts, beyond the direct services I observed. This, as noted already, was the goal of the coalition that formed at the restart of family detention. I was not expecting such a blunt response to this question, but I was not entirely surprised by it either.

Meg's role with the project had recently changed, as had many others'. Over the years, new organizations had taken over the work of the Dilley project, while RAICES remained responsible for the efforts at Karnes. In Dilley, few staff remained living at the ranch house, while most others, like Meg, moved out to separate apartments in town or to San Antonio. It felt strange that staff were shifting away from not only the communal living structure they had for so long but also that they were moving physically farther away from the facility, in part because somewhat counterintuitively, it felt like their role in the center was becoming more entrenched. It was clear that the organizations that had been involved in this aid work had begun to think more seriously about long-term legal service engagement. In other words, thinking about family detention as something temporary had clearly changed.

This was, of course, a divergence from those early intentions around the project, as a temporary response to a crisis. These facilities, so many expressed, would be closed, most likely from legal challenges to either their legitimacy or the abuses, including denials of rights, that occurred within them every day. This informed the essence of these projects, those that depended greatly on unpaid labor. As the years went by, it astounded many that they were still able to find new groups of volunteers every week, groups that would fly to Texas, rent hotel rooms, pay their own meals and gas and everything else. And yet, although this continuity was an encouraging fact, the simultaneous reminder that this was still needed was increasingly discouraging. This caused advocates to question why the facilities seemed so difficult to shutter.

In lieu of definitive answers to this, I might suggest a couple of reasons for what was believed, at the time, to be a kind of immovability. With the earlier iteration of family detention in 2005, at the T. Don Hutto facility in Texas, a refrain familiar within the first Trump administration was deployed for different ends. Schrag (2020, 87) notes about the time:

> Because some of the female immigrants were arriving with their children, ICE arranged for the detention of those children along with their mothers. It contracted with [CoreCivic] to convert one of its private prisons for convicted adult criminals into a detention center for the immigrant families. . . . DHS would later tell the immigrants' advocates that it had created the family jail in response to those advocates' complaints about separating families, and that they were very proud to have been able to keep families together.

Considering what would come during that first Trump presidential era with respect to new border policies and practices, the idea of keeping families together took on new significance. It was a phrase that was emblazoned on T-shirts and protest signs, deployed as the conceptual framework for activist campaigns both within and beyond these advocacy communities. "Keep families together" became a kind of rallying cry that responded to the mass separations of family members as they attempted to cross the Mexico-U.S. border, spurred likely in part by the graphic stories and photographic depictions of young children, even babies, being taken sometimes violently from the arms of their parents. Then, after the fact, many watched the heart-wrenching videos and read of the stories of young children crying as they were reunited with their mothers after months, sometimes years, unable to recognize their faces (Jordan et al. 2018). Although most legal advocates remained devoted to ending the practice of family detention, the many upsetting changes to the treatment of asylum-seeking families, like the more extensive operationalization of family separation, complicated the aims of these projects and others like them. New harms like these divided attention as well as complicated the language they might use to contest such diverse practices.

Yet, there were other elements at play in the ongoing existence of the facilities that more directly implicated legal advocates. The co-optation of legal labor by various facility administrators was used to effect a more positive portrayal of both the relationship between administration and legal advocates as well as what the facility offered detainees. Of course, facility administration did not provide legal services to detainees. As this book has shown, extensive legal care services were provided not only through a combination of voluntary and nonprofit efforts, but they were also offered in an environment that was often hostile to those providers and obstructive of their work. Legal advocates were neither welcomed nor supported, in substantive, consistent ways, in these environments by administration. There were individual staff within these spaces, working on behalf of the private prison corporations or other associated organizations, that did support the presence of these advocates. Those facility staff members helped detainees meet with legal advocates, and some of those, from health-care professionals to guards to asylum officers, expressed their respect for these legal advocates and regard for the necessity of legal aid. These individuals, however, did not reflect the norm across the spectrum of administrative actors. Broadly, legal advocates faced constant, ever-changing barriers to conducting their work and were frequently treated with enmity by administrative figures, at times experiencing actual retribution for their work and the challenges they leveled at the administration. Their care, a form of resistance issuing from tensions and differences in ethical and practical commitments, was often treated as a threat.

Ultimately, though, their efforts effectively improved the processing functions of these facilities, which was where the more troubling nature of their presence lay. Their work helped construct a world in which a detained mother might comment that she was grateful for what she was provided in detention. With the help of legal advocates, most detained families were released into the United States, after typically brief periods, to continue their asylum cases. Advocates established an effective process that led most to positive results and successful court appeals of negative decisions. They advocated for timely releases of detainees and provided them with necessary information about legal processes after detention. They also contributed much beyond strictly asylum operations, advocating for appropriate interpretation services and medical and childcare. Their work certainly did not "make these places good," as, I would contend, such sites cannot be made good because they will always run counter to human rights and dignity, no matter the quality of their management. What advocates did in their work, however, was make these places more "livable," as carers are meant to do, recalling again Tronto and Fisher's characterization of care as "everything that we do to maintain, continue, and repair 'our world' so that we can live in it as well as possible" (Tronto 1993, 103). The problem appeared to be that making this little world more livable, in a way, aided its continued existence precisely because of the opportunities it afforded others to view it as good. In other words, making it more livable potentially subverted the goal of ending the practice. And yet, because they were caregivers, they could not easily extricate themselves from this work. Like medical professionals who swear the Hippocratic oath to "do no harm," these advocates also implicitly followed this because of their awareness of the harm that would unfold if they were not there. Not only detainees but also administrators of all sorts within the facility came to rely on their care, sometimes using that care toward ends at odds with these projects.

In "'A Prison Is Not a Home': Notes from the Campaign to End Immigrant Family Detention," Bob Libal, Lauren Martín, and Nicole Porter (2012), reflecting on efforts to end the previous era of family detention, pose a simple question: What is the alternative? Legal advocates associated with these projects often responded to this question by citing "alternatives to detention" strategies, like case management programs or even ankle monitoring devices, as both more reasonable for the care of migrants as well as exceedingly more cost effective than incarceration. Advocates were quick to contend that detention was not only entirely unnecessary but also often unavoidably harmful, and that was especially so for those whose lives were already more precarious, like children, those who were ill, or those suffering from trauma. Such well-supported claims also confirmed how the larger communities in and around detention, those complex "social ecologies," matter (Ryo and Peacock 2018a). Along this same line of thinking, and considering the thrust of this book, I would pose another question: What is the alternative to legal advocates giving care in this way? This is effectively the "sticky" question for these projects. Staff and longtime volunteer participants with whom I spoke were aware, from the data provided before their existence in these spaces, of what harm would befall detainees were they not there, and not just entirely but nearly every day. As mentioned previously, this understanding was shaped by memories and experiences of the facility in Artesia, New Mexico. Even in recognizing its unstable operations, the machinery at work inside—from deprivations of health care to denials of legal rights in asylum interviews—could be frighteningly effective at causing immense harm. Without being observed or challenged, these abuses could take place without any recognition as such. Administrative actors proved the ease with which they deported migrants who had either little understanding of or effectively no recourse to change the complex legal processes in which they had entered.

The stakes for legal care were substantial, and advocates knew this at an intimate level. This explained why a staff attorney slept with their cell phone resting on their pillow, waiting for a call that their client might be in the process of being put on a bus to be deported at 2:00 a.m., when advocates were not allowed to be in the facility, just so that they could hurriedly contact the administration to try to stop them. It was why advocates who attended interviews were asked to take extensive notes on what was said and done in that space, and why volunteers were cautioned not to say or do things that might upset those decision-makers who had the power to refuse our presence. All of this—knowing the critical difference that their care made and what their absence could set into motion—left advocates somewhat caught within a system that simultaneously did not value their work as necessary care and took credit for the benefits that their presence afforded. This was, as any advocate would be quick to note, incomparable to how detainees were "caught" within this same system, but I would suggest that without recognition of the ways they were entrapped, in a sense, as well, such problems around legal care in similar contexts have the potential to become more deeply embedded in structures inflicting violence.

MOMENTUM

I return to that early claim, that if care practices are not taken seriously or attended to, there is a risk of their erosion (Mol, Moser, and Pols 2010a). In looking at these spaces through not only a lens of care but also one of friction, we can see an instructive interplay. Friction, literally, if allowed to continue unabated, causes things to wear down but sometimes unevenly. The mechanisms of power that upheld the institution of family detention may not have been eroded, significantly, by the on-the-ground direct services of legal advocates—though this is debatable when considering those in collaboration with off-the-ground litigation work—but it's clear that legal advocates were most certainly worn down by their ongoing commitments amid that friction. Attending to the contours and constraints of care across such landscapes is vital for stopping, or at least slowing, the movement toward erosion before it starts, especially given that care "can be done within and for worlds we might find objectionable" (Puig de la Bellacasa 2017, 6).

At the end of my research, legal advocates' work seemed to continue to unfold on this kind of uncertain, unbounded terrain. Gloria Anzaldúa (1987) spoke poignantly of the very landscape, which she described as a wound, along which these facilities existed. The long, open wound of the Mexico-U.S. border, she eloquently stated, is a "vague and undetermined place created by the emotional residue of an unnatural boundary" (25). She also reminded us that before a scab can form on that or any wound, it will hemorrhage. Sometimes these detention centers felt like wounds that might never really close; the predictable frictions between administrative changes, looming private interests, and constant, albeit fluctuating flows of people seeking safety and security would almost guarantee to keep them fresh and painful. And yet, in these fleeting encounters, a strange kind of hope could take root, as it was meaningful to have someone there, tending to the wound, even if there was no apparent end to the hemorrhage. This, as I've argued, was a political act of resistance not without complications or ambiguities, but it inspired, among other things, sentiments of hope.

Hope may not be best understood as connected to a specific outcome, in this case, in part because it cannot be tied to *just* an upholding or extension of legal rights. Something like a right to access legal counsel is circumscribed by practices and practical conditions, shaped by the passing moments and uneven contexts in which these things unfold. Carolyn Sufrin (2017, 54) demonstrates how this plays out with medical care in jails, noting, "Health care rights for prisoners are not only adjudicated in courtrooms, but through everyday human relationships and practices of care. After all, rights are not prepolitical entitlements but are configurations of social, political, and institutional arrangements, made meaningful through human interaction." As evidenced here, even while the upholding of legal rights is being pursued, hope is not placed solely within them. In observing how advocates' care and accompaniment moved with their detained clients, it might be more productive to think about hope as similarly mobile. Hope, like rights, is construed through the context in which it arises, and in an act of refusal, it found a home in family detention.

CONCLUSION

At the Crossroads

On the night of the 2016 presidential election, sitting with a group of detained mothers filling out intake paperwork, I, along with the on-duty guard, watched the results begin to slowly trickle in on a TV in the Karnes visitation space. We sat there mostly silently, sometimes both of us shaking our heads. In that unfolding scene, we both seemed to share a sense of concern, only exchanging serious looks and frustrated huffs. As I drove back to my apartment in San Antonio that night, I listened to more results shared on the radio, still hopeful that things would turn around despite the fact that it appeared Donald Trump, someone who had expressed such often-racist, odious vitriol for immigrants, would be named our next president.

The following morning, somber and exhausted, I made my way into the Dilley facility to begin another day. I ran into Maggie, the project staff attorney, looking similarly tired and upset. I asked her how she was feeling, to which she replied, "Ugh, OK, I guess." "Because of the election results?" I asked. No, not even that, she explained; it had to do with a client. A client, Mariel, for whom the team had been working extremely hard to get a negative decision overturned, had had another appeal denied. In the middle of the night, the night of the election, Mariel called Maggie to tell her that ICE officers were trying to "remove her" from the facility, meaning initiate deportation. Mariel resisted as she frantically called Maggie, and officers told Mariel that if she continued to resist, they would arrest both her and Maggie. "It was kind of a stressful night," she said. "Everybody just kept talking about the election. I was getting texts about it all night, but I was just trying to make sure someone didn't get deported."

All of this came after an unsettling event earlier in the week in which, for the first and only time while I was in the field, the project team in Dilley had asked a volunteer to leave. In a passing conversation among volunteers and project staff about the upcoming election, one in which Maggie casually expressed support for then-candidate Clinton, the volunteer unexpectedly rounded on Maggie, stating that given the candidate's support of, as she claimed, "partial-birth abortions," Maggie must obviously not care about her advocacy work; as the volunteer put it, she "didn't care about the slaughtering of babies." Clearly, then, this volunteer angrily stated, Maggie must also not care about these mothers, at the center, or their children. The volunteer, a self-identified Trump supporter, would go on that same day, in conversation with project attorney Allie after the incident, to refer to specifically the women project attorneys as "sleazy lawyers," implying that they were engaged in seditious tactics in their work with asylum seekers. This kind of outlandish accusation was something I personally never encountered with volunteers. While Maggie was admittedly shocked, she explained that she had to just keep working, to ensure another family wasn't suddenly deported.

The aftermath of the first election of Donald Trump was expressed in spaces by these sorts of characteristic contrasts. Although there were some immediate effects, like this sort of ill-informed, personally motivated encounter—which was, as I explained, extremely unexpected and abnormal—and others that would become more common, like the increase of asylum-seeking families being illegally turned away by officials at ports of entry, significant shifts in policy as a result of the change in administration would take a bit longer to take shape. In the moment, though, advocates, especially project staff, continued to remain fixed on immediate concerns, like protecting a family threatened with deportation in the middle of the night or ensuring the speedy release of clients with severe medical care needs. Realistically, their care, so constrained by everyday urgency, couldn't afford the space to concern itself with these larger machinations or immaterial slander. They had to keep moving, keep transcribing client statements for negative decision appeals, keep prepping clients for upcoming interviews, keep training new volunteers. Volunteers, likewise, needed to remain "grounded," focused on the work in the moment, as they pored through the microdetails of clients' experiences to help them survive this legal stage, this place.

The story at the heart of this book doesn't just concern the micro-operations of legal norms. Importantly, this book should also not be seen as offering a history of the effects of one presidential administration or another, or even about particular immigration policies or practices. The specific context, of legal advocates working with asylum seekers in family detention, is only part of the story here. Additionally, although this may be the first that explores legal care in detention, it needn't be the only story to do so, and I look forward to future studies of such work in other contexts. This is, after all, a crucial part of recognizing ethnography as indeed storytelling (Götsch and Palmberger 2022).

On a broader scale, my research maps onto the work of other scholars who've aimed to keep track of the "rebel archive" (Lytle Hernandez 2017), including those like Jennifer Cullison (2020, 7) who record those who have "resisted, particularly, immigrant caging." This is a story about the everyday realizations of care in confinement, especially about care as it is practiced and interpreted in unexpected hands: those of voluntary, pro bono legal actors. This is a necessary rejoinder to other crucial work that has documented the experiences of parents and children subjected to family detention (Terrio 2024). What I've tried to represent are the diverse materializations of advocates' care while also making a case for why it warrants our attention and appreciation. It does only in part because it helps us better understand mechanisms of resistance and relationships that unfold in detention, as I contend care is central to the construction of each of those things.

This concluding chapter will think about this work—that which, necessarily, was never meant to be a permanent fixture—in a way that advocates were effectively unable or challenged to do because of this constant state of crisis. It will step out of the facility, widening the gaze to encompass not only the conceptual implications of legal care but also thinking about the larger landscape of detention and legal advocacy. I consider other ways in which violence and wounds mark the experience of moving throughout these spaces—extending the "pains of imprisonment" (Shammas 2017)—while also thinking through how care can be conscripted to produce such effects. Engaging with and beyond care, as possessing potential for both harming and helping, is simultaneously complicated and vital; this is especially relevant as we continue in an era fraught with material and symbolic violence toward migrant communities facing strained caregiving resources. Movement forward must involve a full accounting of the collateral consequences of institutional and structural harm, including those affective, experiential dimensions and impacts on those who struggle to tend the wounds. Recognition necessarily entails how care shapes and is shaped by frictions, together determining the contours of resistance.

PAST AS PROLOGUE

In *The Sanctified Church*, anthropologist Zora Neale Hurston (1981, xix) remarked that "ghosts hate new things precisely because once the conditions that call them up and keep them alive have been removed, their reason for being and their power to haunt are severely restricted." Understanding the apparent continuity of what might be deemed "family detention" calls us to question exactly why its specter remains, especially given both detention's remarkable ineffectiveness as any sort of deterrent (Hiemstra 2019) as well as the profound, documented harm it inflicts. In 2014, with the restart of family detention and upon learning of the Obama administration's plans to open the facility in Dilley, over 150 national, international, and local organizations signed a letter in strong opposition (AILA 2014). In it, they identified five main reasons why family detention should not be allowed to continue, including that it inhibited access to real justice, through fair hearings, and harmed the physical and mental well-being of those detained. It was also unnecessary in that "alternatives to detention (ATD), including community-support programs, are humane, effective, and far less costly than detention." Furthermore, the practice undermined attempts to address increasing incarceration and uphold international human rights (2–5). These arguments were thoroughly supported with evidence from scholarly and nonscholarly sources, including data from the Department of Homeland Security and Department of Justice. Some of these arguments about family detention would be repeated in 2017 by the former (and first) director of the Office of Detention Policy and Planning during the initial term of the Obama administration, Dora Schriro (2017), who described her own emic perspective on the issue as one of both a "practitioner" and "errant ethnographer." In her critical reflections on observing various ICE detention facilities she even likened officers' treatment of detainees to anthropologist Horace Miner's (1956, 467) famous "Body Ritual of the Nacirema": "[The fictitious researcher's] observations of the Nacirema people were without context. His lack of knowledge about and empathy for the actors he observed and his inability to understand their actions left him clueless. I thought it strikingly similar to our government's handling of foreign-born persons in its custody."

Although it continued, much changed with respect to family detention since the completion of my research, and the saga remains ongoing. As noted in the introduction, while the modern instantiation of family detention was reinstituted during the Obama administration, the first Trump administration effected even greater violence on asylum-seeking families, far beyond what many would have predicted. It is important to recognize the ongoing effects of specifically the Trump administration on the individuals described in this book, as well as the shifts in these environments as the United States has transitioned through administrations. The four years of the first Trump administration brought about vast expansions of incarcerations and separations of asylum-seeking migrant families (Flagg and Calderón 2020), additional limitations to asylum, and the institution of new mechanisms to refuse entry, such as the "Remain in Mexico" policy or Migrant Protection Protocols. Furthermore, as of late 2024, over one thousand children that were separated from their parents at the border, because of "zero tolerance" measures, have yet to be reunited with their family members (Human Rights Watch 2024). This continued even despite the establishment of a specific cooperative federal task force that began its efforts in 2021 ("Fact Sheet: A Review").

In March 2021, officials in the Biden administration announced that the two South Texas family detention facilities—Dilley and Karnes—would cease to detain asylum-seeking families (Ainsley 2021). Instead, they explained, the facilities were being rebranded as "reception centers," wherein migrant families would stay for much shorter time while being tested for COVID-19 and arranging travel to their new homes. The third family facility, in Berks County, Pennsylvania, abruptly released all its remaining detained families, though the future function of the facility itself remained unclear. At the time, some advocates expressed relief at these changes, as it meant that families would not be required to undergo asylum processes while detained, sometimes for long periods. Many, however, continued to express their frustrations and skepticism, asking why the facilities remained open at all, particularly when local communities and programs could support these families with their needs. These advocates pointed to the fact that while the function and language around these facilities had been reformulated, even in positive ways, they were nonetheless still spaces from which asylum-seeking families could not willingly leave. On the heels of this debate, activist, filmmaker, and formerly incarcerated Japanese American Dr. Satsuki Ina (2021) penned an article on the matter, reminding President Biden that whatever you wish to call them, a "cage is still a cage."

Following what was the effective conclusion of family detention with the reconfiguration of these centers, in mid-June 2024 the Biden administration announced that the South Texas Family Residential Center in Dilley would be closing for good (Sanchez 2024b). Then, however, with the reelection of former president Trump in late 2024, the announcement was made by incoming "border czar" and former director of ICE Tom Homan, who led the former administration's "zero tolerance" policies, that the practice of family detention might indeed be restarted, though it was unclear if this new instantiation would target the same demographic or other status groups (Miroff 2024). Then, in February 2025, the administration announced that it would likely restart the practice of family detention, reopening the Dilley facility and repurposing, yet again, the Karnes facility for this (Ainsley 2025). This did, in fact, occur in March 2025, with these facilities detaining migrant families, though not exclusively those seeking asylum. The Dilley facility, since renamed the "Dilley Immigration Processing Center," attracted both renewed media and public attention in 2026 through its incarceration of a young boy and his father, as well as ongoing serious deprivations of proper care for detainees. Even before this announcement in February 2025, however, at the end of the first week of Trump's second term, a friend and former long-serving staff member of the Dilley project who went on to work as an organizer in Texas described how they were reminded of their years in Dilley. The urgency, the sense of chaos, the mess of trying to organize amid unpredictable changes to laws and policies, the challenge of managing potential volunteers wanting to help but not knowing how or through which avenues: all these elements characterized those years of family detention's expanded return.

Answering the question of why the specter of family detention continues to haunt is a challenge, as there could be many reasons why different administrations repeatedly turn to this particular form of migrant incarceration, including, as with migrant detention on a larger scale, as a spectacle (Mainwaring and Silverman 2017). What's clear is that shifting away from the practice of family detention is inhibited, in part, by care itself. Care is quite intentionally and inextricably linked with the modern instantiation of family detention. While detention-as-deterrent operates counterintuitively alongside, facility administrators at various scales of authority meaningfully wield care-adjacent language; care is also embedded within the physical structures of the facilities. This expression of an interest in the well-being of asylum-seeking families, indeed promoted as a primary function of the facilities, is not only a form of misdirection, but it's also used as a tool to challenge, even refuse the work of other sorts of caregivers, like legal actors, and avoid serious accounting for harms caused. Identifications with care reinforce justifications and broader support for their continued institutional existence. As a result, it's important to recognize that part of the conditions that continue to call family detention up and keep it alive, as Hurston says, has to do with material and symbolic weaponizations of care, including competition with and co-optation of other caregiving efforts.

Another part of responding to this challenge involves recognizing that although data support the overarching argument that detention doesn't accomplish what supporters or administrators claim and that it, in fact, causes substantial harm to communities, shifting something like public sentiment around the use of migrant detention may well be less influenced by "facts" than by "feelings." Paula Ioanide (2015), for instance, illustrates how emotion, and the manipulations of others' emotions, plays an integral role in how racist policies and attitudes persist despite significant social changes (e.g., moves toward "color-blind" politics). In fact, Ioanide argues, facts about particular groups of color come to be less important than other groups' feelings in terms of organizing support for racist politics. This has been especially prevalent in this most recent "post-truth" political era in which many researchers have documented politicians' weaponization of unsupported claims about marginalized communities through primarily emotional appeals, while also promoting similarly baseless or blatantly fabricated "alternative facts" (Barrera et al. 2020; Miller 2018). With this, as with care, it's necessary to think through the ways in which feelings are mobilized to support various forms of detention, including that of migrant families. In this sense, the "conditions" that might lead to reinstitutions of family detention are flexible, allowing elected or would-be politicians significant opportunities to shape public concerns around containment of perceived crises through fluctuating, albeit constant, detention regimes. Recognizing the contours of these fabricated constructions is critical for restricting their haunting power.

MINDING THE GAP

The past few decades have seen the rise of many nonprofit or pro bono projects aimed at providing various forms of legal services to detainees, often due to the "justice gap" (Harris 2018) that separates migrants from guaranteed legal assistance with their cases, unlike other incarcerated individuals (Eagly and Shafer 2016). This is obviously critical. As Stenken (2012, 212) notes, "the absence of a system of public legal defense in immigration court may affect someone in more drastic ways than a criminal sentence. If people lose their removal hearing, or lose their residency status for minor legal infractions, they may be returned to a country where they face persecution or torture." The stakes for the legal cases of asylum seekers and refugees are especially high. This has only increased with the kinds of significant changes to asylum adjudication made over the past several years, in part making it much harder for applicants to secure legal representation in a reasonable length of time (Schrag, Ramji-Nogales, and Schoenholtz 2023). One long-standing program, the Florence Project, is a legal assistance program established in 1989 that has prepared detainees for pro se representation (or self-representation) mostly through know-your-rights presentations and basic legal orientations and advice for detainees.[1] The government has replicated this project's efforts, to some degree, through their Legal Orientation Programs, funded historically by the Department of Justice's Executive Office of Immigration Review, which provide not legal advice but rather basic information to detainees about processes. In other contexts, scholars have shown how such programs are used by legal advocates to serve underrepresented migrant detainees (Bautista, Bressler, and Bosworth 2019; Macías-Rojas 2016).[2] These programs, like so many others related to the care of migrant communities, however, are currently under attack by the Trump administration (García 2025), and their future remains uncertain. This continues a wider trend in which folks operating in a variety of "helping" working roles or caring professions, from nurses to educators and, as I've suggested, legal actors, are experiencing existential threats (Greene 2021, 186).

Scholars and activists alike have stressed the urgency for further volunteer or pro bono legal assistance for migrant communities, including the need for more funding support, as a lack of funding is a major concern (Haas 2023; Lukens 2024; VERA 2024). The past several years especially have seen a rise in pro bono legal representation efforts and assistance projects across the country; unfortunately, this has expanded alongside the rise of both the incarceration of migrants and a

1. "Our History," *Florence Project* (blog), accessed April 23, 2020, https://firrp.org/who/history/.

2. Such Legal Orientation Programs existed in the Dilley and Karnes facilities during my fieldwork, and their role in these centers was effectively unclear. Their representatives did not use the same spaces as the legal advocacy teams, and they seemingly had little cross-contact. Variously, representatives for these programs would provide Dilley and Karnes advocates with lists of names of current detainees, including their necessary "A" numbers assigned at entry, to help the projects establish contact with them for legal assistance. Their sharing of these lists appeared inconsistent; it also was unclear how these groups were able to collect this sort of information at the facility, whereas the legal advocacy projects struggled to be given access to this. It is an unfortunate fact that I was not able to get more information about these representatives during my research, but their relative invisibility in these spaces essentially affected this. I would not make claims about their effectiveness or collaborations with these facility administrators based on these limited encounters and observations.

greater, often unmet need for legal support amid growing backlogs of cases (Pedroza, Potochnick, and Santillano 2025; Sanchez 2024a; TRAC 2023). Some of the projects are locally or regionally based, such as Texas Rio Grande Legal Aid or the Amica Center for Immigrant Rights, while others provide services nationwide, like the American Immigration Council's Immigration Justice Campaign.[3] One program, with which I also volunteered remotely during and after my field research, was the Southeast Immigrant Freedom Initiative, a project of the Southern Poverty Law Center.[4] This program, until recently, served as the "only program primarily dedicated to legal representation" for those detained in Georgia, Louisiana, and Mississippi (Lukens 2024), states that detain particularly high numbers of migrants (Immigration and Customs Enforcement 2024) and also have serious track records of mistreatment in detention (see, e.g., American Civil Liberties Union 2024 and Warsi 2023). Although offering varying services, these projects unite over a common aim: to provide necessary legal assistance or information to those in migrant detention, as ongoing studies continue to show both the significant underrepresentation of migrants, due in part to a growing shortage of relevant lawyers and increases in detention and deportation processes, as well as the crucial effects of representation, in and out of detention (Eagly and Shafer 2015; National Immigrant Justice Center 2024; Sandoval 2024; TRAC 2017).

In the past several years, Americans have observed countless shifting atrocities visited on migrant communities, and yet alongside this, one aspect of my field observations has remained relatively unchanged: legal advocates offering a unique kind of care, to varying degrees and in diverse capacities, to those incarcerated in detention facilities. It is my ultimate contention that these actors are, and should be recognized as, caregivers. As I have demonstrated, caring for detainees was invariably shaped by the frictions and ambiguities that mark this sort of strange environment and its fleeting encounters. Legal advocates navigated these

3. See https://www.trla.org/; https://amicacenter.org/about-us/; https://immigrationjustice.us/.

4. "Southeast Immigrant Freedom Initiative (SIFI) | Southern Poverty Law Center," accessed April 23, 2020, https://www.splcenter.org/our-issues/immigrant-justice/southeast-immigrant-freedom-initiative-en.

terrains through relationality and flexibility, tinkering with the care they operationalized on uncertain grounds while reconfiguring their own expressions of power and resistance. In moving beyond this specific context, it's important to continue to think about the different ways that the concept of legal care might help us better understand encounters between legal actors and migrant communities, especially those impacted by incarceration. It's also of critical importance to take seriously the various kinds of obfuscations of social relations and forms of precarious existence that result from only thinking about immigration in terms of legal processes and statuses (Sangaramoorthy 2023). I challenge others to consider what sorts of complicated, layered social relations come out of legal encounters, especially those that rely in significant ways on volunteer or pro bono labor. How are legal actors both informing and impacted by the challenging navigations around legal violence through care? This adds greater dimension to our gaps in understanding around the form and effects of such relational encounters.

Speaking to other relevant gaps, while in an earlier chapter I shared advocates' reflections on the "untranslatability" of the experience of being in this place and doing this work, this is precisely what my book has attempted to do: to find a way to translate this somewhat mystifying experience. And yet, in the end, I also share this ineffable sentiment. The strangeness of the experience, the contradictions and unanswered questions make this text feel a bit like a failure in that what I've recounted and how I've analyzed those conversations and observations do not properly translate all that occurred. Such is the challenge of the ethnographic endeavor, thus fueling the ongoing insecurities around the accuracy of our representations. I find David Zeitlyn's (2014) characterization of anthropology as an "ekphrastic" process particularly useful in this case. Zeitlyn describes ekphrasis as a "verbal account or evocation of a typically non-present image or object," arguing that thinking of our work as such helps us to better understand the sometimes necessarily incomplete facsimiles we create out of our observations while also striving to narrow representational gaps. The places at the heart of this book's story are, in truth, especially ripe for misrepresentations, as, with other carceral facilities, they existed in a nearly invisible manner. This sense of "invisibility" is even more characteristic of migrant detention centers, something further reinforced by their shadowy, murky legal existence (Just Future Project 2018). As noted earlier, in doing research on and around such spaces, carceral ethnography has been challenged by various barriers, and we see this today shift to new forms, like those effected by global pandemics (Berg, León, and Tosh 2022). Making space for this reality, as simply part of the anthropological challenge of representation and thus offering an incomplete facsimile of life and culture in these facilities, allows for the simultaneous truths of an untranslatable experience and an affective portrait of care, and necessarily also violence, in detention.

VIOLENCE, CARE, AND BEYOND

In 1969, Hannah Arendt argued that "no one engaged in thought about history and politics can remain unaware of the enormous role violence has always played in human affairs, and it is . . . rather surprising that violence has so seldom been singled out for special consideration" (12). Anthropologists and other social scientists have since given substantial attention to the subject, and for good reasons. Although scholars have shown how "violence" is not a simple construction with clear boundaries (Greenberg 2019), it is generally agreed on that what might be interpreted as violence is "highly revelatory of basic social processes" (Jones and Rodgers 2019, 299). While as social scientists, there is still a need to unpack all the ways that legal violences, specifically, take shape, especially as we witness ongoing changes to legal structures that expand exclusions of migrants, among other marginalized groups, it's important to also think about how much we are attending to the forms of care that are built in resistance. Likewise, at least in some cases we can't fully comprehend practices of care without taking violence into consideration. While this book has very intentionally centered care, it most certainly is also a story about violence, primarily the violence of incarceration and exclusionary legal processes. It's about how asylum seekers, while the principal targets of this violence, are not its only recipients. Legal caregivers are also subject to this, albeit in different ways, thus also residing along that violent continuum, expanding the reach of harm beyond what we might initially consider. In fact, it is their practices of caregiving that, in this case, bring them into contact with violence. These things must be explored together: we cannot adequately understand the care they give without discussing the harm, yet discussing just that harm offers only a partial view, effectively denying the various material forms of resistance.

Engagements with unexpected operative modes of care, especially with unrecognized caregivers, offer opportunities to rethink the ways we constitute the boundaries of care. They allow us to critically evaluate how care might be practiced in a given context while also thinking about the ways in which violence masquerades as care (even when unintentionally realized by earnest caregivers). They further help us see the harm that can be caused when something isn't identified as care work, both for the recipient and the giver. Care scholars remind us that "we need to think beyond care as a very particular array of moral sentiments and social arrangements" (Ticktin 2016, 266), including how tensions and frictions around care inscribe asymmetries and ambiguities (Coe 2019). These reflections have significantly informed the substance of care represented here; thinking otherwise about the subject would have severely limited my interpretation of the modes and moments through which care was brought into being. Thus, I agree that "the job of the [care] researcher is both 'describing practices to do with care' and 'wondering what care is'" (Coopmans and McNamara 2020, 7, also citing Mol et al. 2010a).

This book has considered how "spaces of care" are created, even within those that objectively cause harm. As I observed, advocates used various tactics to move through spaces that were often resistant, sometimes outwardly hostile to their presence. I've suggested the importance of looking at the affective, sensorial dimensions of carceral spaces specifically, as this informs a more complete understanding of their sometimes counterintuitive—like becoming accustomed to a sense of disorientation—and other times contradictory affects—like a sense of the passing of time as both slow and fast. Concepts like "embodied space" and a more thoughtful attention to feelings help us understand these affects in a more effective way. Thinking about how a particular carceral space's simultaneously symbolic and linguistic, explicit and implicit identifications—in this case, with care—is also important for making sense of the ability of outside actors, like legal advocates, to engage in supportive practices with such "captive" groups.

Previous chapters have depicted the kinds of narrative care work that advocates engaged in for various purposes. Of course, as legal "brokers," advocates inevitably participated in the exclusionary legal processes inherent to asylum law; as was noted, this was recognized by advocates in varying degrees. They did this primarily through shaping detained families' experiences into narrative terms both meaningful and legible to official adjudicators, asylum officers, and judges. In a way, these practices straddled a muddy line between care work and harm, and even if not always explicitly recognized, advocates felt this conflict. At the same time, their narrative care was also defined by practices of counterstorytelling and counternarrative; these were made manifest variously, but all represented expressions, sometimes reclamations, of power through reimagined stories.

In making sense of the uneven terrain that characterized such spaces, it was necessary to consider the material ways that advocates' legal care in everyday encounters in detention was construed through both exceptional and mundane frictions leading to contestations of power between advocate caregivers and administrative "others." Taking these encounters as evidence of care-at-work helps us make sense of the kinds of tensions and complicated management of inherently fraught relationships advocates navigated to maintain the flow of care. This was made evident in ways according to different spaces within these facilities, again illustrating the importance of thinking of and through spatial affects. Varying encounters reflected multiple practical modes of legal accompaniment, especially in spaces where their care was more substantively constrained. In the being-with in different spaces, advocates deployed alternative strategies for resistance, sometimes through acts of witnessing or documentation. These were often subtler forms of care, illustrations of what might be interpreted as more implicit, quieter practices of activism.

Throughout this book, I have highlighted the importance of taking seriously the collateral or spillover consequences of engaging in such work, including how those effects can and do extend beyond expected boundaries. In doing so, I've considered how even legal caregivers experience "hauntings" from their care work, again demonstrating similarities with other forms of care labor. Of course, hauntings or specters communicate more than simply personal experiences of trauma; they help us better understand the various configurations and extensions of power. This is instructive for understanding the operations of powerful institutional and structural forces, even in the aftermath of care. I've argued that part of the challenge embedded within this kind of work is the way in which advocates' care was simultaneously contested, constrained by facility administrators, while also co-opted by those very same entities. This sort of confusing relationship blurred the boundaries of who was giving care and who was operationalizing harm, putting advocates' work into a sort of trap in which dependencies flourished and the ultimate aim of legal advocates—that of ending the practice of family detention—was complicated.

The idea that hope, something that fuels the continuation of care amid precarity, can be somewhat mobile, rather than fixed or dependent on a specific outcome, was an important if unexpected outcome of conversations with legal advocates. This sort of itinerant or "nomadic" hope became evident in these unpredictable settings, realized most clearly, again counterintuitively, by those advocates who were aware of the serious challenges that lie ahead for detained clients. In a way, then, the work being done by advocates became a site of hope, one where albeit temporary victories and a moment of respite existed within reach, breathing a sort of hopeful life into otherwise relentlessly cruel legal realities.

The work of abolitionists has had a major impact on the ways I imagine future engagements with care in and around detention, as they have also informed my consideration of the boundless potential of a kind of mobile hope. Abolitionists offer vital perspectives on the need for border and migrant carceral abolition (e.g., Akers Chacón 2021; García Hernández 2019), which cannot and should not be decoupled from abolitionist aims and movements beyond those impacting primarily migrant communities. Abolitionist thinking also necessarily encourages a kind of "vigilant imagination" (Snider 2022), something so indispensable for not only ridding ourselves of harmful, destructive policies and practices related to immigration and incarceration but also for making space for hope amid apparent disasters. This sort of "abolitionist imaginary" (Gordon 2011, 8) indeed

> recognizes that transformative time doesn't always stop the world, as if in an absolute break between now and then, but is a daily part of it, a way of being in the ongoing work of emancipation . . . [and is] key to anticipating, inhabiting, making the world you want to live in now, urgently, as if you couldn't live otherwise, peacefully, as if you have all the time in the world.

In returning to the idea of haunting, in relation to considering what the future holds, this imaginative mode of thought might help us better understand something like justice as similarly haunting: "Understanding justice as spectral produces a reckoning with the difficult question of how one might live as 'justly' as possible with ghosts while recognizing that a full and satisfactory justice might remain hauntingly elusive" (Govindrajan 2022, 40). In this way, we needn't only be haunted by the thought of continuities of violence but also by a long thread linking us with the promise of justice.

TENDING WOUNDS

Sociologist Avery Gordon (2011, 17) presciently reminds us that

> as imprisonment . . . becomes the destiny of abandoned and "surplus" populations, we, the non-imprisoned, become more and more dependent on the work it does for us in managing our putative right to a safe and prosperous future. This is a deeply sacrificial and immoral situation and it is also a dangerous one because such intolerance grotesquely deforms and deeply scars all of us. To avoid this haunted future, to eliminate the conditions that are producing it, we would do well to remember that social death is a relational idiom of power. It is as much, perhaps even more, for us than for "them."

Although, I would argue, families detained in these sorts of facilities are not necessarily subject to the same kinds of "social death" explored by scholars in relation to other carceral spaces, this book demonstrates that detained families were ineluctably exposed to forms of deep social exclusions. Theirs is a different story from those experiencing longer-term, nonadministrative imprisonment, but those exclusions were representative of similar relational expressions of power, ones intended to reinforce racist social boundaries and promote conflicted narratives of protection. With respect to family detention specifically, two seemingly directly counterposed narratives were deployed: (1) detention-as-deterrent or punishment, protecting a "native" populace from the perceived external threat posed by asylum seekers and (2) detention-as-care, protecting asylum-seeking families from more vague existential threats, often contrasted specifically with the arduousness of the journey to the United States (see, e.g., Santiago 2018). In these ways, family detention shares the institutionalized violence of imprisonment as well as its operationalization of security-in-containment. As Gordon says, this deforms and scars us all.

I frequently thought about the idea of wounds, and scars, after I initially left the field in July 2017. Just a month after I left, I found myself at a clinic in the middle of Yellowstone National Park. A couple of weeks after that first year of fieldwork ended, my partner and I were married in a casual ceremony at my childhood home in a small town in North Texas. With only a brief period left before our return to the Northeast, we embarked on a honeymoon road trip, touring a few national parks in the western states. It was during that trip that I began to feel significant physical pain, first starting near my chest on the right side of my body. Both of us worried, we stopped into the Old Faithful Medical Clinic in Yellowstone, a building that stood just near the famous geyser and looked like an old log cabin. I saw several doctors that day, none of whom could detect any cause for my pain, even after sending me over the border into Idaho to a proper emergency room. It would be the first of many medical appointments that would take place over the next few years, all with the same results: nothing appeared wrong. The pain I would come to experience was also widely varying, shifting unpredictably all throughout my body, shaping my life in almost immeasurable ways. Before fieldwork, I had not had such experiences; after fieldwork, it felt like my body became a sort of alien being, something I could no longer understand or control.

At the time, nothing made sense, but I tried to manage the pain and confusion. Now, through the distance of time, I see things a bit more clearly. What I have come to understand about this challenging period of my life, as a budding researcher, and the concomitant experience of pain, involves a recognition of the ways that ethnographers can be scarred by their work, especially when done in violent spaces on sensitive subjects, thus being themselves wrapped up within the wider expression of collateral effects. I've described this as a kind of "vicarious wound" in ethnographic research (Routon 2025) that can register in sometimes less detectable forms. The physical pain I felt after fieldwork, I learned, was entwined with the emotional pain I experienced, and suppressed, in the field. This was partly caused by my desire to offer as much assistance as possible to asylum seekers as well as to the interlocutor communities of advocates that meant so much to me and my work. The deeply impactful, emotional environment that I depict here impacted me as well, but this went unrecognized because of my (misinformed) assumptions about potential expressions of trauma and their delayed material manifestations. Like my interlocutors, I experienced visceral wounds from my time in family detention, but also like them, I found myself ignoring them to prioritize care for detained families.

This harmed me, in complex, psychosomatic ways, and helped me further realize the necessity of recognizing care labor. It also left me with newfound reflections on the complicated relationship between care and ethnographic research, including an appreciation for what we can better understand of ethnography when looked at through the lens of care. Pain, of course, went with the territory of family detention. In my conversations with volunteers and staff of these projects about their experiences, some would themselves use the language of wounds: of having been wounded by different encounters or stories, of having borne witness to the creation of new wounds for those in detention, or sometimes feeling as if they had played a role in manifesting others' wounds. This language lends itself to important broader discussions about the various pains caused to not only those incarcerated but also communities around them, as the carceral world casts its long shadow (Longazel, Berman, and Fleury-Steiner 2016).

As an engaged anthropologist, it is important to think about how such wounding extends to our own work as well. I follow other engaged, activist, and applied scholars who've spoken on the responsibilities on the part of the researcher working with migrant communities to support, advocate, and accompany (Nuñez-Janes, Ovalle, and Plancarte 2018; Gomberg-Muñoz 2018; Yarris 2021), sometimes acting effectively as a "researcher–cum–social worker" (Horton 2016). I agree that it's especially important to think on the ways that we must be attuned to the effects of conducting research in emotionally fraught environments, especially those shaped around "crisis" (Backe 2017) and the challenges and opportunities of working within activist coalitions (Heyman 2011). I have taken this as part of my responsibility in working with caregiving communities that serve migrants as well in that while I work alongside those caregivers, I also think about how they require support, advocacy, and accompaniment, albeit sometimes in different forms: in essence, how I might use my position to help tend to their wounds. My accompaniment with advocates involved making space for them to tell their stories, to offer a kind caring attention to them. It involved recognizing how the violence of detention and legal processes impacted them while also making room for other types of encounters, other experiences and forms of relationality that were built simultaneously in their work. The complexity of what occurred there is the story, so sharing their part is integral. It was also clear that at least some advocates perceived that setting aside space for their own storytelling was healing in a way, as this was recounted on numerous occasions to me. This was an unexpected and unintended consequence of my separate role as a researcher. But I was not just a researcher; I was an ethnographer, someone who, as a consequence of our disciplinary approach, was intimately familiar with the space and their work, and was thus someone who understood that sometimes indescribable experience. Although this proximity was at times challenging for me to navigate, it offered depth to my relationships with advocates and related communities of care and continues to inform my praxis as an engaged ethnographer.

ENDINGS

On a Sunday afternoon in 2019, I found myself at another orientation meeting, with a large group of volunteer advocates (some of whom I recognized from years prior), in a conference room at the Best Western Plus Inn and Suites in Dilley. Kayla, then an attorney working for the Dilley project, stood at the end of the long, wide table, explaining in detail what volunteers should expect when going into the facility the following day. "Everything here in detention is changing, every day," she said boldly. "The government is hell-bent on making the process for asylum seekers as difficult as possible. Some of you might have come here thinking you wouldn't be thrown right into things, but I'm here to tell you that you can do it. Remember, *it's always us or no one.* We are fighting for a chance for these clients to fight their own case."

The meeting rolled along as Kayla explained all the expectations of their roles in a most effective presentation style, demonstrating, for instance, how to instruct clients on acting out scenes for greater interview effect. New volunteers stared with attention and jotted notes while she offered many examples of the sorts of things they might encounter in the work, including its inherent difficulties. She talked about how they might communicate legal paradigms to clients and navigate those exclusionary limitations of asylum while also offering the kind of attention and respect those people, and their stories, deserved. "I want you to be a human being," she said clearly. "Be sympathetic, listen, absorb all they're telling you. Then, take a step back and plug that story into this stupid, ruthless system. You have to do both: be a human being and step back to plug their story into this system."

This apparent paradox—of "being human" while engaging in an inhumane process—was of the sort that characterized advocates' everyday operations and the deeply felt challenges in their navigation. More broadly, their work faced the paradoxical challenge of how to maintain their care of and for detained families while situated in an objectively ambiguous position within these structures. Migrant incarceration itself is paradoxical, lying at the "conceptual and material crossroads between the domestic and foreign, the intimate and geopolitical, the detention center and the prison" (Mountz et al. 2012, 536). This liminal existence encourages frictions, and "much of what we know about these tensions comes from advocates doing the work of documentation against obscurity, publicity against silence, and challenge against impunity" (536). Sufrin (2017, 5–6) further reminds us that the "violent realities within jails and prisons lead to a tacit assumption that relations of care are impossible. And yet, the emerging equivalence between the carceral net and the safety net has created opportunities for care and discipline not only to coexist, but to shape each other in unexpected ways." Although the often more ephemeral space of the migrant detention center, like that in this story, is not a prison or a jail, migrant detainees effectively have no such safety net when it comes to critical legal aid. In this context, the universal care located in legal advocates' work functioned as a kind of "new safety net," as Sufrin describes the jail. At the same time, those same assumptions about relations of care in detention shape our perceptions of those spaces as well. Recognizing that legal assistance rises to the level of critical care, and thus should be guaranteed to detainees, as well as how complex relations of care inform and are informed by these spaces are, I would argue, vitally important. This helps us better understand everyday frictions and contestation in and around carceral space, while also hopefully shifting who we see as necessary caregivers. Legal advocates in family detention did their work and moved through these spaces with a care not beholden to "dreaming up a world without lack" but rather seeking to "lighten what is heavy" such that "even if it fails it keeps on trying" (Mol, Moser, and Pols 2010b, 14). Through it all, they too resided in the struggle and remained, with devotion, in the fight.

REFERENCES

Abel, Richard L. 1995. *Politics by Other Means: Law in the Struggle against Apartheid, 1980–1994*. Routledge.

Agamben, Giorgio. 1998. *Homo Sacer: Sovereign Power and Bare Life*. Stanford University Press.

Agier, Michel, and David Fernbach. 2011. *Managing the Undesirables: Refugee Camps and Humanitarian Government*. Polity.

Agustín, Laura María. 2007. *Sex at the Margins: Migration, Labour Markets and the Rescue Industry*. Zed.

Ahmed, Sara. 2014. "Affective Economies." *Social Text* 22 (2): 117–39.

AILA. 2014. "Letter to President Obama Opposing Family Detention." September 25. https://www.aila.org/library/letter-to-obama-opposing-family-detention.

Ainsley, Julia. 2021. "In Court Filing, ICE Says It Is Effectively Ending Use of Family Detention." *NBC News*, March 6. https://www.nbcnews.com/politics/immigration/court-filing-ice-says-it-effectively-ending-use-family-detention-n1259818.

Ainsley, Julia. 2025. "Trump Administration Preparing to Restart Immigrant Family Detention." *NBC News*, February 7. https://www.nbcnews.com/politics/national-security/trump-administration-preparing-restart-immigrant-family-detention-rcna191230.

Akers Chacón, Justin. 2021. *The Border Crossed Us: The Case for Opening the US-Mexico Border*. Haymarket Books.

Alber, Erdmute, and Heike Drotbohm, eds. 2015. *Anthropological Perspectives on Care: Work, Kinship, and the Life Course*. Palgrave Macmillan.

American Civil Liberties Union. 2024. "New Report Exposes Rampant Abuse in Louisiana ICE Detention Facilities." ACLU, August 26. https://www.aclu.org/press-release/new-report-exposes-rampant-abuse-in-louisiana-ice-detention-facilities.

American Immigration Council. 2019. "A Primer on Expedited Removal." February 3. https://www.americanimmigrationcouncil.org/research/primer-expedited-removal.

American Immigration Council. 2024. "Fact Sheet: Asylum in the United States." January 15. https://www.americanimmigrationcouncil.org/research/asylum-united-states.

Anzaldúa, Gloria. 1987. *Borderlands/La Frontera*. Aunt Lute.

Arendt, Hannah. 1969. "Reflections on Violence." *Journal of International Affairs* 23 (1): 1–35.

"The Artesia Report." 2024. *Innovation Law Lab*. Accessed June 6. https://perma.cc/4CU6-WBWY.

Augustine-Adams, Kif, and D. Carolina Núñez. 2021. "Sites of Translation: The Credible Fear Process in United States Immigration Detention." *Georgetown Immigration Law Journal* 35 (2): 399.

Auyero, Javier. 2012. *Patients of the State: The Politics of Waiting in Argentina*. Duke University Press.

Backe, Emma L. 2018. "A Crisis of Care: The Politics and Therapeutics of a Rape Crisis Hotline." *Medical Anthropology Quarterly* 32 (4): 463–80.

Backe, Emma Louise. 2017. "Engagements with Ethnographic Care: Ethnographer as Activist." *Anthropology News*.

Bailey-Hall, Miara L., and Emily P. Estrada. 2022. "Private Immigration Detention without the Immigrants: The Subtle Use of Controlling Images in the Contemporary Era." *American Behavioral Scientist* 66 (12): 1645–68.

Baillot, Helen, Sharon Cowan, and Vanessa E. Munro. 2009. "Seen but Not Heard? Parallels and Dissonances in the Treatment of Rape Narratives across the Asylum and Criminal Justice Contexts." *Journal of Law and Society* 36 (2): 195–219.

Barrera, Oscar, Sergei Guriev, Emeric Henry, and Ekaterina Zhuravskaya. 2020. "Facts, Alternative Facts, and Fact Checking in Times of Post-Truth Politics." *Journal of Public Economics* 182.

Barrett, Dierdre, ed. 2016. *Trauma and Dreams*. Harvard University Press.

Bauer, Shane. 2018. "Today It Locks Up Immigrants. But CoreCivic's Roots Lie in the Brutal Past of America's Prisons." *Mother Jones*.

Bautista, Joann, Katie J. Bressler, and Nora R. Bosworth. 2019. "Immigration Detention: Perspectives from Maine Law Students Working on the Ground at the Laredo Detention Center in Texas." *Maine Law Review* 71:1.

Beckett, Greg. 2019. "Staying with the Feeling: Trauma, Humility, and Care in Ethnographic Fieldwork." *Anthrodendrum*, June 22. https://anthrodendum.org/2019/06/22/staying-with-the-feeling-trauma-humility-and-care-in-ethnographic-fieldwork/.

Berg, Ulla, Sebastian K. León, and Sarah Tosh. 2022. "Carceral Ethnography in a Time of Pandemic: Examining Migrant Detention and Deportation during COVID-19." *Ethnography* 25 (3).

Biehl, João Guliherme. 2005. *Vita: Life in a Zone of Social Abandonment*. University of California Press.

Biehl, João Guliherme. 2012. "Care and Disregard." In *A Companion to Moral Anthropology*, edited by Didier Fassin. Wiley-Blackwell.
Blanco, Maria del Pilar, and Esther Pereen, eds. 2013. *The Spectralities Reader: Ghosts and Haunting in Contemporary Cultural Theory*. Bloomsbury.
Boehm, Deborah, and Susan Terrio. 2019. *Illegal Encounters: The Effect of Detention and Deportation on Young People*. New York University Press.
Bonds, A. 2009. "Discipline and Devolution: Constructions of Poverty, Race, and Criminality in the Politics of Rural Prison Development." *Antipode* 41:416–38.
Boris, Eileen, and Rhacel Salazar Parreñas. 2010. *Intimate Labors: Cultures, Technologies, and the Politics of Care*. Stanford University Press.
Bosworth, Mary. 2017. "Penal Humanitarianism? Sovereign Power in an Era of Mass Migration." *New Criminal Law Review: An International and Interdisciplinary Journal* 20 (1): 29. https://doi.org/10.1525/nclr.2017.20.1.39.
Bosworth, Mary, and Andriani Fili. 2016. "Immigration Detention in Greece and the UK." In *Detaining the Immigrant Other: Global and Transnational Issues*, edited by Rich Furman, Douglass Epps, and Greg Lamphear. Oxford University Press.
Bourdieu, Pierre. 1986. "The Forms of Capital." In *Handbook of Theory and Research for the Sociology of Education*, edited by Maureen T. Hallinan. Springer.
Burnett, John. 2014. "Amid Wave of Child Immigrants, Reports of Abuse by Border Patrol." NPR. https://www.npr.org/2014/07/24/334041633/amid-wave-of-child-immigrants-reports-of-abuse-by-border-patrol.
Burridge, Andrew, and Nick Gill. 2016. "Conveyer-Belt Justice: Precarity, Access to Justice, and Uneven Geographies of Legal Aid in UK Asylum Appeals." *Antipode* 49 (1): 23–42.
Calhoun, Craig. 2010. "The Idea of Emergency: Humanitarian Action and Global (Dis)order." In *Contemporary States of Emergency: The Politics of Military and Humanitarian Interventions*, edited by Didier Fassin and Mariella Pandolfi. Zone.
Castañeda, Michelle, and Molly Crabapple. 2023. *Disappearing Rooms: The Hidden Theaters of Immigration Law*. Duke University Press.
Caswell, Lina M., and Emily Ruehs-Navarro. 2023. "Unaccompanied Undocumented Immigrant Children and the Structural and Legal Violence of the U.S. Immigration System." In *Children Crossing Borders: Latin American Migrant Childhood*, edited by Alejandra Josiowicz and Irasema Coronado. University of Arizona Press.
Chiovenda, Andrea, and Melissa Chiovenda. 2018. "The Specter of the 'Arrivant': Haunting of an Interethnic Conflict in Afghanistan." *Asian Anthropology* 17 (3).
Chishti, Muzaffar, and Faye Hipsmann. 2016. "Increased Central American Migration to the United States May Prove an Enduring Phenomenon." Migration Policy Institute, February 18. https://www.migrationpolicy.org/article/increased-central-american-migration-united-states-may-prove-enduring-phenomenon.
Cho, Eunice Hyunhye. 2021. "More of the Same: Private Prison Corporations and Immigrant Detention under the Biden Administration." ACLU, October 5.
Clifford, James. 1997a. "Museums as Contact Zones." In *Routes: Travel and Translation in the Late Twentieth Century*, 188–219. Harvard University Press.

Clifford, James. 1997b. *Routes: Travel and Translation in the Late Twentieth Century.* Harvard University Press.

CLINIC. 2019. "Local Organizations Speak Out against Locking Infants in Detention Centers." August 9. https://www.cliniclegal.org/stories/local-organizations-speak-out-against-locking-infants-detention-centers.

Coe, Cati. 2019. *The New American Servitude: Political Belonging among African Immigrant Home Care Workers.* New York University Press.

Comfort, Megan. 2008. *Doing Time Together: Love and Family in the Shadow of the Prison.* University of Chicago Press.

Conley, John M., and William M. O'Barr. 1990. *Rules versus Relationships: The Ethnography of Legal Discourse.* University of Chicago Press.

Conradson, David. 2003. "Spaces of Care in the City: The Place of a Community Drop-In Centre." *Social & Cultural Geography* 4 (4): 507–25. https://doi.org/10.1080/1464936032000137939.

Cook, Joanna, and Catherine Trundle. 2020. "Unsettled Care: Temporality, Subjectivity, and the Uneasy Ethics of Care." *Anthropology and Humanism* 45 (2): 178–83.

Cooper, Jessica. 2018. "Trapped: The Limits of Care in California's Mental Health Courts." *Social Justice* 44 (1): 121–41.

Coopmans, Catelijne, and Karen M. McNamara. 2020. "Care in Translation: Careful Research in Medical Settings." *East Asian Science, Technology and Society: An International Journal* 14 (1): 1–14. https://doi.org/10.1215/18752160-8193729.

CoreCivic Inc. 2024. "Detention Services." https://www.corecivic.com/safety/detention-services.

Cornejo, Kency. 2024. *Visual Disobedience: Art and Decoloniality in Central America.* Duke University Press.

Costantini, Cristina. 2015. "'Drink More Water': Horror Stories from the Medical Ward of a Texas Immigration Detention Center." Fusion. https://fusion.tv/story/165837/dilley-detention-center-horror-stories-from-the-medical-ward/.

Coutin, Susan B. 2000. *Legalizing Moves: Salvadoran Immigrants' Struggle for U.S. Residency.* University of Michigan Press.

Cullison, Jennifer. 2020. "Valley of Caged Immigrants: Punishment, Protest, and the Rise of the Port Isabel Detention Center." *Tabula Rasa.*

Cunningham, Clark D. 1992. "Lawyer as Translator, Representation as Text: Toward an Ethnography of Legal Discourse." *Cornell Law Review* 77:1298–387.

Cvetkovich, Ann. 2012. *Depression: A Public Feeling.* Duke University Press.

Danze, Alicia, Rebecca Maria Torres, and Caroline Faria. 2021. "Contesting Invisibility of Immigrant Detention Landscapes in Texas." In *The Routledge Handbook of Development and Environment,* 128–42. Routledge.

Dayan, Colin. 2011. *The Law Is a White Dog: How Legal Rituals Make and Unmake Persons.* Princeton University Press.

De Certeau, Michel. 1984. *The Practice of Everyday Life.* University of California Press.

DeGenova, Nicholas. 2016. "Detention, Deportation, and Waiting: Toward a Theory of Migrant Detainability." Global Detention Project Working Paper 18. Global Detention Project.

DeGenova, Nicholas, and Nathalie Mae Peutz. 2010. *The Deportation Regime: Sovereignty, Space, and the Freedom of Movement*. Duke University Press.

Del Bosque, Melissa. 2014. "As Feds Lock Up More Immigrant Families, Abuse Allegations Grow." *Texas Observer*, November 4. https://www.texasobserver.org/grow-number-abuse-cases-immigrant-family-detention-facilities/.

Delgado, Richard. 1989. "Legal Storytelling for Oppositionists and Others: A Plea for Narrative." *Michigan Law Review* 87:2411.

Department of Homeland Security Press Office. 2015. "Fiscal Year 2015 Six Month Border Security Update Statement by Secretary Johnson." DHS.gov, April 24. https://www.dhs.gov/archive/news/2015/04/24/fiscal-year-2015-six-month-border-security-update.

Derrida, Jacques. 1994. *Specters of Marx: The State of Debt, the Working of Mourning, and the New International*. Routledge.

Detention Watch Network and Heartland Alliance's National Immigrant Justice Center. 2018. "ICE Lies: Public Deception, Private Profit." January.

Douglas, Mary. 1971. "Do Dogs Laugh? A Cross-Cultural Approach to Body Symbolism." *Journal of Psychosomatic Research* 15:387–90.

Dow, Mark. 2005. *American Gulag: Inside U.S. Immigration Prisons*. University of California Press.

Dow, Mark. 2007. "Designed to Punish: Immigrant Detention and Deportation." *Social Research* 74 (2): 533–46.

Dowling, Julie A., and Jonathan Xavier Inda, eds. 2013. *Governing Immigration through Crime: A Reader*. Stanford University Press.

Dunbar-Ortiz, Roxanne. 2021. *Not a Nation of Immigrants: Settler Colonialism, White Supremacy, and a History of Erasure and Exclusion*. Beacon.

Eagly, Ingrid V., and Steven Shafer. 2015. "A National Study of Access to Counsel in Immigration Court." *University of Pennsylvania Law Review* 164:1–91.

Eagly, Ingrid, and Steven Shafer. 2016. "Access to Counsel in Immigration Court." *American Immigration Council*, September 28. https://www.americanimmigrationcouncil.org/research/access-counsel-immigration-court.

Ewick, Patricia, and Susan S. Silbey. 1995. "Subversive Stories and Hegemonic Tales: Toward a Sociology of Narrative." *Law and Society Review* 197.

"Fact Sheet: A Review by the Family Reunification Task Force on the Second Anniversary of Its Establishment." 2023. Department of Homeland Security, February 2. https://www.dhs.gov/archive/news/2023/02/02/fact-sheet-review-family-reunification-task-force-second-anniversary.

Farmer, Paul. 2005. *Pathologies of Power: Health, Human Rights, and the New War on the Poor*. University of California Press.

Fassin, Didier. 2005. "The Truth from the Body: Medical Certificates as Ultimate Evidence for Asylum Seekers." *American Anthropologist* 107:4.

Fassin, Didier. 2007. *When Bodies Remember: Experiences and Politics of AIDS in South Africa*. University of California Press.

Fassin, Didier. 2011. "*Noli Me Tangere*: The Moral Untouchability of Humanitarianism." In *Forces of Compassion: Humanitarianism between Ethics and Politics*, edited by Erica Bornstein and Peter Redfield. School for Advanced Research.

Fassin, Didier. 2012. *Humanitarian Reason: A Moral History to the Present*. University of California Press.

Fassin, Didier. 2016. *Prison Worlds: An Ethnography of the Carceral Condition*. Polity.

Fassin, Didier, and Patrick Brown. 2015. *At the Heart of the State: The Moral World of Institutions*. Pluto Press.

Fassin, Didier, and Estelle D'Halluin. 2007. "Critical Evidence: The Politics of Trauma in French Asylum Policies." *Ethos* 35 (3): 300–329.

Fassin, Didier, and Mariella Pandolfi. 2010. *Contemporary States of Emergency: The Politics of Military and Humanitarian Interventions*. Zone.

Fassin, Didier, and Richard Rechtman. 2009. *The Empire of Trauma: An Inquiry into the Condition of Victimhood*. Princeton University Press.

Feldman, Ilana, and Miriam Ticktin, eds. 2010. *In the Name of Humanity: The Government of Threat and Care*. Duke University Press.

Flagg, Anna, and Andrew R. Calderón. 2020. "500,000 Kids, 30 Million Hours: Trump's Vast Expansion of Child Detention." Marshall Project, October 30. https://www.themarshallproject.org/2020/10/30/500-000-kids-30-million-hours-trump-s-vast-expansion-of-child-detention.

Fobear, Katherine. 2015. "'I Thought We Had No Rights': Challenges in Listening, Storytelling, and Representation of LGBT Refugees." *Studies in Social Justice* 9 (1): 102–17.

Foucault, Michel. 1977. *Discipline and Punish: The Birth of the Prison*. Translated by Alan Sheridan. Vintage Books.

Furman, Rich, Douglas Epps, and Greg Lamphear. 2016. *Detaining the Immigrant Other: Global and Transnational Issues*. Oxford University Press.

Galli, Chiara. 2023. *Precarious Protections: Unaccompanied Minors Seeking Asylum in the United States*. University of California Press.

Garcia, Angela. 2010. *The Pastoral Clinic: Addiction and Dispossession along the Rio Grande*. University of California Press.

García, Uriel J. 2025. "Justice Department Restarts Legal Aid Programs for Detained Immigrants." *Texas Tribune*, February 4. https://www.texastribune.org/2025/02/04/texas-immigrant-legal-aid-federal-program-department-justice/.

García Hernández, César Cuauhtémoc. 2019. *Migrating to Prison: America's Obsession with Locking Up Immigrants*. New Press.

Gill, Nicholas. 2009. "Longing for Stillness: The Forced Movement of Asylum Seekers." *M/C Journal* 12 (1). https://journal.media-culture.org.au/index.php/mcjournal/article/viewArticle/123.

Gilmore, Ruth Wilson. 2007. *Golden Gulag: Prisons, Surplus, Crisis, and Opposition in Globalizing California*. University of California Press.

Goffman, Erving. 1959. *The Presentation of Self in Everyday Life*. Bantam Doubleday Dell.

Golash-Boza, Tanya. 2010. "The Criminalization of Undocumented Migrants: Legalities and Realities." *Societies without Borders* 5 (1): 81–90.

Golash-Boza, Tanya M. 2019. "Punishment Beyond the Deportee: The Collateral Consequences of Deportation." *American Behavioral Scientist* 63:1331–49.

Gomberg-Muñoz, Ruth. 2018. "Come to Terms: Accomplices." *Journal of the Anthropology of North America* 21 (1): 25–27.

Gómez, Laura. 2018. "Deaths of Migrant Kids Underscore Risks of *Hieleras*." *Arizona Mirror*, December 28. https://www.azmirror.com/2018/12/28/deaths-of-migrant-kids-underscore-risks-of-hieleras/.

Gonzales, Alfonso. 2013. *Reform without Justice: Latino Migrant Politics and the Homeland Security State*. Oxford University Press.

Good, Anthony. 2006. *Anthropology and Expertise in the British Asylum Courts*. Routledge-Cavendish.

Gordon, Avery F. 2008. *Ghostly Matters: Haunting and the Sociological Imagination*. University of Minnesota Press.

Gordon, Avery F. 2011. "Some Thoughts on Haunting and Futurity." *Borderlands* 10:2.

Götsch, Barbara, and Monika Palmberger. 2022. "The Nexus of Anthropology and Narrative: Ethnographic Encounters with Storytelling Practices." *Narrative Culture* 9 (1): 1–22.

Govindrajan, Radhika. 2022. "Spectral Justice." In *The Promise of Multispecies Justice*, edited by Sophie Chao, Karin Bolender, and Eben Kirksey. Duke University Press.

Granfield, Robert. 1992. *Making Elite Lawyers: Visions of Law at Harvard and Beyond*. Routledge.

Greenberg, Max A. 2019. *Twelve Weeks to Change a Life: At-Risk Youth in a Fractured State*. University of California Press.

Greene, Daniel. 2021. *The Promise of Access: Technology, Inequality, and the Political Economy of Hope*. MIT Press.

Greenhouse, Carol J., Elizabeth Mertz, and Kay B. Warren. 2002. *Ethnography in Unstable Places: Everyday Lives in Contexts of Dramatic Political Change*. Duke University Press.

Gupta, Akhil. 2012. *Red Tape: Bureaucracy, Structural Violence, and Poverty in India*. Duke University Press.

Haas, Bridget Marie. 2023. *Suspended Lives: Navigating Everyday Violence in the US Asylum System*. University of California Press.

Hall, Alexandra. 2012. *Border Watch: Cultures of Immigration, Detention and Control*. Pluto Press.

Hamilakis, Yannis. 2018. *The New Nomadic Age: Archaeologies of Forced and Undocumented Migration*. Equinox Publishing.

Hamington, Maurice. 2004. *Embodied Care: Jane Addams, Maurice Merleau-Ponty, and Feminist Ethics*. University of Illinois Press.

Hannaford, Dinah. 2023. *Aid and the Help: International Development and the Transnational Extraction of Care.* Stanford University Press.

Haraway, Donna. 2016. *Staying with the Trouble: Making Kin in the Chthulucene.* Duke University Press.

Harris, Lindsay M. 2018. "Contemporary Family Detention and Legal Advocacy." *Harvard Latinx Law Review* 21.

Hayden, Dolores. 1995. *The Power of Place: Urban Landscapes as Public History.* MIT Press.

Heidbrink, Lauren. 2014. *Migrant Youth, Transnational Families, and the State: Care and Contested Interests.* University of Pennsylvania Press.

Henderson, Lynne. 1987. "Legality and Empathy." *Michigan Law Review* 85 (7): 1574–653.

Hernández, C. C. G. 2015. "Naturalizing Immigration Imprisonment." *California Law Review* 103 (6): 1449–514.

Heyman, Josiah. 2011. "An Academic in Activist Coalition: Recognizing and Bridging Role Conflicts." *Annals of Anthropological Practice* 35:136–53.

Heyman, Josiah. 2024. "Accompaniment as Moral and Political Practices: Possibilities and Challenges." In *Accompaniment with Im/migrant Communities: Engaged Ethnography,* edited by Kristin E. Yarris and Whitney L. Duncan. University of Arizona Press.

Hiemstra, Nancy. 2019. *Detain and Deport: The Chaotic U.S. Immigration Enforcement Regime.* University of Georgia Press.

Hinton, Devon E. 2009. "Introduction to the Special Section: Nightmares of Trauma Victims—Cross-Cultural Perspectives." *Culture, Medicine, and Psychiatry* 33: 216–18.

Hochschild, Arlie Russell. 1983. *The Managed Heart: Commercialization of Human Feeling.* University of California Press.

Hollan, Douglas. 2009. "The Influence of Culture on the Experience and Interpretation of Disturbing Dreams." *Culture, Medicine, and Psychiatry* 33:313–22.

Hollan, Douglas. 2019. "Who Is Haunted by Whom? Steps to an Ecology of Haunting." *Ethos* 47:4.

Horton, John, and Peter Kraftl. 2009. "Small Acts, Kind Words, and 'Not Too Much Fuss': Implicit Activisms." *Emotions, Space and Society* 2 (1): 14–23.

Horton, Sarah. 2016. *They Leave Their Kidneys in the Fields: Illness, Injury, and Illegality among U.S. Farmworkers.* University of California Press.

Horton, Sarah. 2024. "'Being-With,' 'Doing For,' and 'Doing With': An Accompaniment Approach to Applied Research." In *Accompaniment with Im/migrant Communities,* edited by Kristin E. Yarris and Whitney L. Duncan. University of Arizona Press.

Huey, Laura, Kevin Walby, and Aaron Doyle. 2006. "Cop Watching in the Downtown Eastside." In *Surveillance and Security,* edited by Torin Monahan. Rutgers University Press.

Human Rights First. 2022. "Inadequate Access to Legal Representation, Rushed Timelines Impede Meaningful Opportunity to Seek Asylum under New Asylum Processing Rule." September 14. https://humanrightsfirst.org/library/inadequate-access-to-legal-representation-rushed-timeline-impede-meaningful-opportunity-to-seek-asylum-under-new-asylum-processing-rule/.

Human Rights Watch. 2009. *Locked Up Far Away: The Transfer of Immigrants to Remote Detention Centers in the United States.* https://www.hrw.org/report/2009/12/02/locked-far-away/transfer-immigrants-remote-detention-centers-united-states.

Human Rights Watch. 2017. *Systemic Indifference: Dangerous and Substandard Medical Care in U.S. Immigration Detention.* https://www.hrw.org/report/2017/05/08/systemic-indifference/danger-substandard-medical-care-us-immigration-detention.

Human Rights Watch. 2024. "US: Lasting Harm from Family Separation at the Border." Human Rights Watch, December 16. https://www.hrw.org/news/2024/12/16/us-lasting-harm-family-separation-border.

Hunleth, Jean. 2019. "Zambian Children's Imaginal Caring: On Fantasy, Play, and Anticipation in an Epidemic." *Cultural Anthropology* 34 (2): 155–86. https://doi.org/10.14506/ca34.2.01.

Hurston, Zora Neale. 1981. *The Sanctified Church.* Turtle Island.

Ibsen, Alexander Z. 2013. "Ruling by Favors: Prison Guards' Informal Exercise of Institutional Control." *Law & Social Inquiry* 38:342–63.

ICE (Immigration and Customs Enforcement). N.d. "PREA." Accessed March 16, 2021. https://www.ice.gov/detain/prea.

Immigration and Customs Enforcement. 2024. "ICE Enforcement and Removal Operations Statistics." https://www.ice.gov/spotlight/statistics.

Ina, Satsuki. 2021. "A Cage Is Still a Cage: President Biden Must End U.S. Detention of Children and Families." *Time,* March 11. https://time.com/5945307/biden-end-detention-migrant-children/.

INCITE! Women of Color against Violence. 2007. *The Revolution Will Not Be Funded: Beyond the Non-Profit Industrial Complex.* South End Press.

Ioanide, Paula. 2015. *The Emotional Politics of Racism: How Feelings Trump Facts in an Era of Colorblindness.* Stanford University Press.

James, Deborah, and Evan Killick. 2012. "Empathy and Expertise: Case Workers and Immigration/Asylum Applicants in London." *Law and Social Inquiry* 37 (2): 430–55.

Jones, Gareth A., and Dennis Rodgers. 2019. "Ethnographies and/of Violence." *Ethnography* 20 (3): 297–319. https://www.jstor.org/stable/26775257.

Jones, Reece. 2017. *Violence Borders: Refugees and the Right to Move.* Verso.

Jordan, Miriam, Katie Benner, Ron Nixon, and Caitlin Dickerson. 2018. "As Migrant Families Are Reunited, Some Children Don't Recognize Their Mothers." *New York Times,* July 10. https://www.nytimes.com/2018/07/10/us/politics/trump-administration-catch-and-release-migrants.html.

Just Future Project. 2018. "What Is a Shadow Prison?" https://ajustfuture.org/what-is-a-shadow-prison/.

Kaplan, Amit. 2022. "'Just Let It Pass By and It Will Fall on Some Woman': Invisible Work in the Labor Market." *Gender & Society* 36 (6): 838–68.

Keats, Patrice A. 2005. "Vicarious Witnessing in European Concentration Camps: Imagining the Trauma of Another." *Traumatology* 11 (3): 171–87.

Kehr, Janina. 2018. "Colonial Hauntings: Migrant Care in a French Hospital." *Medical Anthropology* 37 (8): 659–73.

Khan, Aisha. 2022. "The Carceral State: An American Story." *Annual Review of Anthropology* 51:49–66. https://doi.org/10.1146/annurev-anthro-041420-013930.

Kirmayer, Laurence J. 2009. "Nightmares, Neurophenomenology and the Cultural Logic of Trauma." *Culture, Medicine, and Psychiatry* 33:323–31.

Kisiara, Otieno. 2015. "Marginalized at the Centre: How Public Narratives of Suffering Perpetuate Perceptions of Refugees' Helplessness and Dependency." *Migration Letters* 12 (2): 162–71.

Kittay, Eva Feder, and Ellen K. Feder, eds. 2002. *The Subject of Care: Feminist Perspectives on Dependency*. Rowman & Littlefield.

Kleinman, Arthur. 2024. "Paul Farmer and the Audacity of Accompaniment: Reflecting on Paul Farmer's Extraordinary Legacy." Think Global Health, February 21. https://www.thinkglobalhealth.org/article/paul-farmer-and-audacity-accompaniment.

Kohn, Steffen. 2016. *Mediating Mobility: Visual Anthropology in the Age of Migration*. Columbia University Press.

Lakhani, Sarah. 2013. "Producing Immigrant Victims' 'Right' to Legal Status and the Management of Legal Uncertainty." *Law & Social Inquiry* 38 (2): 442–73.

Lakhani, Sarah. 2014. "From Problems of Living to Problems of Law: The Legal Translation and Documentation of Immigrant Abuse and Helpfulness." *Law & Social Inquiry* 39 (3): 643–65.

Laliberté, Nicole, and Carolin Schurr. 2015. "Introduction." *Gender, Place & Culture* 23 (1): 72–78.

Laughland, Oliver. 2016. "US Detention Facility Restricts Use of Crayons for Migrant Children." *The Guardian*, November 17.

Lawson, Victoria. 2007. "Geographies of Care and Responsibility." *Annals of the Association of American Geographers* 97 (1): 1–11.

Libal, Bob, Lauren Martín, and Nicole Porter. 2012. "'A Prison Is Not a Home': Notes from the Campaign to End Immigration Family Detention." In *Beyond Walls and Cages: Prisons, Borders, and Global Crisis*, 253–65. University of Georgia Press.

Linde, Charlotte. 1993. *Life Stories: The Creation of Coherence*. Oxford University Press.

Livingston, Julie. 2012. *Improvising Medicine: An African Oncology Ward in an Emerging Cancer Epidemic*. Duke University Press.

Longazel, Jamie, Jake Berman, and Benjamin Fleury-Steiner. 2016. "The Pains of Immigrant Imprisonment." *Sociology Compass* 10:989–98.

López Ricoy, Ana, Abigail Andrews, and Alejandra Medina. 2022. "Exit as Care: How Motherhood Mediates Women's Exodus from Violence in Mexico and Central America." *Violence against Women* 28 (1): 211–31.

Low, Setha M. 2009. "Towards an Anthropological Theory of Space and Place." *Semiotica* 175:21–37. https://doi.org/10.1515/semi.2009.041.

Loyd, Jenna M., and Alison Mountz. 2018. *Boats, Borders, and Bases: Race, the Cold War, and the Rise of Migration Detention in the United States.* University of California Press.

Lukens, Michael. 2024. "Opinion: The Need for More Immigration Attorneys in the Deep South Was Already Urgent. After the SPLC Layoffs, It's a Full-Blown Crisis." Prism, July 15. https://prismreports.org/2024/07/15/deep-south-immigration-attorney-crisis-splc-layoffs/.

Luz Ibarra, María de la. 2013. "Frontline Activists: Mexicana Care Workers, Subjectivity, and the Defense of the Elderly." *Medical Anthropology Quarterly* 27 (3): 434–52.

Lytle Hernandez, Kelly. 2017. *City of Inmates: Conquest, Rebellion, and the Rise of Human Caging in Los Angeles, 1771–1965.* University of North Carolina Press.

Macías-Rojas, Patrisia. 2016. *From Deportation to Prison: The Politics of Immigration Enforcement in Post–Civil Rights America.* New York University Press.

Mainwaring, Cetta, and Stephanie J. Silverman. 2017. "Detention-as-Spectacle." *International Political Sociology* 11 (1): 21–38.

Malkki, Liisa. 1996. "Speechless Emissaries: Refugees, Humanitarianism, and Dehistoricization." *Cultural Anthropology* 11 (3): 377–404.

Malkki, Liisa. 2015. *The Need to Help: The Domestic Arts of International Humanitarianism.* Duke University Press.

Mares, Sarah. 2020. "Mental Health Consequences of Detaining Children and Families Who Seek Asylum: A Scoping Review." *European Child Adolescent Psychiatry* 30:1615–39.

Martin, Lauren. 2012a. "'Catch and Remove': Detention, Deterrence, and Discipline in US Noncitizen Family Detention Practice." *Geopolitics* 17 (2): 312–34.

Martin, Lauren. 2012b. "Governing through the Family: Struggles of US Noncitizen Family Detention Policy." *Environment and Planning* 44:866–88.

Martin, Lauren. 2015. "Noncitizen Detention Spatial Strategies of Migrant Precarity in US Immigration and Border Control." *Annales de géographie* 702–3:231–47.

Martinez-Aranda, Mirian G. 2020. "Collective Liminality: The Spillover Effects of Indeterminate Detention on Immigrant Families." *Law & Society Review* 54 (4): 755–87.

Matoesian, Gregory M. 2001. *Law and the Language of Identity: Discourse in the William Kennedy Smith Rape Trial.* Oxford University Press.

Mattingly, Cheryl. 2010. *The Paradox of Hope: Journeys through a Clinical Borderland.* University of California Press.

McCulloch, Jude, and Sharon Pickering. 2009. "The Violence of Refugee Incarceration." In *The Violence of Incarceration*, edited by Phil Scraton and Jude McCulloch. Routledge.

McKinley, Michelle. 1997. "Life Stories, Disclosure, and the Law." *PoLAR* 20 (2): 70–82.

McNeillie, Natalie, and John Rose. 2021. "Vicarious Trauma in Therapists: A Meta-ethnographic Review." *Behavioural and Cognitive Psychotherapy* 49 (4): 426–40.

Menjívar, Cecilia, and Leisy Abrego. 2012. "Legal Violence: Immigration Law and the Lives of Central American Immigrants." *American Journal of Sociology* 117:5.

Menjívar, Cecilia, and Shannon Drysdale Walsh. 2019. "Gender, Violence and Migration." In *Handbook on Critical Geographies of Migration*, 1–16. Edward Elgar.

Merry, Sally Engle. 1990. *Getting Justice and Getting Even: Legal Consciousness among Working-Class Americans*. University of Chicago Press.

Merry, Sally Engle. 2006. *Human Rights and Gender Violence: Translating International Law into Local Justice*. University of Chicago Press.

Merry, Sally Engle. 2007. Introduction to *The Practice of Human Rights: Tracking Law between the Global and the Local*, edited by Mark Goodale and Sally Engle Merry. Cambridge University Press.

Mertz, Elizabeth. 2007. *The Language of Law School: Learning to "Think like a Lawyer."* Oxford University Press.

Millbank, Jenni. 2009. "'The Ring of Truth': A Case Study of Credibility Assessment in Particular Social Group Refugee Determinations." *International Journal of Refugee Law* 21 (1): 1–33. https://doi.org/10.1093/ijrl/een040.

Miller, Lucy. 2018. "Feelings Trump Facts: Affect and the Rhetoric of Donald Trump." In *Affect, Emotion, and Rhetorical Persuasion in Mass Communication*, edited by Lei Zhang and Carlton Clark. Routledge.

Miner, Horace. 1956. "Body Ritual among the Nacirema." *American Anthropologist* 58:503–7.

Minian, Ana Raquel. 2024. *In the Shadow of Liberty: The Invisible History of Immigrant Detention in the United States*. Viking.

Miroff, Nick. 2024. "Trump's Top Border Adviser Says He Will Bring Back Family Detention." *Washington Post*, December 24. https://www.washingtonpost.com/immigration/2024/12/26/immigration-border-tom-homan-trump/.

Miyazaki, Hirokazu. 2004. *The Method of Hope: Anthropology, Philosophy, and Fijian Knowledge*. Stanford University Press.

Mol, Annemarie. 2008. *The Logic of Care: Health and the Problem of Patient Choice*. Routledge.

Mol, Annemarie. 2010. "Care and Its Values: Good Food in the Nursing Home." In *Care in Practice: On Tinkering in Clinics, Homes, and Farms*, edited by Annemarie Mol, Ingunn Moser, and Jeannette Pols. Transcript Verlag.

Mol, Annemarie, Ingunn Moser, and Jeannette Pols. 2010a. *Care in Practice: On Tinkering in Clinics, Homes, and Farms*. Transcript Verlag.

Mol, Annemarie, Ingunn Moser, and Jeannette Pols. 2010b. "Care: Putting Practice into Theory." In *Care in Practice: On Tinkering in Clinics, Homes, and Farms*, edited by Annemarie Mol, Ingunn Moser, and Jeannette Pols. Transcript Verlag.

Mountz, Alison. 2010. *Seeking Asylum: Human Smuggling and Bureaucracy at the Border*. University of Minnesota Press.

Mountz, Alison. 2012. "Mapping Remote Detention: Dis/location through Isolation." In *Beyond Walls and Cages: Prisons, Borders, and Global Crisis*, edited by Jenna M. Loyd, Matt Mitchelson, and Andrew Burridge. University of Georgia Press.

Mountz, Alison, Kate Coddington, R. Tina Catania, and Jenna M. Lloyd. 2012. "Conceptualizing Detention: Mobility, Containment, Bordering, and Exclusion." *Progress in Human Geography* 37:522–41.

Mountz, Alison, and Nancy Hiemstra. 2013. "Chaos and Crisis: Dissecting the Spatiotemporal Logics of Contemporary Migrations and State Practices." *Annals of the Association of American Geographers* 104 (2): 382–90.

"MSNBC Town Hall Participant Yells Question Out of Turn to Hillary Clinton." 2016. YouTube, April 25. https://youtube.com/watch?time_continue=1&v=Nh8MzdG0AcM&feature=emb_logo.

Mulla, Sameena. 2014. *The Violence of Care: Rape Victims, Forensic Nurses, and Sexual Assault Intervention.* New York University Press.

Munn, Nancy. 1992. "The Cultural Anthropology of Time: A Critical Essay." *Annual Review of Anthropology* 21:93–123.

Murphy, Michelle. 2015. "Unsettling Care: Troubling Transnational Itineraries of Care in Feminist Health Practices." *Social Studies of Science* 45 (5): 717–37. www.jstor.org/stable/43829053.

Murray, Marjorie, Sofía Bowen, Marisol Verdugo, and Jona Holtmannspötter. 2017. "Care and Relatedness among Rural Mapuche Women: Issues of *Cariño* and Empathy." *Ethos* 45 (3): 367–85.

National Immigrant Justice Center. 2023. "Obstructed Legal Access: June 2023 Update." June 20. https://immigrantjustice.org/staff/blog/obstructed-legal-access-june-2023-update.

National Immigration Justice Center. 2024. "Access to Counsel." https://immigrantjustice.org/issues/access-counsel.

National Immigration Law Center. 2016. "Blazing a Trail: The Fight for Right to Counsel in Detention and Beyond." https://www.nilc.org/wp-content/uploads/2016/04/Right-to-Counsel-Blazing-a-Trail-2016-03.pdf.

Nayak, Meghana. 2015. *Who Is Worthy of Protection? Gender-Based Asylum and US Immigration Politics.* Oxford University Press.

Noguchi, Yuki. 2019. "Unequal Outcomes: Most ICE Detainees Held in Rural Areas Where Deportation Risks Soar." NPR, August 15. https://www.npr.org/2019/08/15/748764322/unequal-outcomes-most-ice-detainees-held-in-rural-areas-where-deportation-risks.

Nuñez-Janes, Mariela, Mario Ovalle, and Stephanie Plancarte. 2018. "Creating Sanctuary: Practices of *Acompañamiento*." https://culanth.org/fieldsights/creating-sanctuary-practices-of-acompanamiento.

Office of the Vice President. 2014. "Remarks to the Press with Q&A by Vice President Joe Biden in Guatemala." June 20. https://obamawhitehouse.archives.gov/the-press-office/2014/06/20/remarks-press-qa-vice-president-joe-biden-guatemala.

Patler, Caitlin, and Tanya Maria Golash-Boza. 2017. "The Fiscal and Human Costs of Immigrant Detention and Deportation in the United States." *Sociology Compass* 11 (11): e12536.

Paulsen, Krista E. 2009. "Ethnography of the Ephemeral: Studying Temporary Sciences through Individual and Collective Approaches." *Social Identities* 15 (4): 509–24.

Peak, Kenneth J. 2023. "The Inmates World: The 'Keepers' and the 'Kept.'" In *Introduction to Criminal Justice*. Sage.

Pedroza, Juan, Stephanie Potochnick, and Robert Santillano. 2025. "The 2016 United States Election and Financial Support to Migrant-Serving Legal-Aid Organizations." *International Migration Review*. https://doi.org/10.1177/01979183241309573.

Perkinson, Robert. 2010. *Texas Tough: The Rise of America's Prison Empire*. Metropolitan Books.

Peterie, Michelle. 2024. *Immigrant Detention and Social Harm: The Collateral Impacts of Migrant Detention*. Routledge.

Pierce, Jennifer. 1995. *Gender Trials: Emotional Lives in Contemporary Law Firms*. University of California Press.

Pierce, Jennifer. 1999. "Emotional Labor among Paralegals." *Annals of the American Academy of Political and Social Science* 561:127–42.

Polychroniou, Ariadni. 2021. "Towards a Critical Reconstruction of Modern Refugee Subjectivity: Overcoming the Threat-Victim Bipolarity with Judith Butler and Giorgio Agamben." *Open Philosophy* 4 (1): 252–68.

Pottinger, Laura. 2017. "Planting the Seed of a Quiet Activism." *Area* 49 (2): 215–22.

Preston, Julia. 2014. "Detention Center Presented as Deterrent to Border Crossings." *New York Times*, December 15. https://www.nytimes.com/2014/12/16/us/homeland-security-chief-opens-largest-immigration-detention-center-in-us.html.

Preston, Julia. 2015. "Judge Orders Release of Immigrant Children Detained by the U.S." *New York Times*, July 25. https://www.nytimes.com/2015/07/26/us/detained-immigrant-children-judge-dolly-gee-ruling.html.

Puig de la Bellacasa, María. 2012. "'Nothing Comes without Its World': Thinking with Care." *Sociological Review* 60:197–216.

Puig de la Bellacasa, María. 2017. *Matters of Care: Speculative Ethics in More than Human Worlds*. University of Minnesota Press.

Rabben, Linda. 2016. *Sanctuary and Asylum: A Social and Political History*. University of Washington Press.

RAICES T. N.d. "To: Immigration and Customs Enforcement: End the Crayon Ban at Karnes Family Detention Center." Mijente. Accessed March 16, 2021. https://action.mijente.net/petitions/end-the-crayon-ban-at-karnes.

Redfield, Peter. 2013. *Life in Crisis: The Ethical Journey of Doctors without Borders*. University of California Press.

Reed, Adam. 2003. *Papua New Guinea's Last Place: Experiences of Constraint in a Postcolonial Prison*. Berghahn.

Rhodes, Lorna A. 2001. "Toward an Anthropology of Prisons." *Annual Review of Anthropology* 30:65–83.

Rhodes, Lorna A. 2004. *Total Confinement: Madness and Reason in the Maximum Security Prison*. University of California Press.

Richardson, Miles. 1982. "Being-in-the-Plaza versus Being-in-the-Market: Material Culture and the Construction of Social Reality." *American Ethnologist* 9: 421–36.

Richland, Justin. 2008. *Arguing with Tradition: The Language of Law in Hopi Tribal Courts*. University of Chicago Press.

"The Right to Be Heard from Immigration Prisons: Locating a Right of Access to Counsel for Immigrant Detainees in the Right of Access to Courts." 2018. *Harvard Law Review* 132 (2): 726–47.

Rosenblum, Marc R., and Isabell Ball. 2016. "Trends in Unaccompanied Child and Family Migration from Central America." Migration Policy Institute Fact Sheet, January. https://www.migrationpolicy.org/sites/default/files/publications/UnaccompaniedMinors-Factsheet-FINAL.pdf.

Routon, Erin. 2024. "A Reliable Narrator." *Anthropology News*, April 30.

Routon, Erin. 2025. "A Vicarious Scar: Secondary Trauma and Ethnographic Care in Fieldwork." *American Ethnologist*, February 6.

Rozakou, Katerina. 2012. "The Biopolitics of Hospitality in Greece: Humanitarianism and the Management of Refugees." *American Ethnologist* 39 (3): 562–77.

Ryan, Dermot A., Fiona E. Kelly, and Brendan D. Kelly. 2009. "Mental Health among Persons Awaiting an Asylum Outcome in Western Countries: A Literature Review." *International Journal of Mental Health* 38 (3): 88–111.

Ryo, Emily. 2017. "Fostering Legal Cynicism through Immigrant Detention." *Southern California Law Review* 90:999–1053.

Ryo, Emily. 2018. "Representing Immigrants: The Role of Lawyers in Immigration Bond Hearings." *Law & Society Review* 52:503–31.

Ryo, Emily, and Ian Peacock. 2018a. "Beyond the Walls: The Importance of Community Contexts in Immigrant Detention." *American Behavioral Scientist*, July 19.

Ryo, Emily, and Ian Peacock. 2018b. "The Landscape of Immigration Detention in the U.S." *American Immigration Council*, December.

Sakuma, Amanda. 2015. "The Failed Experiment of Immigrant Family Detention." MSNBC, August 3. https://www.msnbc.com/msnbc/failed-experiment-immigrant-family-detention.

Sampson, R. C., and G. Mitchell. 2013. "Global Trends in Immigration: Detention and Alternatives to Detention: Practical, Political and Symbolic Rationales." *Journal on Migration and Human Security* 2 (3): 98–102.

Sanchez, Sandra. 2021. "Denial of Asylum Often Depends on the Region in Which Migrants Live, Report Finds." Border Report, December 17. https://www.borderreport.com/immigration/denial-of-asylum-often-depends-on-the-region-in-which-migrants-live-report-finds/.

Sanchez, Sandra. 2024a. "Fast-Growing Number of Asylum Seekers Face Shortage of Immigration Lawyers, Study Finds." Border Report, February 7.

Sanchez, Sandra. 2024b. "ICE to Close Nation's Largest Migrant Detention Center in South Texas." Border Report, June 21. https://www.borderreport.com/immigration/migrant-centers/ice-to-close-nations-largest-migrant-detention-center-in-south-texas/.

Sanchez, Sandra. 2024c. "Report: Disparate Swings in Asylum Outcomes by US Immigration Judges." Border Report, December 6. https://www.borderreport.com/immigration/report-disparate-swings-in-asylum-outcomes-by-us-immigration-judges/.

Sandoval, Edgar. 2024. "A New Challenge for Asylum Seekers: Lawyer Shortages." *New York Times*, May 19. https://www.nytimes.com/2024/05/19/us/migrants-lawyer-shortages.html.

Sangaramoorthy, Thurka. 2023. *Landscapes of Care: Immigration and Health in Rural America*. University of North Carolina Press.

Santiago, Leyla. 2018. "Migrant Mother Gabriela Hernandez Is Almost Relieved to Be in Detention after a Hellish Journey through Mexico." GEO Group, May 11. https://www.geogroup.com/geo-news/migrant-mother-gabriela-hernandez-is-almost-relieved-to-be-in-detention-after-a-hellish-journey-through-mexico/.

Sarat, Austin, and Stuart A. Scheingold. 2004. *Something to Believe In: Politics, Professionalism, and Cause Lawyering*. Stanford Law and Politics.

Sarat, Austin, and Stuart A. Scheingold. 2005. *The Worlds Cause Lawyers Make: Structure and Agency in Legal Practice*. Stanford Law and Politics.

Saunders, Natasha, and Tamara Al-Om. 2022. "Slow Resistance: Resisting the Slow Violence of Asylum." *Millenium, Journal of International Studies* 50 (2): 524–47.

Scheper-Hughes, Nancy, and Philippe Bourgois. 2004. "Introduction: Making Sense of Violence." In *Violence in War and Peace: An Anthology*, edited by Nancy Scheper-Hughes and Philippe Bourgois. Blackwell.

Schoenholtz, Andrew I., Philip G. Schrag, and Jaya Ramji-Nogales. 2014. *In Lives in the Balance: Asylum Adjudication by the Department of Homeland Security*. New York University Press.

Schrag, Philip G. 2020. *Baby Jails: The Fight to End the Incarceration of Refugee Children in America*. University of California Press.

Schrag, Philip G., Jaya Ramji-Nogales, and Andrew I. Schoenholtz. 2023. "The New Border Asylum Adjudication System: Speed, Fairness, and the Representation Problem." *Harvard Law Journal* 66 (3): 571–642.

Schriro, Dora. 2017. "Weeping in the Playtime of Others: The Obama Administration's Failed Reform of ICE Family Detention Practices." *Journal on Migration and Human Society* 5:2.

Sehlikoglu, Sertaç, and Aslı Zengin. 2015. "Introduction: Why Revisit Intimacy?" *Cambridge Journal of Anthropology* 33 (2): 20–25.

Shah, Silky. 2024. *Unbuild Walls: Why Immigrant Justice Needs Abolition*. Haymarket Books.

Shammas, Victor L. 2017. "Pains of Imprisonment." In *The Encyclopedia of Corrections*, edited by K. R. Kerley. Wiley.

Sheringham, Olivia Yvette, and Helen Taylor. 2022. "On Stories, Storytelling, and the Quiet Politics of Welcome." *Acme: An International Journal for Critical Geographies* 21 (3): 284–302.

Slack, Jeremy, Daniel E. Martínez, Scott Whiteford, Josiah Heyman, and Murphy Woodhouse. 2018. *The Shadow of the Wall: Violence and Migration on the U.S.-Mexico Border*. University of Arizona Press.

Smith-Khan, Laura. 2017. "Telling Stories: Credibility and the Representation of Social Actors in Australian Asylum Appeals." *Discourse and Society* 28 (5): 512–34.

Snider, Madison. 2022. "The Vigilant Imagination of Abolition." Simpson Center for the Humanities, February 11. https://simpsoncenter.medium.com/the-vigilant-imagination-of-abolition-e042cc8abf6f.

Solzhenitsyn, Aleksandr Isaevich. 1974. *The Gulag Archipelago, 1918–1956: An Experiment in Literary Investigation*. Harper & Row.

Speed, Shannon. 2019. *Incarcerated Stories: Indigenous Women Migrants and Violence in the Settler-Capitalist State*. University of North Carolina Press.

Stenken, Christopher. 2012. "Detention and Access to Justice: A Florence Project Case Study." In *Beyond Walls and Cages: Prisons, Borders, and Global Crisis*, edited by Jenna M. Loyd, Matt Mitchelson, and Andrew Burridge. University of Georgia Press.

Stevenson, Lisa. 2014. *Life beside Itself: Imagining Care in the Canadian Arctic*. University of California Press.

Stoler, Ann Laura. 2008. "Imperial Debris: Reflections on Ruins and Ruination." *Cultural Anthropology* 23 (2): 191–219.

Stumpf, Juliet. 2006. "The Crimmigration Crisis: Immigrants, Crime, and Sovereign Power." *American University Law Review* 56 (2): 367–419.

Sufrin, Carolyn. 2017. *Jailcare: Finding the Safety Net for Women behind Bars*. University of California Press.

Sykes, Gresham. 1958. *The Society of Captives: A Study of Maximum Security Prison*. Princeton University Press.

Tamboukou, Maria. 2021. "Narrative Rhythmanalysis: The Art and Politics of Listening to Women's Narratives of Forced Displacement." *International Journal of Social Research Methodology* 244 (2): 149–62.

Taylor, Charles. 2002. "Modern Social Imaginaries." *Public Culture* 14 (1): 91–124. https://muse.jhu.edu/article/26276.

Terkel, Studs. 2003. *Hope Dies Last: Keeping the Faith in Difficult Times*. New Press.

Terrio, Susan. 2024. *Forced Out: Migrant Mothers in Search of Refuge and Hope*. New York University Press.

Thornton, Leslie A., and David R. Novak. 2010. "Storying the Temporal Nature of Emotion Work: Bearing Witness to the Lived Trauma of Others." *Health Communication* 25 (5): 437–48.

Ticktin, Miriam Iris. 2011. *Casualties of Care: Immigration and the Politics of Humanitarianism in France*. University of California Press.

Ticktin, Miriam. 2016. "Thinking beyond Humanitarian Borders." *Social Research: An International Quarterly* 82 (2): 255–71.

Tonry, Michael, and Joan Petersilia. 1999. *Crime and Justice, Volume 26: Prisons*. University of Chicago Press Journals.

TRAC. 2017. "Who Is Represented in Immigration Court?" October 16. https://trac.syr.edu/immigration/reports/485/.

TRAC. 2021. "Asylum Success Varies Widely among Immigration Judges." https://trac.syr.edu/reports/670/.

TRAC. 2023. "Immigration Court Docket Growth Crushes Pro Bono Representation Efforts: TRAC." May 12. https://trac.syr.edu/reports/716/.

TRAC. 2024. "Asylum Success Still Varies Widely among Immigration Judges." November 25. https://trac.syr.edu/reports/752/.

Tronto, Joan C. 1993. *Moral Boundaries: A Political Argument for an Ethic of Care*. Routledge.

Trundle, Catherine. 2020. "Tinkering Care, State Responsibility, and Abandonment: Nuclear Test Veterans and the Mismatched Temporalities of Justice in Claims for Health Care." *Anthropology and Humanism* 45:202–11.

Tsing, Anna Lowenhaupt. 2005. *Friction: An Ethnography of Global Connection*. Princeton University Press.

Tyler, Imogen, Nick Gill, Dierdre Conlon, and Ceri Oeppen. 2014. "The Business of Child Detention: Charitable Co-option, Migrant Advocacy, and Activist Outrage." *Race & Class* 56 (1): 3–21.

USCIS (U.S. Citizenship and Immigration Services). 2019a. "Affirmative Asylum, Credible Fear, and Reasonable Fear." https://wwww.uscis.gov/sites/default/files/USCIS/Resources/Resources%20for%2020Congress/USCIS_OLIA_March_2019_Hill_Conference_Asylum_Overview.pdf.

USCIS (U.S. Citizenship and Immigration Services). 2019b. "Interview—Introduction to the Non-adversarial Interviewing." December 20. https://www.uscis.gov/sites/default/files/document/foia/Interviewing_Intro_to_the_Non_Adversarial_Interview_LP_RAIO.pdf.

Vargas Reyes, Erika, Lupe Lopez, and Whitney L. Duncan. 2024. "*Convivencia*: Storytelling as Accompaniment, Activism, and Care." In *Accompaniment with Im/migrant Communities*, edited by Kristin E. Yarris and Whitney L. Duncan. University of Arizona Press.

Vélez Young-Alfaro, Morghan. 2017. "Students as Threats: Schooling inside a Youth Prison." *Anthropology & Education Quarterly* 48:301–17. https://doi.org/10.1111/aeq.12201.

VERA. 2024. "Advocated and Lawmakers Rally to Demand Right to Counsel in Immigration Court and $150M for Legal Services Funding." VERA Institute of Justice, March 14. https://www.vera.org/newsroom/advocates-and-lawmakers-rally-to-demand-right-to-counsel-in-immigration-court-and-150m-for-legal-services-funding.

Vogl, Anthea. 2013. "Telling Stories from Start to Finish: Exploring the Demand for Narrative in Refugee Testimony." *Griffith Law Review* 22 (1): 63–86.

von Werthern, M., K. Robjant, Z. Chui, R. Schon, L. Ottisova, C. Mason, and C. Katona. 2018. "The Impact of Immigrant Detention on Mental Health: A Systematic Review." *BMC Psychiatry* 18. https://doi.org/10.1186/s12888-018-1945-y.

Wacquant, Loïc. 2002. "The Curious Eclipse of Prison Ethnography in the Age of Mass Incarceration." *Ethnography* 3 (4): 371–97.

Wacquant, Loïc. 2009. *Prisons of Poverty*. University of Minnesota Press.

Walsh, James P. 2013. "From Border Control to Border Care: The Political and Ethical Potential of Surveillance." In *Governing Immigration through Crime: A Reader*, edited by Julie A. Dowling and Jonathan Xavier Inda. Stanford University Press.

Warsi, Zeba. 2023. "Hundreds of Immigrants Have Reported Sexual Abuse at ICE Facilities. Most Cases Aren't Investigated." PBS, July 21. https://www.pbs.org/newshour/nation/hundreds-of-immigrants-have-reported-sexual-abuse-at-ice-facilities-most-cases-arent-investigated.

Washington, John. 2017. "These Jurisdictions Have Become 'Asylum Free Zones.'" The Nation, January 18. https://www.thenation.com/article/archive/these-jurisdictions-have-become-asylum-free-zones/.

Wexler, L. 2007. "The Non-legal Role of International Human Rights Law in Addressing Immigration." *University of Chicago Legal Forum*, 358–404.

Widra, Emily. 2024. "States of Incarceration: The Global Context 2024." Prison Policy Initiative, June. https://www.prisonpolicy.org/global/2024.html.

Wilson, Thomas M. 2024. *Borders, Boundaries, Frontiers*. University of Toronto Press.

Wolch, Jennifer. 1990. *The Shadow State: Government and Voluntary Sector in Transition*. Foundation Center.

Woolley, Agnes. 2017. "Narrating the 'Asylum Story': Between Literary and Legal Storytelling." *Interventions* 19 (3): 376–94.

Yarris, Kristin E. 2021. "ICE Offices and Immigration Courts: Accompaniment in Zones of Illegality." *Human Organization* 80 (3): 214–23.

Yarris, Kristin E. 2024. "Accompaniment in Activist Spaces: Solidarity at Ethnography's Edges with an Immigrant Bond Fund." In *Accompaniment with Im/migrant Communities*, edited by Kristin E. Yarris and Whitney L. Duncan. University of Arizona Press.

Yarris, Kristin E., and Whitney L. Duncan. 2024a. "Introduction: Accompaniment as Ethnographic Engagement." In *Accompaniment with Im/migrant Communities*, edited by Kristen E. Yarris and Whitney L. Duncan. University of Arizona Press.

Yarris, Kristin E., and Whitney L. Duncan, eds. 2024b. *Accompaniment with Im/migrant Communities: Engaged Ethnography*. University of Arizona Press.

Young, Eliot. 2020. *Forever Prisoners: How the United States Made the World's Largest Immigrant Detention System*. Oxford University Press.

Zaman, Jawziya F. 2017. "Why I Left Immigration Law." Dissent Magazine, July 12. https://www.dissentmagazine.org/online_articles/left-immigration-law.

Zeitlyn, David. 2014. "Antinomies of Representation: Anthropology as an Ekphrastic Process." *HAU: Journal of Ethnographic Theory* 4 (3): 341–62. https://doi.org/10.14318/hau4.3.022.

INDEX

ABOUT THE AUTHOR

Erin Routon is an assistant professor of anthropology at the University of Houston in Houston, Texas. She also teaches advanced social scientific writing for Harvard Extension School. Her research, activism, and teaching center social justice causes related to immigration and incarceration, particularly in the United States and Latin America. She is a member of the Abolitionist Anthropology Working Group and has worked as a volunteer with various immigrant advocacy organizations and projects across the United States.

FSC
www.fsc.org
MIX
Papier | Fördert gute Waldnutzung
FSC® C083411

Kolibri 360 GmbH
Ferdinand-Jühlke-Straße 7
99095 Erfurt, Deutschland
produktsicherheit@kolibri360.de